'OH DAMN THE CHLOROFORM!'

Published under licence by Brown Dog Books and
The Self-Publishing Partnership Ltd, 10b Greenway Farm, Bath Rd, Wick, nr.
Bath BS30 5RL

www.selfpublishingpartnership.co.uk

ISBN printed book: 978-1-83952-476-9
ISBN e-book: 978-1-83952-477-6

Cover design by Luke Storkey
Internal design by Andrew Easton

Printed and bound in the UK

This book is printed on FSC certified paper

MIX
Paper from
responsible sources
FSC® C013604

'OH DAMN THE CHLOROFORM!'

ADELAIDE BARTLETT'S FAMILY OF SECRETS

and

THE PIMLICO MYSTERY

ROSE STORKEY

BROWN
DOG
BOOKS

In loving memory of my sister, Gill (Gillian Rosmé Roberts, née Cantle) and my parents, Nel (Clarice Nellie Cantle, née Gully) and Ivor John Cantle

For Luke, Gemma, Harry and Leo

'It appears to me impossible that I should cease to exist, or that this active, restless spirit, equally alive to joy and sorrow, should be only organised dust.'

Mary Wollstonecraft, *Letters Written During a Short Residence in Sweden, Norway and Denmark* (London: J Johnson, 1796). A personal travel narrative by Mary Wollstonecraft (1759–97). Mary, the highly influential British feminist, advocate of women's rights, philosopher and author, wrote those words after her second attempt to end her life.

CONTENTS

PREFACE: SCATTERED LIVES AND 'ORGANISED DUST'   13

PROLOGUE   19

PART ONE: BLOODLINES   25
1 Enter Adolphus   26
2 Being 'Henry Desbury'   28
3 'Desdemona to the Moor' – Maria Margaret Bearcock   41
4 Chamberlains, Newalls – and Young Henry William Desbury   47
5 Henry William Desbury: Older, not Wiser   59
6 Rodolphus Hampton d'Escury (known as Rodolphe)   64
7 'Deep Sorrows and Afflictions'   70
8 'Something Extraordinary'   80
9 Women, a Will and a Baby   83
10 Walter Henry Prout de Thouars d'Escury and the Murder of Sarah   89
11 Helen d'Escury and Modestus Felix de Thouars d'Escury   94

PART TWO: CLARA AND ADOLPHE'S CHILDREN   97
12 Henry Edouard de Thouars   98
13 Adelaide de la Tremoille de Thouars d'Escury   103
14 Frederick George de Thouars   108
15 Clara de la Tremouille   112

PART THREE: THE HUSBAND, THOMAS EDWIN BARTLETT (EDWIN)   115
16 Home and Away   116
17 Bed and Bored   126
18 What Adelaide Did   132

PART FOUR: ADELAIDE AND EDWIN ENDURE   139
19 Illness and Loss   140
20 Dyson Fills the Vacuum   148

PART FIVE: PIMLICO   161
21 The Accommodating Mrs Doggett   162
22 The Desperate Times, December 1885   165
23 The Poison   174

PART SIX: DEATH AND DENIAL   183
24 Enter the Registrar of Births, Marriages and Deaths   184
25 The Post-mortem and the Fall-out   192
26 Trying to Get to the Bottom of it All   197
27 'To Disprove the Strange Statements Promulgated'   215

PART SEVEN: THE OLD BAILEY, LONDON   231
28 Two then One   232
29 Prosecution, Defence, Judge and Jury   235
30 Bearing Witness   243
31 Finishing Off   281

PART EIGHT: 'UNREBUKED TO FREEDOM'   315
32 Correspondence and Opinions   316
33 Doctor Alfred Leach   332
34 Adieu, to You and You and You   339

PART NINE: TIME FOR GEORGE DE THOUARS   351
35 A Stick-up and a Lock-up   352
36 Straight Out of Pentridge   364

PART TEN: GOODBYE GEORGE DYSON   371
37 'Misconducted Himself'   372

PART ELEVEN: BEING 'JOHN BERNARD WALKER'   375
38 A Scientific American   376

WRAPPING UP   394

ILLUSTRATIONS and PHOTOGRAPHS   407
FAMILY TREE   412
WIDER FAMILY DETAILS AND RELATIONSHIPS   413
ENDNOTES   417
ACKNOWLEDGEMENTS   433
BIBLIOGRAPHY   435

PREFACE

SCATTERED LIVES AND 'ORGANISED DUST'

Adelaide de la Tremoille de Thouars d'Escury became simply 'Mrs Adelaide Bartlett' but there was nothing straightforward about her life. Nor about her husband Edwin's demise; his end came at 85 Claverton Street, Pimlico, London, a very short walk from the swirl and stench of the River Thames.

The drip, drip, drip of revelations about the couple caused sensations, literally, among women and men. Many queued to gain entry to the Inquest concerning Edwin's death or subsequently to his widow's trial for murder. Many were left out in the street, craning their necks excitedly, hoping to spot witnesses or – best of all – get a glimpse of Adelaide. Sensational stories transfixed a soaring number of Victorian newspaper readers in 1886 as they pored over the shocking details. The more that people were fed about the couple and about Edwin's death, the less any sense could be made of the jarring contrasts between his mundanity and Adelaide's mystique. And what to make of their close friend, the Reverend George Dyson?

All was not what it seemed, yet how to fathom the truth – sometimes boring – and what was false – often endlessly fascinating? The tragedy, relationships and red herrings have intrigued true/fact crime sleuths ever since.

The Pimlico Mystery/Pimlico Poisoning Case: same unwholesome ingredients, different labels. Hard-working Edwin Bartlett's descent into illness and depression; enigmatic Adelaide's trial. Sex or the lack of it; a foreigner, a grocer, a reverend; a love triangle, poison, lies and secrets; a sudden, surely painful death; a young, bewitchingly attractive widow.

By some process Adelaide was chosen to marry Edwin or she chose him; whichever, in the end all lives come down to dust. Biographical stories about the dead are, bluntly, 'organised dust'.

Why did I want to write about Adelaide and the 'scattered lives' of her extended family? My late father, Ivor Cantle, was an amateur criminologist from the 1950s until his death in 1980; my sister Gillian and I grew up with murder in the blood – or rather, on the dining table. Books and bulging files; newly-delivered birth, marriage and death certificates; photographs of long-dead suspects and victims; Victorian and Edwardian memorabilia.

Our long-suffering mother, Nel, appeared to bear it all with a mixture of good grace and occasional interest, only asking that the dining table be cleared for meals. A low point came when, on a family day trip, Ivor knocked at the door of a long-dead man's relative. Gill and I grumbled away about our embarrassing father as we waited in the back of the car. He returned with a shocking story of a death-bed confession.

I still wonder why and when Ivor became interested in researching alleged murders, particularly cases which involved poisons. He may have heard about the 'Napoleon killed by poison' theories when in the British Army on the island of Saint Helena in the Second World War.

Adelaide Bartlett's life and trial was one of my father's favourite 'cases'. Goodness knows how my mother really felt about it all, but with her usual kindness she gave Kate Clarke the 'Adelaide' file after Ivor's death. Kate, in her book *The Pimlico Murder: The Strange Case of Adelaide Bartlett* (Souvenir Press Ltd, 1990) acknowledged Ivor's 'Adelaide' endeavours.

I admire how much he achieved as a researcher pre-internet, coping with the disappointment when not receiving a reply, or getting a negative response, after months of waiting for letters. My father researched cases with great care, spending much of his spare time pondering motives and methods; crafting correspondence to elicit facts from people near and far; sending off suspects' handwriting for analysis. In the twenty-first century I can choose from billions of hard facts and soft hunches, many available with just a click.

Top of Ivor's case list sat the one involving Constance Kent from Road/ Rode, a village not many miles from our home. Research concerning Constance and her family led him around the world, figuratively not literally.

My searches, in the virtual world, for Adelaide and the family took me around the globe and back through the nineteenth century, driven on initially by a question which has always hung around the case.

WHO WAS ADELAIDE'S FATHER?

Studying Adelaide's eyebrows, her curly hair, and comparing them with Lord Alfred Paget's was something my father and I did. Ivor's research into Adelaide and her family led him to believe Lord Alfred Paget (member of the British aristocracy, and Chief Equerry, Clerk Marshal to Queen Victoria) to be Adelaide's birth father. I and others followed that line and have only recently found it to be incorrect: Lord Paget has no part in the story of Adelaide.

We sleuths thought that Adolphe, the man who married Adelaide's mother, was cuckolded by her, but no – he tricked others. This book tells the strange stories of her birth father and of her extended family, this is about much more than 'just' Adelaide and Edwin's lives. I explore bloodlines and blood lines in the extended family and in the headline-making lives of others caught up in the Pimlico Mystery. I track a surprising range of births, marriages and deaths, alleged criminals and guilty ones, all around the world and through the nineteenth century, You will meet Adelaide's nineteenth-century siblings and half-siblings: offspring from the same father yet with contrasting lives. These people scattered; some shattered others or were shattered by events. Sadnesses, injuries and cruelties. Happiness in everyday lives was rarely recorded and one can only hope that people in Adelaide's family felt it sometimes.

Going back several centuries for information about supposedly 'ordinary' people turns up little – except among rogues, victims/survivors and the mentally ill – unless 'gold dust' in the form of letters, diaries and memoirs is uncovered. With regard to women (of any class), unless they had fame, finances, notoriety, or involvement with a crime, information about them was rarely recorded.

Newspaper reporters' and editors' subjective views of people and events provide the backdrop here, usually with a masculine gaze, and precious little about how women felt about themselves or others. Apart from Adelaide's story, few facts are known publicly about the women in her family in the nineteenth century. Unless relatives know more about them, the women's stories from her extended family have gone forever.

'BUT WHAT A WEAK BARRIER IS TRUTH'

With respect for the living and the dead I sought the truth about their lives, but of course the truth lies in so much more than facts. The truth involves each individual's experiences of a situation, their feelings and motivations. I recall other words from Mary Wollstonecraft: 'what a weak barrier is truth when it stands in the way of a hypothesis'.[1]

I kept reminding myself: theories have a place but keep an open mind about what happened, follow facts and opinions, hold the unearthed up to the light before making deductions – and in many instances, just putting it out there. I dipped into my imagination and a few poems emerged in response to the prose. I consider them slightly better than

George Dyson's poem 'My Birdie' – but it is not a competition and they would not win one.

YOU COULDN'T MAKE IT UP

Alfred Hitchcock[2], hugely influential film maker and 'Master of Suspense', described the Pimlico Mystery as one of 'the strangest stories' he had ever heard, with 'many elements of a great film play'. But he did not know the half of it, not knowing Adelaide's *actual* 'backstory'.

I prefer to read fact/true crime books rather than crime fiction (brilliant as that can be and hugely appreciated by millions of readers). Why do I choose the former? Having spent a working life in social work and management, my abiding interest is in the vagaries of the human condition, what really happens, and its impact upon individuals and families.

THE STRANGENESS OF TRUTH

Things that make people 'tick' and the strangeness of truth: how utterly bizarre many lives turn out to have been; lives exposed through genealogy, social history and criminal records. Evidence features here from the era of massive increase in both newspaper titles and circulation figures (particularly after the repeal in 1855 of a tax on newspapers). Reports of violence and passion in Adelaide's family have not been embellished by me in the re-telling. The main sources are family history records, newspapers, true crime books and archived material, including the transcript of a trial and prison records. Other sources include maps, photographs and drawings.

Most of the people in this story were not poor. But of course, as many do, they suffered through illness, bereavement and want; yearning for love and excitement. Some struggled in situations of their own making, others as 'victims' on the receiving end of duplicitous behaviour.

Hold on for a strange trip through time and around the globe, starting out in wintery Pimlico, London and soon heading back to a summer's day in the west of England.

To avoid repetition, details from numerous England Census records (which were collected from 1801 every ten years, with the exception of 1941) are shown as, for example, 'in 1851'.

Throughout, I have used capital letters liberally, for emphasis, eg Reverend, Trial.

PROLOGUE

PIMLICO, LONDON, 1885

If you were getting set to kill your husband with poison, would you deliberately rent rooms in the home of a registrar of births, marriages and deaths? Or was the choice innocently made, in ignorance of that fact; an arrangement made solely with the landlady? Or was there no dastardly plan?

PIMLICO, NEW YEAR'S MORNING, 1886

Adelaide's tight fist raps on the Doggetts' bedroom door; her call, 'Come down, I think Mr Bartlett is dead' awakens the Registrar of Births, Marriages and Deaths for Belgravia. The deeply shocked Mr Doggett clatters downstairs, sees the man flat on his back on a chair-bed, feels the bare breast, blurts out to Adelaide: 'perfectly cold' with death ... he must have been dead for 'two or three hours'. Doggett catches his breath ... he's only seen Mr Bartlett once to exchange pleasantries – and now this.

Fred Doggett knows he must remember the time: '4.10 a.m. by the clock on the drawing-room mantelpiece,' he informs a court in April.

Edwin Bartlett: dead. Adelaide Bartlett – born Adelaide de la Tremoille de Thouars d'Escury: alive, starting the new year, 1886, as a widow. Merry, a murderer – or mortified?

ROAD/RODE, 1820

Adelaide, illustrious names flowing out behind her like a bridal train, is nowhere near being born. Her father, hidden in plain sight, won't sire her until much murkier water has flowed under London bridges. To get anywhere near to understanding Adelaide, we need to find her father. And ages before he meets Clara, who gives birth to Adelaide, there is Eleanor.

July 1820, West Country, England. Eleanor Caroline Hampton and three of her brothers have just been baptised in Road, a village straddling the Somerset and Wiltshire county border.

Eleanor is given pride of place here, in recognition of the love which her children will feel when bestowing her names (and variations of them) on their children. Eleanor's life leads the way to mysteries in which people's names change for many reasons, some expected but most unanticipated. Names lost and taken on through marriage, a need or an urge for falsehood, flight from dangers to freedom, escape from trauma. Names frequently misheard and wrongly spelt, by census enumerators for example.

And the spelling of this village's name changed slightly, Rode to Roda to la Rode to Road to Rode[3] over many centuries, forth and back, on the whims of locals and officials.

Road, the village which will forever be associated with one of the most infamous child murders of the nineteenth century. Road in Somerset – but Road Hill House where the family lived is just a short walk up the road into the next county, Wiltshire. In 1860, Francis Savill Kent, age three, was cruelly murdered, possibly by suffocation. Someone slashed his throat and thrust his body into an outside privy. The case was a challenging one for local police: against their wishes Detective Inspector Jack Whicher was called in from Scotland Yard, London. The child's half-sister, Constance Kent, aged sixteen: arrested by order of the local magistrates, released at the committal hearing. Five years later she confessed to the murder, was charged and received the mandatory death sentence. Her sentence commuted to life imprisonment,

Constance served the full twenty years in English prisons.

Subsequently she lived in Australia as 'Emilie Kaye' until her death, aged one hundred. The murder of young 'Savill' and Constance's confession (true or false) were sensational stories that put Road (now Rode) on the map. International interest in the murder has continued – particularly after the publication of Kate Summerscale's incisive, enthralling *The Suspicions of Mr Whicher: A Shocking Murder and the Undoing of a Great Victorian Detective.*[4]

'FROM DAILY NUISANCE TO NATIONAL OBSESSION'

Road/Rode was one of so many villages in which people struggled to survive during the nineteenth century. The push/pull effect of increasingly large-scale food production through mechanisation and involving imports/ exports, removed working-class jobs and emptied people's pockets.

'The procurement of food escalated from daily nuisance to national obsession'[5] and social upheaval hugely affected rural areas. In desperation, the hungry – if they had any energy left – made decisions, hoping that escaping would lead to work. Taking paths and dirt roads away from the countryside, off into towns and cities they went; often in family groups comprising three generations. Between 1815 and 1846, British governments made a succession of Corn Laws as protectionist measures, with tariffs and other trade actions against cheap foreign imports of wheat and other grains, (collectively known as 'corn').

In 1837, Queen Victoria's reign began. The Anti-Corn Law League was formally established in Manchester in 1839 to build a mass movement, including the middle classes, to oppose landlords. Later that year Victoria proposed marriage to Albert (royal protocol, not a leap year) and the wedding was held in February 1840. The land-owning aristocracy went on reaping huge benefits from the ever-rising selling prices resulting from the Corn Laws; working people continued to suffer from prohibitive food prices and consequent lack of food.

WHAT IN THE WORLD?

What else was happening? The World Anti-Slavery Convention met for the first time in June 1840, as part of various campaigns for the abolition of slavery worldwide. Women, denied full access to these proceedings in London, could only watch and listen. One knock-on effect: Lucretia Mott and Elizabeth Cady Stanton returned home to north-eastern America resolving to hold a convention. And that led to the forming of a society in the US to advocate for the rights of women and suffrage. Other examples of women's relegation to the role of spectators will appear throughout this story.

The ongoing Industrial Revolution in North America, Western Europe and Britain from around 1760 had initiated the mass movement of rural workers to seek employment in towns and cities across Great Britain. Those who had toiled in fields and left them needed to be fed now by those remaining in the countryside. However, rural workers flocked in ever-greater numbers to ever-expanding urban areas as the Corn Laws cut into their lives.

The Hamptons of this story were probably not desperate; with the rural decline it is likely that, before the rot set in, they decided to try using their skills in other places, in new roles.

The first 'modern' Census in the United Kingdom was held in 1841. Censuses are like permanent molehills across a green field, throwing up materials which, for the historian, the genealogist and the plain curious, contain diamonds and gold. Before that Census the Hamptons had upped sticks from Road and headed eastwards to London. Many individuals and families moved, hoping for a better life; many hopes died. But by 1841, the Hamptons were doing well in the capital. Eleanor Caroline Hampton, 'Ellen', age twenty, a stock maker, lived with her parents, Hannah and Robert, at 55 Bunhill Row, St Luke's parish, Finsbury, in the Borough of Islington. Their house was opposite Bunhill Fields – the name a corruption of Bone Hill Fields. This was an ancient site for internments, and the unconsecrated ground had been used by religious Dissenters for burials, mainly since 1665, time of the Great Plague of London epidemic. Over 100,000 bodies lie there, disarranged.

Unlike so many other people in this story who moved from place to place within London and elsewhere, through necessity or choice, Hannah and Robert Hampton lived at 55 Bunhill Row for more than ten years.

No job was noted for Eleanor's mother but women had more than enough to do – it just didn't pay. Eleanor's father, a spinner in Road, left the declining wool trade behind him and became an engineer, perhaps involved in the burgeoning demand for railway development. Their London home was just a few streets north of the newly built Bishopsgate station.

Eleanor Caroline Hampton now makes a public appearance as 'Helena Caroline' marrying Adolphus Collot de Thouars d'Escury. (She will be referred to as Eleanor throughout.)

Adolphus, whoever he is, leads us to Adelaide on twisting roads from who knows which country. His daughter Adelaide, whoever she is, does not hove into view until several hearts have been torn and lives shattered. The extraordinary stories of her relatives, their intrigues and tragedies, show us what Adelaide is made from, are the backdrop to what she becomes.

PART ONE
BLOODLINES

Chapter 1

ENTER ADOLPHUS

Adolphus: what was he like and how might he be recognised on the street? Which countries and how many women had he left behind by the 1840s?

In December 1843, working at Mr James Greene's school at Herstmonceux, Sussex, 'Mr D'Escury', tested pupils at the half-yearly examinations of 'the young gentlemen' in 'Arithmetic, English Composition, Elocution, Latin, and French'. The examinations were 'agreeably varied by a French comedy, the characters ... sustained by Messrs D'Escury, Huggett' etc.[6]

It is extremely likely that 'Mr D'Escury' was Adolphus, shortly to be noted as a teacher of mathematics and languages. Someone may know the year and country of his birth and where he lived before that sighting in southern England.

In December 1844 at the parish church of St Luke's, Finsbury, near where they resided in Bunhill Row, 'Adolphus Collot de Thouars d'Escury' (a professor of languages) married 'Helena Caroline Hampton'.

HARD TIMES

Throughout the 1840s in Europe, England and Ireland, blight decimated potato crops. The food crises and deaths led to terrible misery and unrest, adding to the revolutionary fervour rising up across much of mainland

Europe. This was at the time when many Europeans began to have the benefit of education, the opportunities it could bring, and the desire for liberty and rights. Famine separated and destroyed many families, particularly in the south and west of Ireland. Particularly between 1845 and 1849 there was *Gorta Mór*, in Irish, meaning the Great Famine or the Great Hunger, with ensuing diseases including typhoid fever, typhus, dysentery, smallpox and (from 1849) Asiatic cholera. The worst year was 1847, remembered as *Blianin an Drochshaoil*, the Famine Year. Hard lives in hard times.

Between 1845 and 1855 over two million people were displaced through hunger and poverty, over 95 per cent of them boarding ships to cross the Atlantic – many dying en route. Ireland, ruled directly from Parliament in Westminster, London since 1801, was greatly affected by the Corn Laws and harm continued after their repeal in 1846. Complexities of the dire situation for the Irish people arose not only from the potato blight and a monoculture but also from politics, colonialism and prejudice. Demands by the Irish for land reform (drafted during the Great Famine) were not conceded to by the government in Britain until the Irish Land Acts from the 1870s onwards. Prejudice against the Irish will be seen to be part of Adolphus' make-up – and he was not alone in that.

In London, Eleanor and Adolphus lived near her parents for at least part of the time. She gave birth to their first three children in 1845, '47 and '48. It is not known whether any were born in France yet, if nothing else, that country featured in their thoughts and words during adulthood.

It will become obvious that 1848 and 1849 were traumatic years for this woman and her children, a time of significant disruption; all of them caught up in frightening events in their no longer private lives.

Chapter 2

BEING 'HENRY DESBURY'

LECKHAMPTON

At odds with the idyllic Georgian splendours of nearby Cheltenham, a violent attack took place in the summer of 1848 at leafy Leckhampton, in the English county of Gloucestershire. Looming over the village: the Devil's Chimney, a limestone rock formation high on a hill.

DESPICABLE DESBURY

Adolphus is brought to life in newspaper reports as 'Henry Desbury'. Violent, intelligent, detestable and manipulative; apprehended after a vicious assault on 21 June 1848 and in court on several occasions that summer.

'POSSESSED OF HANDSOME FEATURES'

The *Cheltenham and Gloucestershire Advertiser*, 5 July 1848, had details on Henry Desbury's case when he was up before the magistrates on remand. 'Mrs Desbury', Maria Margaret, had been too ill to attend before – and now fainted twice while giving evidence.

'She was very respectably dressed, possessed of handsome features, and her whole demeanour was very prepossessing.'

Maria Margaret's story was extracted bit by bit: she was the prisoner's wife; temporary abode at Mrs Lane's, 15 Ambrose Street, Cheltenham. With a friend, Mrs Elizabeth Ellis, she went on 21 June to Desbury's lodgings at 1 St Philip's Terrace, Leckhampton between 7 and 8 am in the morning. She knocked on the door, a woman in nightclothes opened it. Maria Margaret asked to see her husband. The reply: 'NO.' Maria Margaret asked if the woman was his wife, but received no answer.

This other woman ran upstairs ahead of her and just as Maria Margaret reached the third step from the top, Henry Desbury came out of a bedroom and threw an earthenware night commode at her head 'with great force'. She screamed out 'murder' and heard a roar from Henry. 'Where is my knife?' he bellowed and at these words down she fell, senseless. A man named Kennedy was nearby and when the assailant fetched a knife, Kennedy 'gave him a hit on the side of the head, and prevented him from leaving until the surgeon and policeman arrived'.

Police Constable Thomas produced the bonnet worn by 'Mrs Desbury'; it was saturated with blood. Police Sergeant George Seyes deposed that the prisoner (when on his way to custody in the police station house) declared that he was not married to Maria Margaret.

Presumably Desbury had not reckoned on her resourcefulness and determination. She held an ace up her sleeve – or rather, in her bag that day. She had brought with her from London their marriage certificate and now gave it to Sergeant Seyes, who showed it to Desbury. Caught in a proverbial cleft stick, Desbury changed his story, saying that actually, she really was his wife. The police needed to investigate, find out which of the couple told the truth about what sort of couple they were …

'A MULATTO'

Charged with intent to murder, he was brought up again before the Cheltenham magistrates after several remands. The *Hampshire Advertiser* of 15 July 1848 referred to his colour and possible origins, saying he was 'a mulatto' (a term today generally only used in its historical contexts) – referring to those born of one white and one black parent, or of a mulatto parent or parents. The newspaper reported (perhaps erroneously) that Henry Desbury was 'formerly of Southampton', a large port on the south coast of England.

Business at Monmouth having been concluded early, Judges Platt and Rolfe attended a service in Gloucester Cathedral. The interrelationship between the legal system and the Church of England entailed this traditional, formal attendance of judges at special services in the cities and towns on the circuit.

Next morning, Thursday 10 August, the judges wanted to get on with the job – and they arrived before Gloucester's great and good expected them. The local civic functionaries were at sixes and sevens because 'the business of the Courts was commenced two hours earlier than the time fixed, much to the inconvenience of persons summoned to the Assizes. On the names of the city magistrates being called over, the Mayor was absent, and thus was fined 5/- by Baron Platt'.[7] Having penalised the Mayor for lateness, Platt was more than ready to preside.

'BROKEN ENGLISH'

'Henry Desbury ... a foreigner of a very dark complexion'[8]

Horrific details of his physical attack on this young woman, and the convoluted tale he told, were covered in Dickensian detail by regional and national newspapers. The scene: the Oxford Circuit, day two of Gloucestershire Summer Assizes at Gloucester, 11 August 1848, before Mr Baron Platt. The Prosecutors were Messrs Piggott and Skinner.

Unrepresented, Henry Desbury 'who appeared like a foreigner' stood up, 'held a written defence in his hand' and made his case 'in a most skilful manner'.

Having no lawyer, the bravado of his self-defence booms loud and clear down the centuries. His passionate speech was described as being in 'broken English' – the accent perhaps, but his vocabulary and fluency surpassed that of many English-speaking people of any era.[9]

He declared that he and Maria Margaret married in January last; he left her after some differences in March and became a teacher of languages in Cheltenham, hence his new life in Leckhampton.

Evidence from witnesses at Desbury's court appearances that summer revealed the aftermath of his violence: Maria Margaret had severe head wounds. Plasterer Thomas Tibbles, who lived nearby, was fetched to assist, then her friend, Mrs Ellis, rushed off to find a medical man. The *Hampshire Advertiser,* 15 July 1848, had the disgusted Tibbles asking Desbury, 'if he was not ashamed of himself?'. Desbury was defiant: 'No', he 'would have done it again if he had anything else in his hand'. He told Tibbles to 'take his wife out of doors or to a public house and let her bleed there'. Pushing her out of his home, Desbury ran back in, shouting 'Where is my knife?''.

That was the point at which Maria Margaret had lost consciousness. Two surgeons deposed as to the nature and extent of the injuries. Mr Robert Askwith of Huntley Lodge had arranged for Maria Margaret to be taken for treatment; Mr David Hartley, from the hospital in Cheltenham, found her 'perfectly insensible' through concussion. She had three contused wounds from a blunt instrument and 'lay in a dangerous state' for several weeks. Constable James Thomas produced the victim's clothing (covered in blood), a quantity of her hair and pieces of white ware – the alleged weapon being a commode pan. The bedroom door that the prisoner allegedly slammed against her head was left covered in her blood for several days, until after the evidence was noted down by the police. Only then was the door washed down. Goodness knows what the children living in the house made of all the uproar and bloodshed. Of course, Desbury had not been living there alone.

'THREW THE AFOREMENTIONED PANS AT HER HEAD'

Sergeant Seyes told of Desbury's words when taken into custody. He 'acknowledged committing the offence' but denied that Maria Margaret was his wife; they had lived together in London and when he saw her enter his house in Leckhampton he thought 'she was going to kill his children, and in order to save them, he threw the aforementioned pans at her head'. However, when Sergeant Sayes showed him a marriage certificate, Desbury had changed his story, 'the unfortunate woman was his wife' – he made no further mention of the children.

The reporter described Maria Margaret as 'a young woman, possessing great personal attractions' who 'while giving her evidence, fainted several times from weakness' and had to be seated. She declared: 'I am the wife of the prisoner.'

Henry's declarations: he had been a lieutenant in the Dutch Royal Navy; in 1830 on leave of absence in Paris, he 'took a part in the attack on the Tuileries, had his left arm shot off and received various other injuries'. Allegedly involved in two revolutions, he said he had a rank equal to lieutenant conferred on him 'by Louis Philippe, besides the cross of the Legion of Honour.' (Henry was referring to the man who was the French king from 1830–48, Le Roi Citoyen or Citizen King, also called Louis Philippe, Duc d'Orleans.)

Many newspapers conveyed to readers the florid language emanating from the outrageous defendant in the dock. Desbury used various ploys, including flattery, saying he could have had, 'a Jury of half Anglaise and half foreigners; nay, if I demanded it I could be tried by a jury composed of all foreigners. But, gentleman, were the choice offered to me, I would condemn, I would despise it, and would choose a jury composed entirely of true Britons.'

'Gentlemen, in praising the Anglaise I must not include the Irish. The policeman is an Irishman. Search the annals, read the history of that country; is it not one of murder, rapine, bloodshed, and crime? Therefore I ask you not to believe an Irishman on his oath. The police inspector is the man who chooses the degree of crime. Talk about law, gentleman, can a policeman tell the legal difference between murder, manslaughter, or a common assault, any more than a jackass can tell the taste of a kidney-bean from a piece of toasted cheese? Therefore I compare him to that animal. I am accused, gentlemen, of an attempt to murder! God only knows the intentions of the human mind, and no human being can tell the machinations of it.'[10]

Disgraceful levels of prejudice against the Irish were evident in England and other countries; Adolphus/Henry was only one of the many who spoke in vile language against the Irish. In 1836, a future prime minister of Great Britain, Benjamin Disraeli, had said:

The Irish 'hate our order, our civilisation, our enterprising industry, our pure religion. This wild, reckless, indolent, uncertain and superstitious race has no sympathy with the English character. Their ideal of human felicity is an alternation of clannish broils and coarse idolatry. Their history describes an unbroken circle of bigotry and blood.'

Disraeli by Robert Blake.[11]

A JACKASS, A KIDNEY-BEAN, A PIECE OF TOASTED CHEESE

Desbury had lumped in a policeman with a jackass (a male ass or donkey; a stupid person) inferring that such beings did not have enough brain to tell one thing from another. Presumably he was gambling on the Jury not only being prejudiced against the Irish but also against policemen of any rank (there were no policewomen). Enjoying centre stage, he was carried away by his tongue and was on a dangerous path, continuing to voice disdain for his captor and for the 'police inspector'. Seemingly unabashed by such serious charges and undeterred by the evidence presented against him, Desbury brazened on with breathtaking and chilling nerve. Of Maria Margaret he said she was jealous of him and that he had reason to be jealous of her. He put the blame on his 'wife' – Maria Margaret – alleging she 'misconducted herself' and displayed suspicion and jealousy in London and Cheltenham.

Desbury's blustering excuse for his violence was his jealousy. This was reported by many newspapers, to the effect that he alleged she spoke of a dear friend whom, in that moment of passion, he considered a paramour, hence his throwing the basin at her. He said there was no evil intention; throughout the court proceedings he minimised his violence against Maria Margaret, who had obviously been seriously injured and shocked.

His final declaration: he loved her dearly and 'would now rather die than endanger her life.' Weasel words designed to reduce the sentence he was about to be handed down. His words rang hollow and the Court would deal with his deeds.

'THAT IS EXACTLY WHAT I EXPECTED'

The Jury deliberated for a short time and found him guilty of assault with intent to do grievous bodily harm. Mr Baron Platt sentenced him to twelve months' imprisonment – and must have been surprised to hear Desbury pipe up in response: 'That is exactly what I expected.'[12]

Desbury had the last word – and sounded pleased to be correct, rather than sorry for being guilty of committing a shameful crime.

That Friday afternoon, the convicted Desbury was taken back to Gloucester gaol to start his sentence. Mr Baron Platt must have been glad to see the back of him.

INDICTED FOR BIGAMY

Henry Desbury was back, placed in court again next day, Saturday 12 August, and indicted for bigamy.

Bigamy, a word of Latin and Greek origin: the act of entering into a marriage with a person while still legally married to another. It is a crime in many countries and often neither the first nor second spouse is aware of the other. In countries which have laws against bigamy, where there is marital monogamy, consent given by a prior spouse does not make a second marriage legal, and the latter is usually declared 'void'.

Mrs Maria Margaret Desbury was NOT Desbury's lawful wedded wife; he already had one of those.

He asked for the case to be adjourned until the next Assizes, as he wanted witnesses from London and France to be able to attend. Prosecutor Piggott objected on the grounds of cost, as witnesses had already been brought from London and, if not heard now, would have to return at another date. The Judge said that 'a question of expense to the county was as nothing in comparison with the proper defence of a prisoner' which was scrupulously fair – but of course the county's finances were of no concern to judges.

The Governor of the county gaol in Gloucester, Captain Mason, confirmed that the prisoner was correct in saying that the usual rule for such a sentence was a maximum of one letter to and from a prisoner every three months, with no personal visits. Thus the Judge made a Special Order: Desbury could write from prison to the witnesses he wanted in attendance at his bigamy trial, to give evidence in his defence.

The case being rescheduled for the next Assizes. Desbury was taken back to prison to continue his sentence for the violence against Maria Margaret.

The prison record says so much in just a few words:

'Date of Admission [on remand] at Gloucester Prison 21 June 1848, the day of the alleged assault. Number 2575. "Native of Marsailles" [sic] lately living in Cheltenham. Teacher, age forty-one, five foot five inches, black curly hair, very dark eyes, visage long, complexion "very dark, a mulatto". Other marks: "has lost the left arm & has been badly wounded in the left side". Cause of Commitment: "Charged with attempt at Murder".'

When and where was he born? Names of countries and territories changed but the areas that come to mind as possibilities include the Kingdom of Holland; Dutch Indonesia; Belgium; England. Somewhere else in the Dutch or British empires? The subject of his alleged birthplace, Marseilles in France, will be returned to later in connection with one of his sons. The second part of his prison record was written in cross-hatching, black ink horizontally and red ink vertically. In black, the alleged offence of wounding with intent to murder; in red, the alleged offence of marrying Maria Margaret when his first wife was 'then alive'.

Henry Desbury's case had provided many ingredients popular with editors and certain readers: violence, passion, jealousy, a love triangle. The following March, details would emerge of the bitter triangle associated with his bigamous marriage.

Meanwhile that week, the *Cheltenham Journal and Gloucestershire Fashionable Weekly Gazette's* 'Cheltenham Arrivals' included a Mr Dumas at the Fleece Hotel and under 'Fashionable Changes' the comings and goings of various titled and monied personages from local residences. Of course, it did not announce the recovering Maria Margaret and, separately, the pregnant Eleanor and her children leaving town for London or elsewhere …

The so-called Henry Desbury would remain in prison until March 1849, then be put up in court yet again.

'CREOLE'

A reporter described the man he saw in court as a 'Creole' (Creole meaning, at that time, a person of mixed European and black origin).[13]

'FELONIOUSLY INTERMARRIED'

Henry's bigamy trial in March 1849 was held at Gloucestershire Lent Assizes, Mr Justice Coltman (Sir Thomas Coltman) presiding. 'Henry Desbury, a man of colour, aged forty-one, was charged with having on 25 January 1848 feloniously intermarried' – his first wife still being alive.[14]

Also on that page of the local newspaper was a summary of the themes in a speech by Sir Robert Peel MP, former Prime Minister of the United Kingdom. He urged that measures be put in place for economic recovery, as 'the misery of Ireland is proverbial. Her very name calls up hateful associations. Suffering and crime form the stereotyped substance of her history ... Civil strife, rebellion, famine, proscription, pestilence, have reappeared century after century – avengers of the past and unheeded prophets of the future.' Peel's policy proposals included 'the introduction of an improved system of husbandry' [farming] and a large-scale transfer of estates from insolvent to solvent proprietors.

Back from the political to the personal. The most singular feature of this bigamy case, explained Mr Piggott (prosecuting) was that Desbury, after his alleged second 'marriage' lived with both women, pretending that his first wife was actually his cousin's wife. The Judge clarified for the Jury that a lawful spouse could not appear in court to give evidence for or against the partner – 'hence the difficulty of the case.'[15]

Thus Eleanor could not be called as a witness, even in terms of mitigating factors. Whether she wished to or not, she could not be there to help her Adolphus to swim – or to sink him, Maria Margaret's 'Henry'. Evidence from other people would therefore be crucial to the case against the defendant.

'PARADISE LOST'

John Milton's epic work *Paradise Lost* is regarded by many as the greatest English language poem ever written. He wrote this challenging blank verse (published in 1667) at home in Artillery Row, which subsequently became Bunhill Row. His purpose was to 'justify the ways of God to men.' Reflect on the feelings of Adam and Eve in the Garden of Eden: pleasure, lust, temptation and guilt. Back into a true story of similar emotions came the mother-in-law of 'Henry', Hannah Hampton, caught up indirectly in his sinning. She travelled west in March 1849 from her Bunhill Row home, angry and sad for her daughter. Nervous yet determined to give evidence, as was one of her sons, Reuben. They would identify Henry as Adolphus.

Several newspapers mistakenly reported that Hannah had been present at the marriage of her daughter Eleanor with d'Escury, but the *Gloucester Journal* on 31 March 1849 presented a different, credible account with quotes from the prisoner and witnesses. Hannah identified the prisoner as her son-in-law, saying he was 'very much altered, but appears to be the most like him of any one man I have seen. I have not seen him for twelve months. His hair was curled then.' Laughter in court. The prisoner asked if she had been present when her daughter was married (this was Desbury being crafty, because he knew the answer). 'No,' said Hannah. Prisoner, 'Then you have only hearsay that your daughter was married?' Hannah retorted, 'I know a gentleman named Desbury took my daughter away to marry her.' Confusing for the reader perhaps – but think. Hannah may have said, 'd'Escury' – the surname on the marriage certificate of the man who had married Hannah's daughter, Eleanor, in 1844.

Reuben wasn't going to put up with any more of his brother-in-law's nonsense and deposed that he knew the man perfectly well from five years ago and received French lessons from him about two years ago. Positive as to the prisoner's identity? Yes, he 'had lost his left arm, and wore a false one'.[16]

Reuben added that the second 'wife' had been fully cognisant of the fact that his sister (Reuben's sister, Eleanor, the first wife) slept with the prisoner. The latter 'with great ingenuity, examined this witness with the view of shaking his testimony as to his identity'.[17]

However, Reuben's fury fuelled his insistence – and he shook not.

The wind was further taken out of Adolphus/Henry's sails by Mr William Smith of Remington Street, City Road, London, deposing that from November 1847 until May 1848 he lived in the same house as the prisoner, known to him as 'Adolphus d'Escury'. Smith knew the second 'wife' – and she was not the woman who had lived in that house in London.

A confusing case – but building up relentlessly against the accused. A serious situation for Henry/Adolphus because, if found guilty, almost certainly he would get another prison sentence.

Henry claimed he was mistaken for his cousin d'Escury – whose name and pupils he had taken on – but then admitted that he 'represented' himself as his cousin. One local reporter gave the prisoner's explanation that 'his cousin was a man of the same shade of colour as himself, and hence the mistake which he alleged had arisen in his identity'.[18]

'AN EBONY ADONIS'

Further north, the *Durham Advertiser* used an eye-catching headline on 13 April 1849. 'An ebony Adonis' showed the attention gained by Henry Desbury, 'a black man'.

On the same page, a report from a separate court case with insulting, patronising jibes about some of the onlookers:

'There was one blot. The presence of ladies on such an occasion is a scandal to the sex. We can have little respect for women, of what condition soever they be, who suffer a morbid appetite for excitement to overcome all their better and gentler feelings. They certainly have no business in criminal courts, and if a sense of delicacy does not deter them from seeking amusement in such places, we think some regulation should be adopted to prevent their admission.'

Newspapers continued over the decades to make similar disparaging and demeaning statements about women attending court cases – and to recommend control. The same forms of prejudice reared up in 1886 during the trial of Adelaide Bartlett in the Pimlico Mystery.

Chapter 3

'DESDEMONA TO THE MOOR' – MARIA MARGARET BEARCOCK

Desbury's lawful wife Eleanor had become invisible in the eyes of the world, air-brushed out by reason of her very lawfulness. Not allowed to appear in court, ironically, in that she was 'the wife'; not permitted to speak out, declare her status and her side of the story. In this case of alleged bigamy by her law-breaking, 'lawful' husband, humiliated Eleanor had no say.

As already stated, bigamy was, and is, deemed a serious crime in many countries.[19]

On 5 April 1849, the *Cheltenham Chronicle* waxed lyrical about Desbury's 'wife' – but she was not his lawful wife. He still had one of those: Eleanor.

The press cast Maria Margaret as 'Desdemona to the Moor'. This was an apt reference to Shakespeare's play *Othello*, (*The Tragedy of Othello, the Moor of Venice*) with its story of a Moorish general and Iago, his disloyal ensign, and of Desdemona, a Venetian beauty. She elopes with Othello, a man several years her senior; Iago manipulates Othello (now her husband) into believing that she is an adulteress. In the last act, Desdemona is murdered by her estranged spouse, Othello. Clearly, some of its enduring themes, jealousy, racism and love, were well-evident in the Gloucestershire courtroom.[20]

Now to travel back through time and up country lanes to Chatteris, a village in Cambridgeshire, England. Here Maria Margaret had been born in the mid or late 1820s and baptised in 1829. Said to be fifteen and a family servant, by 1841 she was living at Mill End in Chatteris. By the end of 1847, she had left her home village and headed south. It is not known how and why she moved to London (probably the place in which she first encountered 'Henry') but of course millions of people headed to the capital. In the 'Hungry Forties' (a time of potato blight and other food shortages) she, like Eleanor, moved from a rural to an urban life.

A leap into the unknown. And she could never have envisaged the contrasts she was to experience.

HURTS

Maria Margaret's plight in 1848 as a severely injured young woman drew graphic reporting of her being on the receiving end of Henry Desbury's extreme violence. His use of humour in court, and inappropriate appreciation of it by some of his audience, leapt out from the page. Laughter erupted – rather than murmurs of sympathy for the victim. Maria Margaret Bearcock in 1848 and 1849 and also Henry's real mother-in-law, Hannah Hampton, were two of only three or four women in the court, with the men giving free rein to their dominating behaviour and imagined superiority.

'JUST AS BLACK AT ONE TIME AS ANOTHER'

Henry Desbury, described as 'a foreigner, a handsome man of colour ... well dressed, and his demeanour ... subdued and graceful', used humour, ridicule and bombast, perhaps attempting to soften the prejudice against him in court. 'The prisoner said his face was just as black at one time as another'. Laughter ensued. 'I am quite sure, my Lord, that any person who sees me today, will know me next year.'[21]

He thought it very strange that the witness, Mr Facey, parish clerk of St

Luke's Church, Finsbury (who had witnessed the wedding of Adolphus and Eleanor) had not been able to identify Henry (real name Adolphus) when he, Mr Facey, had been taken to peer through the bars in the prisoner's door prior to court. But now Facey felt sure that this man with the black face was the bridegroom that day back in 1844. Facey opened up the Parish Register and showed the Court a Register of Marriage containing the lawful wedding entry.

Next in evidence came a record of a 'marriage' between Henry and Maria Margaret on 25 January 1848 at St Peter's Church, Islington, London. It was shown to the court by Mr Mayer, parish clerk. Henry had dishonestly declared himself to be a 'bachelor' with the rank of 'Lieutenant RN' [Royal Navy]. Maria Margaret was the daughter of John Bearcock, a scrap and iron founder.

'I FREELY FORGIVE MR DESBURY THE INJURY HE HAS DONE ME'

Maria Margaret 'recommended the prisoner to mercy' … 'My Lord, I hope you will not put many questions, for I freely forgive Mr Desbury the injury he has done me.'

Her hope was met, the Prosecutor only wanting to ask one question:

'You were married to the prisoner?'
'I was.'
Thereby lies the rub … they had 'married' – but unlawfully.

'DID SHE ATTEMPT TO UNDECEIVE YOU?'

Questioned by the prisoner, she replied that she went to the first wife, 'Mrs D'Escurie', who informed her that the prisoner was 'single'. He asked now about the alleged first wife: 'Did she attempt to undeceive you, that she was my wife?' To which Maria Margaret replied: 'She always said she was your cousin's wife.' Prisoner: 'Did she know that you were my wife?' Maria Margaret: 'Yes.'

'FOR HER PRETTY FACE ALONE'

The Judge, steering away from obfuscation (names, relationships, lawful and unlawful wives) towards the nub of the matter (a possible motive) asked if Maria Margaret had any fortune. 'None of any consequence,' was her reply. Some people in court laughed. Henry begged his Lordship's pardon, he had forgotten to say that she had no fortune – and thanked the Judge for asking the question. He had taken her 'for her pretty face alone, and nothing else'. Surely people laughed again ...[22]

The prisoner continued: he had requested the case postponement at the last Assizes, hoping that his first wife might be allowed to give evidence (even though he knew she could not, as it was against the law). He wanted witnesses from France but had received no answers to his letters.

After trying to place doubt in the minds of the Jurymen by ridiculing the evidence of Reuben, his brother-in-law, now Desbury put blame at the door of his very own (lawful) wife:

'Was it possible to believe that a wife with three children would allow her husband to bring a poor girl to her very house and live with her as his wife! If there had been any fortune, a wife might be as wicked as her husband and, in the expectation of sharing it, hold her tongue.'

He was slandering Eleanor. By law she – being the wife – was not allowed to be there to refute his accusations.

She had given birth to their daughter while Henry was in prison for the attack upon Maria Margaret. Sneeringly, he was voicing allegations against Eleanor, his lawful wife and suggesting that she was equally at fault. By referring to Maria Margaret as 'poor' and using the word 'fortune' again, he was suggesting that his real wife had kept silent in case she could benefit from said fortune!

The likely truth was that he exerted control (what is now termed coercive control) over both women. In his world, just one person mattered: 'Henry Desbury'.

CONFUSION

The Judge summed up and instructed the Jury that the only question was the identity of the prisoner. They soon returned a 'guilty' verdict.

Reuben Hampton, still furious about the prisoner's treatment of Eleanor, stood up for his absent sister. He asked the Judge if he could be allowed to say something about the second wife (Mary Margaret). She had not slept in the prisoner's house and 'she had seen the first wife and the prisoner go to bed. The prisoner had introduced the second wife to him as his cousin. By some means the first wife found out there was a connection between them, and got jealous, and then the second wife went away'. Unpicking this: the prisoner pretended to Reuben that Maria Margaret was his, the prisoner's, cousin and that there had been 'a connection' – implying sexual intercourse – between the prisoner and Maria Margaret. Quite rightly, Reuben had put the blame back onto Henry Desbury (known to Reuben as Adolphus d'Escury) for lying to both women.

Confusion all round, the arguments circulate; the Judge asked the prisoner if he had anything to say as to why sentence should not be passed. According to numerous papers, of course this voluble prisoner took up this opportunity. 'I can't say I am guilty, my Lord; I need not say, before God, I am not guilty.' At this the Judge had had more than enough of the man and 'said he was afraid if the prisoner did [say more], he would add to his offence. He could not entertain a doubt that the prisoner was guilty'.

'A MITIGATING FACTOR'

Irritation had surfaced but, thank goodness, there was not much more business to do. 'The Judge explained to the Jury that a mitigating factor in the case was that Maria Margaret knew of 'the first wife' and thus was not a woman misled into 'marriage'.

Henry's sentence for bigamy was therefore shorter than usual: six months' imprisonment.[23] No one mentioned it at court but Eleanor, the lawful wife, had been pregnant again during the summer of 1848.

Did anyone support Maria Margaret before and after the two court cases at which she gave evidence, and where could she go after such ordeals?

Her 'marriage' to 'Henry Desbury' having been declared void, one might assume that this severely injured and misused woman disappeared from his life, got well away before his release from the county gaol, Gloucester, in late 1849.

Going on to have two children, her life continued to be one of stark contrasts: strong sunshine and dark clouds.

Chapter 4

CHAMBERLAINS, NEWALLS – AND YOUNG HENRY
WILLIAM DESBURY

What did Adolphus Henry get up to after his release from prison? The 1851 England Census (Sunday 30 March) shows no trace of him – other than indirectly. Head of the household: 'Helen C De Thouars d'Escury' the 'Wife of Professor of Mathematics and Languages', living at 58 Bath Street (a very short walk from her parents' home in the adjoining Bunhill Row) in the Borough of Finsbury. With 'Helen' were Rudolphus – five, Walter – four, Helena – two and Modestus, just one month. Eleanor/Helen had been pregnant with Helena in June 1848 (living with her husband and their sons in Leckhampton, Gloucestershire) when he attacked Maria Margaret.

So on Census day, Adolphus/Henry was elsewhere – either having separated from his wife or perhaps working away from home.

After personal crises for so many people, suffering through the national and international depression of the hungry 1840s, there was in London (for some) a welcome distraction. A huge event symbolising power, change and hope. The Great Exhibition of the Works of Industry of All Nations, usually referred to just as the Great Exhibition, opened on 1 May 1851 in the glistening, gigantic Crystal Palace, erected in Hyde Park, London. It was to bring the world to the capital of England, to the city some thought of as the centre of the world. An international event with some 100,000 objects. To view them all would take visitors on a walk of ten miles – if they had the stamina and attention to see everything on display. Culture and industry were showcased and celebrated on the huge site; so much endeavour had gone into such a short period of time.

The Great Exhibition was proposed by Henry Cole, a polymath by all accounts: public servant, arts patron, educator; commissioner of the artwork for the first commercial Christmas cards, involved in the introduction of the stamp and the Penny Post – just some of his staggering range of interests and achievements. And Cole was yet another person with another name, his scale of living so extensive that it overflowed into a pseudonym, to contain his additional roles. As a writer he was 'Felix Summerly' and one of his designs was a teapot. From the small and personal to massive projects, this was some human being.

'WE MUST HAVE STEAM, GET COLE'

Cole's drive, creativity and interest in industrial design led to the realisation of the Great Exhibition. He headed its planning with Prince Albert, who was having an increasingly influential role behind the throne and hence around the empire. They had a Committee including many of the era's great British men (no women): Wellington, Peel, Gladstone and Cobbett. The Prince had not been popular prior to this, but the Great Exhibition was hugely impressive and a financial success. The surplus money went towards science and arts development and education, primarily the South Kensington institutions which expanded over a large area just south of Hyde Park. Cole's brilliance was highly valued by the prince, who made an apt pun when the project needed impetus: 'We must have steam, get Cole.'[24]

Apart from Queen Victoria, who opened the Great Exhibition and visited several times, Charlotte Bronte who went twice, an old woman who allegedly walked all the way from Cornwall to be there, and the millions of women who visited, history hardly mentions the women who must have been involved in providing this spectacle. Involved with the materials being fashioned into exhibits; among the people labouring in many countries, including France, North America, Russia, India and China and, of course, Britain. Thousands and thousands of people toiled, sweated and put care into tiny and huge exhibits which were then carefully taken out of workplaces, across seas and rough roads before their assembly into wonders of the world.

Massive crowds flocked to the Great Exhibition over the six months; six million people paid to visit, with a peak attendance of almost 110,000 on 7 October. Tempting to speculate if any of the people in the family stories mentioned here were able to experience the first and only truly spectacular event of such scale and complexity in London.

Some of the Chamberlains (more on them later) could afford to wander among the wonders. No joy in a different family: in September 1851 Eleanor and Adolphus' youngest child, baby Modestus Felix, died.

In Britain, the pride and passion evident around the Great Exhibition made it a high point for the fortunate, after the deprivation, upheaval and uncertainties of the Hungry Forties. But the 1850s soon saw a return to instability – and engagement in a war which led to soul-searching and reform.

ANOTHER MARRIAGE, ANOTHER BIRTH (BUT NOT AS ONE MIGHT EXPECT)

One decade over, on to the next – and freedom from prison for Henry. Perhaps the relationship between Henry and Maria Margaret resumed immediately. Either she 'freely forgave' Henry senior for his attack on her (as she told the court) – and for the illegal 'marriage' – or was persuaded into what was then called 'connection'. Another possibility is that he had her under 'coercive control'. Whatever, she gave birth in the summer of 1853 in London to their son, Henry William Desbury. Or, a thought: this one was not Henry's child?

And into the frame, only months before Maria Margaret gave birth, comes yet another young wife or 'wife' for Adolphus/Henry Desbury. In January 1853, Clara Chamberlain wed 'Adolphe'.

INTRODUCING THE CHAMBERLAINS

Susannah Aynsley, child of Mary and John, was sixteen and thus a minor when she married William Robinson Chamberlain at Hornsey Rise, Islington, London, in 1822. By 1841 William was a 'stockbroker', living with Susannah in the parish of St Mary, in the Borough of Finsbury.

Their children included William (born in 1823; more will be heard of him in 1875 and after) and Clara, born in 1834, who went on to become a teacher and beloved mother. The Chamberlains come across as a well-to-do, steady-state, comfortably-off family, enjoying life in 1851 in a desirable area, with neighbours of similar status. William Robinson Chamberlain and son William travelled south each day to their work in the City of London. Susannah ran her own school, employing Clara as an assistant. Conveniently, classrooms were in the Chamberlain's home and the adjoining building. At some stage, Clara learnt French from her mother and from Adolphe, and would go on to teach the language.

Henry Turner lodged there. Born in Sierra Leone, West Africa, a clerk to a timber merchant. Entertain the possibility that he was 'Henry de Thouars', his surname wrongly given (or misheard by the enumerator). By 1851, Clara Chamberlain may have known 'Adolphe' and was learning about Adolphus/Henry Desbury/Henry Turner?/Adolphe, this character who was fluent in French and spoke in articulate but 'broken' English.

Unlikely that he was born as Henry Desbury – and perhaps not born as Adolphus either.

CLARA AND ADOLPHE

On 19 January 1853 as 'Adolphe Collot De Thouars D'Escury', this charming older man wed Clara, nineteen, at Saint Leonard's, Shoreditch, London. Her mother Susannah was one of the witnesses. The Chamberlains, solidly middle-class people, still gainfully employed, now lived in select Southgate Road, De Beauvoir Town, Hackney. Clara's father was recorded as a 'Clerk at the Stock Exchange', Adolphe's father as Adolphe 'Duke of [sic] De Thouars'. Perhaps the Chamberlains felt that their Clara was marrying 'up', wedding the son of a foreign 'Duke'. Her bridegroom described himself as a thirty-five-year-old 'Pensioned naval officer in the French service', a widower. No profession was entered on Clara's marriage certificate; she continued as a school assistant.

So this mysterious time-travelling man, declarer to courts in 1848 that he was forty-one, became 'thirty-five' in 1853. Perhaps 'Adolphe' knew whether he was coming or going. The women in his life (and were there even more by now?) may have been unaware of his punished and unpunished complications – or put up with them. Odds-on they found him intriguing, with his otherness, his 'exceedingly dark complexion', foreign accent, flamboyance, intelligence, panache and humour. Frightening? Cutting words and blows? This complex fellow with a false arm, severe injuries to his body: did he suffer from physical discomfort and mental torment on top of everything else?

The year of 1853 may have been tricky for Adolphe to navigate but it is not fanciful to think he relished the challenge of intrigue and subterfuge. Changing names and ages, charming and bamboozling women. Where was all this heading?

MYSTIFICATION

He had married Clara in January 1853; in July his son, Henry William Desbury, was born to Maria Margaret in west London. His devious behaviour towards Eleanor, Maria Margaret and Clara leads to unanswered questions:

- Had Eleanor died before Clara's marriage, between the 1851 Census and January 1853? If not, Henry/Adolphe was breaking the bigamy law – again.
- Did Maria Margaret, pregnant with Henry Desbury's child, know of his marriage on the other side of London in January 1853 to Clara? The bridegroom was recorded as 'Adolphe Collot de Thouars d'Escury'.
- Did Clara know of the birth of Henry/Adolphe's baby, Henry William Desbury, born in July 1853 to Maria Margaret? It feels inconceivable that Clara would know of the baby's baptism that October in Upper Chelsea, London. At the baptism: father – 'Henry', a 'Gentleman'; mother – Maria Margaret, their surname: Desbury. Baby Henry

William's father was married to Clara – but of course that did not have to be disclosed in church or anywhere else. And the previously married 'Henry' perhaps went between the families.

MECHANISATION

Personal upheavals for some family members – hopefully blissful ignorance for others. But from February 1853 the Crimean War[25] viscerally impacted on the British public, particularly as the spread of telegraph cable installation meant that they were being informed of events taking place thousands of miles away, on the continent. News came in about the realities of war, news at a speed and level of detail never possible before. The populace broadly supported this war – but after the fighting ended in October 1856 the war began to be seen as a failure. After deep reflection, Army reform was demanded – Britain having much to learn about building up and maintaining an effective fighting force.

The industrialised world was changing on all fronts: electrical telegraphy, rail and shipping innovations all had the effect of shrinking, expanding and speeding it up; photography was capturing and revealing it; mechanisation kept forging on with the production of goods, including weaponry. Some people, more people than ever before, including those from the families already mentioned, could go somewhere, either in their own countries or by taking to the high seas. But family members also passed away: Eleanor's father in 1853 and her mother in 1856. Dependant children's lives in all parts of the family were being affected by the illnesses and deaths of adults.

Adolphe's death (of which more later) in 1860 led to even more falling apart. By 1861, Maria Margaret and her young son were living who knows where.

INTRODUCING THE NEWALLS

The *London Gazette* on 10 March 1868 contained belated news from the India Office:

David John Falconer Newall gained promotion in July 1867, moving from the Royal (Bengal) Artillery to be a Major in the Bengal Infantry.

A PROPER MARRIAGE

In October 1868 in London, a certain Maria Margaret, surname 'Desbury' (describing herself as a 'widow', of 48 Norland Square, Notting Hill) married Lieutenant-Colonel David John Falconer Newall (a bachelor living in Jermyn Street) of the Royal Artillery. For him: changes of regiments, rank and now marital status; for Maria Margaret, lifestyle changes on many fronts. Did she know whether Henry/Adolphe was alive or dead? Did she ever talk with David about her previous life? He offered her such a different way of life. Such contrasts between the humiliation and loss she had experienced – through involvement with Henry Desbury – and the life she might now have with an army officer who was steadily going up through the ranks.

Successful and financially secure, he signalled dependability, someone who could be a devoted, attentive husband, taking her into his world of foreign travel. Dangers yes, but pleasures too. Newall, born in 1825 in London, experienced privilege but also the separations which careers brought. His father's career in shipping culminated in a lofty position as a Commander in the incredibly powerful East India Company, which functioned as an agent for the British Crown. Often known as simply 'The Company', it had seized control over huge areas of the Indian subcontinent and Southeast Asia, trading in commodities including tea, cotton, salt and opium. Tea, cotton, salt: seemingly such simple substances yet crucial in trade. (And tea figured centrally in the working life of Edwin Bartlett; more about this later.) The Company, long involved in the circles of trade and politics, politics and trade, had private armies and a navy, totalling over

260,000 men. It came to rule much of India.[26]

It was not at all unusual for an army man, a man of the Raj, to wait until his thirties or forties to marry. David Newall's career, rooted in India from the age of nineteen, was all action on behalf of the British. His military postings in the Royal (Bengal) Artillery involved extensive travel; as with many people who experience the magic and misery of India he was soon hooked, developing a deep love of the country.

In the context of the domination of the East India Company and its army, understandable resentment festered in the indigenous population. In 1857, sepoys (infantry soldiers) had great cause to protest against their conditions and the Indian First War of Independence (in the past, called the Indian Rebellion) took place. The British Government took deadly action; after the bloodshed there was a tightening of control and the declaration of the 'Raj', a word taken from Sanskrit and Hindustani and meaning 'rule'. British systems were imposed on 'British India' and in addition those areas ruled by indigenous leaders were put under British paramountcy. And the entire, huge country became known by the British as their 'Indian Empire'. They did not 'know' it - and imagine the impositions made by the British upon millions of indigenous people.

On 1 November 1858, Queen Victoria's Proclamation was read out in cities and towns across India. 'We have resolved to take upon ourselves the Government of India, heretofore administered in trust for us by the Honourable East India Company.' The navy and private armies of The Company were absorbed into the government machinery. The regime and some systems changed, but Indians were put under even more controls than they had been.

It was ten years later that Newall, on leave from his duties in India, married the woman once described in newspapers (after her humiliating court appearance as key witness) as 'Desdemona to the Moor'.

It is likely that west London was the meeting place of Maria Margaret and David. Unlikely bedfellows, but hopefully a harmonious combination. However, at the time of their marriage there was the matter of her fifteen-year-old child, fathered (presumably) by 'Henry Desbury'.

Seventeen-year-old 'Harry Desbury' was probably Henry William, attending Great Ealing School, Middlesex in 1871; 'Harry', surrounded in his classrooms by many pupils from far afield, including Ireland, France, India and Nicaragua. Founded in 1698, in its nineteenth-century heyday this now-unsung school was as famous as Eton and Harrow and, like all the illustrious schools then, was only for boys. When Henry William threw himself into serious trouble years later, it was said that he'd had a college education – and so this private school would 'fit' the bill.

Maria Margaret, mother of Henry William, had a daughter in 1872. By the following year she, husband David and baby were together in Darjeeling, a town in the Lesser Himalayas of north-eastern India. Ah, Darjeeling! A word known by many in terms of tea production and drinking. Why did they go to Darjeeling? A small town with steep-roofed, balconied houses, it was a favourite hill station since the days of the East India Company. Situated at almost 8,000 feet above sea level, up to it went those who could afford the bliss of cooler air.

'In practice, this meant the women and children, with the men escaping from the scalding heat of the plains for a brief week or two when they could'.[27]

Catherine Falconer Newall was baptised in Darjeeling in 1873. It is, of course, feasible that Henry William (young 'Harry'?) visited them in India.

In 1876, India became part of the British Empire, the largest empire in the world. Queen Victoria was the self-styled Empress; large parts of the country had been called British India since the seventeenth century (shackling it until Partition and the coming of the so-called 'free' India in 1947).

Newall was able to retire and as Major General he had his title and full-pay pension from 1878 for life. Now he could continue writing, in England, about the beloved India. His books showed not only his eagerness to learn about the legends and habitats of the country, but also his strategic thinking as a proponent of the military colonisation of the Indian highlands.

In 1881, Henry William Desbury, twenty-seven, a visitor with no occupation, was in the parish of Doddington, North Witchford, Cambridgeshire. Just five miles from Chatteris, the birthplace of his mother, Maria Margaret.

When Maria Margaret and her husband David eventually left India for England they lived at the impressive residence named Beldornie Tower (now a Grade II listed building) on the Isle of Wight, a few miles off the south coast. Just outside the town of Ryde, its garden separated from the waves by just a low wall, the house faces out across the waters of the Solent to mainland Hampshire. Sadly, Maria Margaret died on 31 January 1886. Said to be fifty-six, she may have been nearer sixty.

Hopefully, during that last January of her life she did not hear the shocking news of an incredible link: that between her difficult past and the sudden ending of a life in London. On the first day of January: the life and death of a Mr Edwin Bartlett.

Equally hopefully, the second half of her life was far, far happier than the first – although it is certain that the behaviour of her only son, Henry William, was a tremendous worry to her and to David Newall. Doubtless the widower heard plenty about his errant stepson after Maria Margaret's death. David died in 1901.[28]

Chapter 5

HENRY WILLIAM DESBURY: OLDER, NOT WISER

'SQUANDERED'

Had Henry William's father 'Henry Desbury' spent time with him and Maria Margaret – or was she a single parent? From 1868 (when Maria Margaret married Newall) young Henry William would have had material privileges and advantages that most people did not – but whether he was ever secure as an adult, in himself and in relationships, is highly doubtful.

MR PARTRIDGE, MAGISTRATE

In 1889, of mature age (mid 30s) Henry William admitted: 'I have lived a good deal with my mother and stepfather … at Beldornie Tower, Ryde, but my mother is dead, and having squandered all my money, I am reduced to beggary.' When the magistrate, Mr Partridge, there at Westminster Police Court in central London, asked him why he had not gone to the casual ward or workhouse, his reply was, 'I know nothing of those sort of places.' Immediately, Henry William's wish for a roof over his head was granted: he was remanded in custody.[29]

PIMLICO

Mr Partridge was the magistrate before whom Adelaide Bartlett and a certain young George Dyson stood in the same court just three years before, in February 1886. Henry William committed his offence just a short walk from where Adelaide had lived with her husband in Claverton Street, Pimlico.

He was produced on remand on 11 February 1889. The next day, the *Southern Echo*, '*An Evening Paper for Hants, Wilts and Dorset*' (English counties) stated that Major General Newall's stepson, Henry William Desbury, thirty-five, threw stones to break a house window in Pimlico. This was a public, embarrassing disclosure of the link between the 'prodigal son' and the Major General. No mention was made of the late father, 'Henry Desbury' but the contrasts are stark between the criminal behaviour of the two Henrys (father and son) and the upstanding army officer, David Newall, stepfather.

'RESULT OF EARLY PRODIGALITY'

This was the headline about Henry William in several newspapers including the *Gloucester Journal*, from the city of his father Henry's incarcerations.[30]

Desbury, shabbily dressed, homeless and destitute, caused damage in order to be taken into custody, breaking windows at the residence of a Mr Crawford, to whom he was 'a perfect stranger'. Presumably one had to offend against a good class of person, break huge, expensive windows of properties in the most prestigious streets, in order to be certain of prosecution. Henry William said he was 'brought up a gentleman', wasted his fortune, was 'discarded' by his stepfather and reduced to staying in 'common lodging-houses, and walking the streets without even being able to afford that shelter'. Before being locked up he spent 'three days and nights wandering about starving'.

The Court was told that several gentlemen asked about him after his initial remand and 'one stated that he was at college with him five years ago, when he appeared extremely well off, and spent his money lavishly'. A solicitor from Ryde attended on behalf of the Newall family, who proposed 'to make a small allowance until [Henry William] obtained some employment … Far from being discarded by his stepfather, he had been shown the greatest kindness'.

The family heard from Henry William just twice after the death of his mother (Maria Margaret, three years before) and Newall let it be known that he had no inkling of his stepson's 'abject destitution' during those years.

Mr Partridge was forming a very dim view of Henry William. 'He seems to have brought it on himself entirely. I shall bind him over in the sum of £30 to appear if called upon.' Henry William left the court with friends.

There was a similar report in the *Isle of Wight Times*[31] – with a headline Newall must have hated:

'THE CASE OF THE REDUCED GENTLEMAN'
The criminal behaviour of his stepson – a man, not a mere boy: a worry and an annoyance for the widower at splendid Beldornie Tower …

MINIOTA, CANADA
Henry William was soon helped to emigrate to Canada. The *Winnipeg Free Press* on 1 November 1890 announced new arrivees in town, including Desbury from Beulah (over 200 miles away, a small place in rural Miniota municipality in Manitoba province) and the retired 'General Newall' (from England) at the Queen's Hotel. Harry Newall, probably a relative of theirs, had become 'mentally unbalanced' and the retired 'General' was needed

in Canada to assist. In which case he had not only his stepson but also the relative to worry about.

Henry William returned to England and to many years of committing his usual offences, stuck in the cycle of unemployment, poverty, criminal damage, police cells, prisons, workhouses … round and round, in and out …

'IN SEARCH OF REST'

This was the headline in 1900, quoting Desbury at court for damaging windows in Belgravia, a select area of central London.[32]

He made sure he spent that Christmas and New Year at Southwark Workhouse. 'Calling: Nil' [i.e. no occupation] age: forty-seven, single; admitted on 15 December and discharged in January.

'IGNORANT OF WORK'

This was how a reporter described Henry William[33] (charged in May with his usual offence) whose 'allowance' had recently ceased. Obviously, the 'short-term' allowance from Newall in 1889 turned into a lengthy one: Newall had died just two months before, in March 1901.

Magistrate Mr Horace Smith, asking why Henry William caused the damage, got the reply, 'Because I have been wandering about destitute and homeless'. Then the magistrate questioned, or instructed him, 'But you could get work or go to the workhouse?' The accused: 'I know nothing about work or workhouses'.

That clinched it – made the magistrate's mind up as to what fitted the crime. 'You will have the experience now of a month's hard labour.'

In 1906, Henry William, age fifty-two, was sentenced to serve twenty-one months with hard labour and carted off to Wormwood Scrubs Prison in west London.

There is no mention of the 'demon drink' (alcohol) in the records kept about him, so alcohol may not have been one of his problems. But it is highly likely that he was the so-called 'William Henry' (as well as the Henry William) Desbury in and out of London workhouses, particularly Southwark and Saint Pancras, until at least 1913. His life must have been so very different from his hopes and from the family's expectations.

Chapter 6

RODOLPHUS HAMPTON D'ESCURY

(KNOWN AS RODOLPHE)

Back to the nineteenth century, to greet a new life. Rodolphus, Eleanor and Adolphus' first child, born on 5 September 1845, birth registered in the St Luke's district, Finchley. He was one of two little children in the house at Leckhampton that morning when their father threw a chamber pot and there was blood everywhere from that woman's head, and shouting and running ... then their father was taken away somewhere and not seen for a long, long time ...

By 1851, Rodolphus lived at 4 Bath Street with his parents, and three younger siblings. Sadly, the maternal grandparents, Robert and Hannah Hampton, nearby in Bunhill Row, died just a few years later.

'Rudolphus H D'Escury' made a successful passport application on 24 July 1860. Was that big step precipitated by the death of his father, just four months before? Or did he not have contact with his father – and whoever he was with? Rodolphus may have travelled to and from France with his parents and siblings when younger, but it is unlikely that a passport was needed for that. Now he had plans to use the precious passport he clutched in his hand.

Perhaps an orphan (as it is likely that his mother Eleanor had died by then) somehow he left London for Portsmouth, already a famous port on the south coast of England. On 25 March 1861 as 'Rodolphus Hampton' (new surname taken from his second forename, his mother's maiden name) he signed up. Rodolphus the Royal Naval seaman, age fifteen, volunteering for 'continuous service'.

ON BOARD THE VESSEL, *VICTORY*

In April 1861, 'Rodolphus Hampton' was one of many Boys' School apprentices on board the *Victory*, the enduringly famous Battle of Trafalgar vessel. By then it was only a flagship used for training and accommodation purposes, anchored out in Portsmouth Harbour, near Gosport town.

Thousands of miles west across the Atlantic, the American Civil War began on 12 April, breaking out when Confederate forces from the southern states attacked Fort Sumner in South Carolina. Seven slave states seceded and formed a new nation, the Confederate States of America. Just weeks after the Fort Sumner attack, four more slave states joined the Confederacy. This war was the culmination of many years of dispute, with deep disquiet over slavery and other stark contrasts. The gulf widening: economic expansion and diversification in the northern states, and the South continuing with immense investments in cotton crops and slaves – people who were primarily regarded as property.

Victorious in the 1860 election, Abraham Lincoln's[34] inauguration as President of the United States on 4 March 1861 was as the nation stood on the brink of war.

Behind the scenes, Lincoln's routine use of blue pills made from mercury chloride had been a worry to some of his inner circle. It was thought that he started taking them to try to shift his constipation and/or depression but the little blue pills changed his behaviour. Violent rages and mood swings: Abraham Lincoln in the metaphorical 'Cave of Gloom' as his colleague on the law circuit, Henry Clay Whitney, described him. Fortunately most of the effects of mercury poisoning are reversible – and it is thought that Lincoln stopped taking the tablets around the start of the war.[35]

ON BOARD THE *AMERICAN EAGLE*

Adding a year to his age, saying he was eighteen, 'Rudolph De Thoures' joined the American Civil War.

He enlisted on 10 September 1862 at Smithtown, having arrived in New York just the previous day. As passenger 'Rodolphe d Thouars' (a clerk who declared himself French-born) he had left London on the *American Eagle*. His birthday – age not mentioned to those around him? – occurred somewhere on the North Atlantic Ocean.

Although this may be a story of an adolescent with a mission, embarking alone on a long journey to a far-off land to fight in a war, there is the possibility that Rodolphe, just seventeen, went into New York seeking work – and got tricked into signing up for the Union cause.

Such was the fate of many, including a German, Joseph Klein, who left his homeland in July 1862 and arrived at Long Island, New York, that September. He later stated he had not even known that there was a war on … Invited to go into the city, Klein was held under guard until he gave in and signed up for the army – thus he was deemed a 'volunteer'. Within twelve hours of setting foot on dry land he was put into the 'blue suit' as a Union soldier. Klein was one of the men who survived the war and he remained in the States for the rest of his life.

Whether a volunteer or coerced, the new recruit from England comes to life in the army description: 'Rudolph', said to have been born in France, a clerk, five feet two inches tall, of dark complexion with black hair and black eyes. Ten days after his enlistment he joined a fighting force, mustering in as a private on 20 September 1862 in the 131st New York Volunteer Infantry [the 131st], originally designated as the 1st Regiment of the Metropolitan Guards. He joined Company K which did much of its recruiting in Smithtown, a town in Suffolk County, New York, on the North Shore of Long Island. Rodolphe and his fellow soldiers came from all over the city and well beyond.[36]

In total, some 50,000 British subjects travelled west across the vast ocean to join the fighting in this war. Both sides recruited from their number and some soldiers would have received bounties for signing up. Money which Rodolphe, for one, probably desperately needed on arrival.

Ironically, African Americans were not allowed to join the Union Army as soldiers until 1863 – and for their troubles were paid lower wages than others. It was not until September 1864 that black soldiers received equal pay.

Huge battles were fought from 1862, with large numbers of deaths from disease and injury. In May of that year, Confederate General 'Stonewall' Jackson and his men took 15,000 boxes of chloroform from the enemies' medical supplies. In 1863, he was anaesthetised with chloroform before his left arm was amputated; he had been shot accidentally by one of his own men at Chancellorsville, Virginia. 'What an infinite blessing,' he said of chloroform, later describing its effect as the 'most delightful physical sensation' he had ever experienced.[37]

'Whether they hailed from farm or city, most Civil War soldiers quickly learned that life in camp was rough, dirty and filled with hardships. Even men accustomed to physical labor found their endurance sorely taxed by long marches, inadequate rations and the discomforts of life in the open.'

James E McBeth, 2nd Lieutenant, Company G of the 131st, gave a first-hand account in a letter home.

'We have marched over 500 miles in thirty-five days so you will see that we haven't been idle. The fact of the matter is that it is killing the men. The hospitals are beginning to fill up very rapidly. My constitution is slowly but surely becoming undermined.'[38]

By 1864 the original Northern aim, of a short war to restore the Union, evolved into planning for the destruction of the Old South – and its slavery – by 'total war'. The slaughter increased.

Then, after all the battles and bloodshed, by spring 1865 all the main Confederate armies had surrendered. When Union cavalrymen captured Jefferson Davis, the fast-retreating Confederate President, resistance collapsed. Most fighting ended that May; then came the collapse of the Confederacy and the beginning of the freeing of four million black slaves.

'ABSENT IN HOSPITAL'

Rodolphe was wounded in action on 27 May 1863 during 'the assault on Port Hudson', Louisiana; there is no record as to what happened to him between then and his being at Company K 'Guard House' somewhere in March and April 1864. By July 1865 he had been 'absent in hospital at Frederick Md since January 5/65', meaning he was in Frederick County, in Maryland, one of the border states between North and South. Frederick's towns had been alternately occupied by both sides, Union and Confederate, as they were at the very crossroads of the American Civil War and it became a major hospital centre. Rodolphe was a patient for six months until mustered out of the army in July 1865 at Savannah, Georgia. This is the official record at the end of young Rodolphe's war:

'DE THOURES, RUDOLPH – Age, eighteen years. Enlisted, September 10, 1862, at Smithtown, to serve three years; mustered in as private, Co. K, September 20, 1862; mustered out with company, July 26, 1865, at Savannah, Ga., as De Thouars; also borne as De Thuses.'[39]

OFFICIAL END

The conflict's official end came the following year, with Johnson's presidential proclamation on 20 August 1866 that 'peace, order, tranquillity and civil order now exist in and throughout the whole of the United States.'[40]

But after the bloodshed, the deaths, divisions and damage to minds, bodies and properties, the realities of life were starkly different. For years to come, deep-seated social issues which triggered the war were still evident – and still are today.

Many survivors never really recovered, as the story of Rodolphe will show. Over 600,000 people died in the war from diseases and the weapons of war. A soldier's chance of surviving the fighting was about one in four and of those who did survive, thousands upon thousands had serious, life-changing injuries.

However, at last Rodolphe and the survivors could return to their homes – if they had one. *His* home had been over three and a half thousand miles away, a journey of many weeks across the North Atlantic. He had only been in America for one day before he went to war.

Now, four and a half years later, the time had come to make a life somehow, somewhere. And to try to bear the pain of his wounded self.

Chapter 7

'DEEP SORROWS AND AFFLICTIONS'

In July 1869 in Manhattan, New York, Rodolphe married well.[41]

The bride was Julia M Harrison, born in 1848 in Kings County, Brooklyn, New York. Her father, James W Harrison, lived on Capitol Hill and had a position in the Government Printing House. No mothers were mentioned in any of the newspaper advertisements announcing such weddings.

Julia gave birth in Washington DC to Helene Caroline, in 1869 or early 1870. The baby's names indicate the regard Rodolphe felt for his (presumably deceased) mother, Eleanor Caroline (probably known as Helene Caroline).

A MARRIED MAN BUT SEPARATED

WASHINGTON DC, 7 August 1870. Rumours began to fly around the city that the previous afternoon a Frenchman of a noble family had committed suicide, shooting himself about an inch below the heart, using a Derringer pistol. He died about two hours later. Said to have been pensioned on account of wounds received in the Civil War, he was described as having been a married man but separated – and living with another woman. She was said to be the cause of the problem between him and his wife.

Rodolphe had been a translator at the Census Bureau, in downtown Washington.

His peacetime in the United States was short: he left the army in July 1865, began to receive a pension in 1869, died on Saturday, 6 August 1870.

The *New York Herald* (8 August) headlined his desperately sad end.

'SUICIDE OF ANOTHER DISTINGUISHED FRENCHMAN'

At 922 Eighth Street near the Washington DC Navy Yard lay a young man who had shot himself in the chest, who said to those rushing in at hearing the shot that he was 'weary of life'. He hoped to put an end to his troubles, which had been 'bitter and agonising' and told the shocked folk: 'I die by my own hand' … 'but I hope the Saviour in heaven will have pity on my soul in consideration of the deep sorrows and afflictions which have followed me'.

The report described his story as one 'that had been told a thousand times over – matrimonial infelicity and consequent infidelity on his part'. It was thought that the 'prompting cause' of his death was widely different from that of 'another distinguished Frenchman', a 'lamented' diplomat (name not given) whose story was known, apparently, to the readers.

And they were given more details about Rodolphe: he shot himself at 3 pm; shocked folk found 'blood splattered around plentifully. He was suffering dreadfully'.

Splashed all over the newspapers, Rodolphe's last letter read:

'WASHINGTON August 6, 1870

'I am going to die. I am sick in mind and body and I want the rest and peace which I pray God I may find in the grave. I hope and trust He will forgive me this last sin in consideration of the anguish which causes it. I have tried hard for the last twelve months to lead an honest, hard-working life for the sake of those I love, and might have succeeded better had I met with a little more kindness from those who ought not to have misunderstood me. I am not an ambassador of France and therefore cannot expect to go to my own native country to lie among the rest of my family, but must be buried as I die, in a strange country, friendless and alone. God bless my wife, baby, family and the few friends I have, and may He, in His infinite mercy, pity and forgive RODOLPHE COLLOT HENRI COMTE DE THOUARS D'ESCURY.

'PS. My earnest, heartfelt thanks to Mr JD Cox, Judge Otto, and to my dear friends, the Marquis de Chambrien and Ousterhe Collett. May God bless and reward them for their kindness and friendship to me. I should like to have them follow me to the grave, that I may not go alone like a dog. May God bless and protect those I love. Let my household furniture be sold, together with everything belonging to me, and the proceeds given to 'Petite'. I want James O'Connor to ask for and receive my month's salary, and give that also to her, for she will have lost her only friend when I die. My pension, if possible, I should like to go to my baby. My life is insured, and Jim O'Connor has my will.'

A GRACE STRONGER THAN HIS BITTERNESS
Look again at Rodolphe's suicide letter: even though he is facing imminent death by his own hand, his words are 'heartfelt' as he says. Crystal clear and eloquent, he seemed to display a grace stronger than his bitterness – bitterness felt through not receiving 'a little more kindness from those who ought not to have misunderstood'.

Why did Rodolphe write 'I am not an ambassador of France'? The use of the word 'ambassador' just seemed to be a reference to the contrast between his situation and that of a high-status representative of his country, whose body might be returned to France. In fact, the deep significance of his inclusion of the word 'ambassador' – and its relevance in terms of Rodolphe's life and death – becomes clearer as more news is uncovered about the deceased young man.

There were more sad twists in his tragic demise – and an actual connection with the French ambassador to the United States. Monsieur Lucien-Anatole Prévost-Paradol had died on 20 July 1870 in Washington – he shot himself the day before. Rodolphe killed himself less than a month later in the same city – in the same way. He thought of himself as a Frenchman, a compatriot of the ambassador.[42]

Details unfolded concerning Prévost-Paradol, a journalist and liberal who had become increasingly unpopular with the Republicans in France. After being installed as envoy in the States, a vote held thousands of miles away caused him great anguish: the Parliament in France voted to declare war on Prussia. Devastated, Prévost-Paradol shot himself on the first day of the Franco-Prussian War (also known as the Franco-German War).

Rodolphe had read all about it.

'THAT I MAY NOT GO ALONE, LIKE A DOG'

In his PS [postscript] Rodolphe gave 'earnest, heartfelt thanks to Mr JD Cox, Judge Otto, and to my dear friends the Marquis de Chambrien and Ousterhe Collett. I should like to have them follow me to the grave, that I may not go alone, like a dog. May God bless and preserve those I love.'

At first glance, the ramblings of a very troubled man, 'name-dropping' in desperation, leaving a mystery to be unravelled. Who were they and how did Rodolphe know them?

Firstly, 'Mr JD Cox': Jacob Dolson Cox, Secretary of the Interior, working for civil service reform in Washington. Summer 1870 was exceptionally hot in the eastern states; in Washington, tempers ran high among public servants. One of JD Cox's aims was to reduce paid-leave days; Rodolphe's 'thanks' to Cox suggest that he (unlike many colleagues) was in favour of the reforms. And he would have known of, admired Cox's war service as a great 'civilian' (no army background) Union general.[43]

Secondly, 'Judge Otto': William Tod Otto, a personal friend of Abraham Lincoln. When the president had lain dying after being shot by John Wilkes Booth on 14 April 1865, Otto was at Lincoln's bedside, holding his hand. The President died the following day. Otto was serving in the Interior Department at the time of Rodolphe's death in 1870.[44]

Thirdly, the 'Marquis de Chambrien' (the newspaper had spelt his name incorrectly): Charles Adolphe de Pineton, Marquis de Chambrun. A French lawyer, opposed to the new Empire in France, he arrived in Washington in early 1865.

His trajectory was such that, through his father-in-law knowing the radical politician Charles Sumner, Chambrun had a 'way in' to the White House. He swiftly joined the inner circle around Lincoln, the relationship helped by the fact that Mary Todd Lincoln, wife of the President, spoke fluent French. Shortly after Lincoln's death, Chambrun wrote an article in French about his recollections of the President, and later of Lincoln and the war.[45]

Fourthly, 'Ousterhe Collett' (a newspaper misspelling): Eustache/Eustace Collett, the artist who sketched two momentous scenes in the nation's history. He was there, a Frenchman, a private in the war, an artist sketching in April 1865. Firstly, General Robert E Lee on horseback, after signing the surrender of some Confederate forces; secondly the McLean House at Appomattox, a village in the State of Virginia typifying the slaveholding south. It was there that the surrender by General Lee had been accepted by General Ulysses S Grant on 9 April 1865.[46]

Fighting continued between some forces. Lincoln was succeeded in April 1865 by Andrew Johnson.

Washington, 1870. James O'Connor, 'Jim',[47] had Rodolphe's Will. Rodolphe had instructed him via the suicide letter to 'ask for and receive' the month's salary of the dead man and give the money to 'Petite'. Rodolphe had also specified that he wanted his furniture and belongings to be sold and the proceeds given to 'Petite'; she 'will have lost her only friend when I die'.

Rodolphe had insured his life and hoped that his pension would benefit his baby.

On 8 August 1870 the *New York Herald* maintained that after Rodolphe's wife left, he lived in his house with another woman – but 'surviving relatives of the deceased refuse to throw any light on the subject'. He had claimed that 'this woman was his sister and not his paramour'. Rodolphe, depicted as a 'Frenchman' who 'came to this country several years ago, and spoke English very fluently' was 'most accomplished and gentlemanly in his deportment'.

Of course, we know that he was fluent in English because he had been born and raised in London, leaving when he was sixteen. Like his father, Adolphus, he was articulate and 'accomplished'.

Rodolphe's Union Army service was mentioned in the newspaper; he 'served with great distinction, displaying on several occasions the most undaunted courage. For his bravery and general good conduct at Vicksburg he received a very unusual honor … a laudatory letter from General Grant himself. In 1868, he was president of the French Republican Club in New York, and worked zealously for the election of General Grant'.

In Washington, recommended by Senator Fenton, Rodolphe obtained a post in the Pension Office. 'Getting into some difficulty with a fellow employee there' he left for New York. Whether or not there was a work 'difficulty', surely the person Rodolphe referred to as 'Petite' was his 'paramour' – whom Rodolphe perhaps lived with in New York.

His final return to Washington was six months prior to his death.

'CAN YOU ADVANCE ME FOURTEEN DOLLARS NOW?'

A friend of the Marquis de Chambrun recommended Rodolphe, and the Marquis took him on as a secretary. On the fateful Saturday, Rodolphe had aimed to return at 5 a.m to do some work. But it was noon when he arrived, apparently very excited. The Marquis saw him reading an article about 'capital punishment' in a French magazine, the *Revue des Deux Mondes*.[48]

Asked by Chambrun as to why he was late, he replied that he felt unwell, but would do the work presently. The Marquis suggested Rodolphe return next day; he promised to do so and (according to many newspapers) asked the Marquis, 'Can you advance me fourteen dollars now? I want it particularly, and will return it at the end of the month'. Not having the full amount on him, the Marquis gave him ten dollars, and Rodolphe left the office.

The next heard of him was that he had shot himself dead. Understandably, the Marquis felt terribly shocked and saddened.

In addition to his suicide note, Rodolphe left another letter. It is startling to see that it was written almost two months before his death. He had not sent it. Stark in its sadness, it reads:

'WASHINGTON D.C. June 17, 1870.
'DEAR MR DE CHAMBRUN – When you will have received this letter I will be dead. I think that you have some friendship for me; certainly I have much for you. I beg, therefore, that you will lend my poor wife sufficient money to have me interred. My wife can repay you and earn enough to support herself and my child. Adieu to your wife and yourself.

RODOLPHE COLLET HENRI,
COMTE DE THOUARS D'ESCURY.
'Lend also to Madame de Doré sufficient to enable her to return to New York and support her there some weeks. My wife will return it to you and I will be most grateful.'

On the envelope he had written that the letter was to be 'given by the Marquis the day after my death to my wife, Julia'.[49]

'THE PARADOL TRAGEDY REVIVED THE GLOOMY RESOLUTION'

Methodical and precise in his instructions to his boss, it is obvious that Rodolphe had contemplated the act of suicide for at least some weeks before even Ambassador Prévost-Paradol's suicide.

But 'he did not carry it [the idea] into effect and probably abandoned it until the Paradol tragedy revived the gloomy resolution' to end his own short life.

'He often spoke about the French Minister's extraordinary death, and agreed that self-killing was most cowardly. The Inquest was held by Coroner Potter this morning, but developed no additional facts of interest. The remains were interred this afternoon in Glenwood Cemetery, attended there by his wife, who seemed deeply afflicted, his father-in-law; Marquis de Chambrun and some twenty others'.

So said the *New York Herald*. And there we have it: Rodolphe not only knew of the Marquis, he worked for him and received a final ten dollars from him, having asked for four more. Would it have made any difference to Rodolphe's state of mind and actions if Chambrun's pocket contained the extra four dollars? Did Rudolphe spend the ten – if so, on what? A pistol or ammunition? He knew the sequence of actions which had led up to Prévost-Paradol's suicide …

The Marquis was one of the people at the cemetery for Rodolphe's laying to rest, fulfilling the deceased young man's wish (expressed in his suicide note) that Chambrun would attend. Rodolphe did not go alone to his grave.

Even English and Scottish newspapers printed the sad news from Washington of the two deaths. The *Guardian* on 24 August 1870 and the *Scotsman* on 25 August wrote that Rodolphe committed suicide by shooting himself in a manner very similar to that of the late French Ambassador.

Who, if anyone, in Rodolphe's family read the news of his death?

In his final letter, was he referring to the horrors of war, his injuries, his personal relationships? All of those may have felt completely overwhelming to Rodolphe, under a burden of sadnesses in his short life.

Chapter 8

'SOMETHING EXTRAORDINARY'

It emerged after Monsieur Prévost-Paradol's death that Chambrun knew him well, had seen his 'great depression of spirits, exhibited nervousness and uneasiness at the difficulties of his new position' as Ambassador.

THE LONG HOT SUMMER OF 1870

As featured in articles after Rodolphe's death, it was a heatwave summer and in Washington, overheating was one of the negative factors in Prévost-Paradol's life that July. On 21st, the *New York Herald* headlined the unfolding events:

'SUICIDE OF THE FRENCH MINISTER'

M Prévost-Paradol shot himself through the heart at 1 am on 20 July 1870; the Inquest was held at his house that day. As was usual, Coroner Potter and the twelve Jurors viewed the body and the wound which led to death. (Potter led the Inquest into Rodolphe's death the following month.)

The first witness was Paul de Jardin, 'Chancellor of the French Embassy'; his face had 'an unusually frightened expression' while he gave his story.

The previous day Prévost-Paradol requested that he accompany him, to buy a pistol. When asked why he wanted one, Prévost-Paradol became very nervous. M de Jardin felt it might be best 'to gratify him' so off they went to Savage's store. When asked by the shop assistant what particular kind of pistol would suit, the Minister said, 'good effective pistols'. Well, twelve dollars a pair or seven dollars each. 'One will suit my purpose,' replied Prévost-Paradol.

By the next morning, the man was dead. De Jardin's first impulse, on being told the news, was to rip open a letter given to him by Prévost-Paradol two days previously. He had been asked not to open it until hearing 'something extraordinary'. Now he *was* hearing something extraordinary, something terrible.

The letter read:

'Monday, June 21 1870

'If any accident should happen to me I pray that you, M de Jardin, will see that my family and servants are sent back to their country. I hope that the measures to be taken will be facilitated by the friends that I have made in the United States.

Prévost-Paradol'

De Jardin realised that the late Ambassador wrote this when he had determined upon his fatal act.

Auguste, the servant (with Chambrun interpreting for him) told the Inquest he heard a pistol shot and his master cried out 'Auguste, viens ici!' (… come here!). Prévost-Paradol died about three-quarters of an hour later.

Next morning, Auguste went to M de Jardin. A question in the newspaper was 'why were the events concealed' for so many hours? Reason given: the servants were said to be 'so overwhelmed … so ignorant of the ways and customs of this strange city, that they did not know how to act'.

M de Jardin rushed to Chambrun's house and woke the Marquis, who immediately exclaimed, 'Prévost-Paradol is dead, is it not so? I know it must be so.' De Jardin, mystified as to why Chambrun knew, guessed this, just nodded and recounted the story from Auguste.

Chambrun (recipient of the 'something extraordinary' letter) and de Jardin went to the late Prévost-Paradol's house; Auguste gave them an envelope. The scribbled note was translated: 'I've killed myself. Come back Berthemy, and stay. Prévost-Paradol.'

They understood the note's meaning. Jules Berthemy had been French Ambassador in Washington from 1866 until Prévost-Paradol's appointment to the role in 1870.[50']

The Jury's verdict was that 'M Prévost-Paradol, Envoy Extraordinary and Minister Plenipotentiary, came to his death by a wound from a pistol in his own hand.'[51]

The newspaper added another piece of the puzzle. 'One of the foreign ministers … a bosom friend … stated … he was subject to considerable fits of temper, during which he lost self-possession'.

Looking back to the very day before he wrote his 'in case of hearing something extraordinary' letter, the newspapers of 20 June 1870 carried news that many old friends deserted Prévost-Paradol when he changed allegiance from the Orleanists to the Napoleon Party.

So the Ambassador had felt under unbearable pressure, with no good end in sight – just as Rodolphe felt. Prévost-Paradol's end and Rodolphe's act: the person they had in common, knew and loved, was Chambrun. And it is highly likely that Rodolphe discussed the Ambassador's death with his employer, Chambrun; had read in the newspapers about the pistol and cartridge purchases, the self-killing, and then the explicit report of the Inquest. Hence Rodolphe's reference in his suicide note to 'an ambassador of France' – and Rodolphe ending his own life in the same painful way.

Chapter 9

WOMEN, A WILL AND A BABY

ADÈLE DE DORÉ

On a happier note, albeit briefly, back to Adèle de Doré.[52]

Adèle's home was in Brooklyn, New York, but she was in Washington at the time of Rodolphe's death. And he had requested that she receive enough money to travel home.

From around 1867 until 1875, Adèle paid for regular advertisements in the *Brooklyn Daily Eagle*. On 26 December 1868:

'CLAIRVOYANTE – removed from 73 to 41 Fulton St, second floor, Mlle A de Doré from Paris, tells all present and future events; lost and stolen goods recovered; prevents persons from all danger, and brings together those who are separated. Lucky numbers given … Ladies 50 cts [cents] to $1; gentlemen $1 to $2.'

In 1872, birthplace given as Paris, age 'thirty', 'Adèle Dedoré' married Ebenezer H Culver. In 1878, name transcribed as 'Adel Dethonars Dedoré', marital status 'unknown', she married Alphonse Prévost.

But she had a marriage before those two. A transcription shows a marriage on 4 May 1868 in 'Saratoga, New York' between 'RCH de

Thomers', twenty-two, born in 1846, and 'Adèle de Doré', born in 1842. His father's surname 'Prince of Falmont', his mother's name 'Helen Caroline Anton'.

Words misheard, inaccurately transcribed – or incorrect information given?[53]

Was that marriage legal? If so, Rodolphe committed bigamy when he married Julia Harrison the following year, 1869.

History repeating itself, son following in his father's footsteps? Rodolphe's father had married bigamously in January 1848.

RODOLPHE'S WILL

Newspaper reports – not wholly accurate – were that Rodolphe had insured his life and that he left a Will bequeathing a total of 5,000 dollars [worth about 100,000 dollars now]; 1,000 dollars to his mistress, the remainder to his wife and brother.

'Rodolphe C de Thouars' signed his Will on 4 August 1870 – just two days before he killed himself. Handwriting firm and clear, instructions explicit and, like his suicide letter, concise.

The clarity of expression may have been the opposite of how he was feeling, if he had a plan to end his life within just a few days. Having insured his life, he had banked on 5,000 dollars – feeling worth more, far more, dead than alive. His Will was proved in May 1871 (see Washington D C Records, 1737-1952, Wills, Boxes 0041-0045, 1869-1871).

Rodolphe left 1,000 dollars to his wife, Julia, and 2,000 dollars to be invested for his 'only child, Ellen Caroline de Thouars' (the clear echoes again of his mother's birth names, Eleanor Caroline, and of his sister's). He left 500 dollars to his sister, 'Helen Caroline', and 500 dollars to his brother, 'Walter Henry Prout; – both 'de Thouars d'Escury'.

And 1,000 dollars to 'Madame Adèle de Doré'…… of whom more later.

'My said brother is now a prisoner in jail for a criminal offence committed in France & is imprisoned.' Rodolphe added that if his brother could *not* receive the legacy, it was to be paid to their sister Helen and invested for Walter's benefit.

The reason why Walter (he would have been about twenty-three years old) was said to be in a French prison in 1870 might remain unknown, but it is yet another link between this family and France. And a link to crime, his father Adolphus/Henry Desbury/Adolphe having been imprisoned (at Gloucester).

Other close relatives of Walter's – the offspring of his father but relatives probably not known by Walter – would be imprisoned in 1880 and 1886 respectively.

EXECUTORS AND GUARDIANS FOR LITTLE 'NELLIE'
Rodolphe had appointed three people as Executors, and guardians of his and Julia's child, later known as 'Nellie'. First, 'Eustache Collett', described as 'a clerk in the US Pension Office, Department of the Interior'; second, James W Harrison, his father-in-law; third, Rodolphe's wife, Julia de Thouars, née Harrison.

Eustace/Eustache Collett, the person who sketched General Robert E Lee and also the 'surrender' house in Appomattox in 1865.

The *Indianapolis News* of 27 September 1870 had its usual, rather dry, column.

'INSURANCE MATTERS'
But that day, the 'Insurance Matters' column had an interesting item from a Washington Correspondent of the *New York Herald*. A twist, the possibility of a significant problem for Rodolphe's chosen beneficiaries.

'An insurance suit is likely to grow out of the late suicide of the Count Henry de Thouard [sic] who, it will be remembered, shot himself in this city not long ago after the sad Paradol tragedy. It appears that a short time before the fatal act of self-destruction the Count insured his life … and what is remarkable, he asked the insurance people at the time whether the money would be paid to his wife in case he committed suicide at any time. He was told that if he should become sick and crazy, and then put an end to his life that the money would be paid, just as if he should die from natural causes.

'A few days afterwards, Thouard shot himself, and the insurance people, on reading over the reports of the tragedy in the Herald, discovered what they considered a bar to the claims of the Count's heirs for the insurance money. This bar is a letter, written weeks before the insurance was effected, to Marquis de Chambrun, in which Count Thouard expressed an intention to commit suicide. The insurance people intend to resist payment, and the heirs of the Count threaten a suit to enforce it.'

Did the insurance company pay out?

In May 1871, the last Will and Testament of 'Rudolph C de Thouars' was proved, Rodolphe's affairs laid to rest … or were they?

Did Adèle de Doré ever receive the 1,000 dollars?

Did Julia ever find out about Rodolphe's marriage to Adèle – the year before Julia and Rodolphe's 'marriage' – or did it remain Adèle and Rodolphe's secret?

No answers are forthcoming at present, but let's look more closely at what sort of wedding took place between those two:

'Comte RCH deThonars, Baron d'Escury, Brooklyn, NY, 22, occupation – none; b. Paris, France. Prince of Falmont*, Helen Caroline Anton** ………………………….. 1st.
Adèle de Doré, Brooklyn, NY, 28; b. Paris, France ……………………………..
2nd.'

.

* Father of bridegroom   ** Mother of bridegroom

Their marriage ceremony was conducted by a Baptist minister in May 1868; as indicated in the record above, this was the bridegroom's first marriage and the bride's second (or was it? - no record found). No witnesses listed; other marriages on the page listed witnesses. And when Adèle married in 1878, she took the 'deThonars' name with her – whatever the correct spelling.[54]

LIFE GOES ON …

The 1880 US Census shows Julia de Thouars, thirty-one, and Helene, 'Nellie', eleven, still in Washington DC.

1892: 'Mme DeDoré' still advertising her services in the *Brooklyn Daily Eagle* as a 'wonderful, natural clairvoyante' from Paris; she unravels 'any mystery; prevents from danger; discovers lost and stolen goods; reunites those separated.'

Julia, society woman and long-time widow of Rodolphe, died in 1922 at 819 Portland Street, the oldest house in Congress Heights, Washington.

MONEY MONEY MONEY

Three financial questions: did Julia and the other named beneficiaries get the money from Rodolphe's estate – or did the insurance company not have to pay out, because his death was by suicide? If Julia did not benefit, perhaps she had money from her parents. One wonders what effect the short life and shocking death of Rodolphe had on Julia's life and on that of their child, Nellie.

Chapter 10

WALTER HENRY PROUT DE THOUARS D'ESCURY AND THE MURDER OF SARAH

Walter, Eleanor and Adolphus' second child, was born in early 1847 at 2 Bunhill Row, London; his baptism was in France on 26 March 1847.

At thirteen, formerly an 'Errand Boy', by May 1860 he was in the 'RW' [Receiving Ward] of St Pancras Workhouse, London, at 4 Kings Road, next to the St Pancras Old Church and churchyard. Those admitted to the institution were there at the mercy of the parish; young Walter was from Kentish Town. Surely it is significant that his father, Adolphus, had died that March and Eleanor, his mother, may have died by then.

Walter was in and out of the workhouse until finally discharged on 24 July – exactly the same day that his older brother made his passport application.

How and why Walter left London and England at some stage within the decade is at yet unknown. Knowledge of his alleged imprisonment in France, before or during 1870, is only discovered through his brother Rodolphe's Will, made that summer.

And, like Rodolphe, Walter ventured much further afield than Europe. Next located in Ravenswood, a small mining settlement in Queensland, Australia, 'Walter Henry Prout D'E'Cury' married 'Sarah Ann Riley' in 1884.

No 'Happy Ever After' though. Soon after the wedding Sarah deserted her husband. Four years later, a murder and yet another trial.

THE MURDER OF SARAH

By 1888, Sarah had taken up with Edmond Duhamel. Strangely, she was murdered on her wedding anniversary in August 1888, four years after her marriage to Walter.

Sarah's throat was cut at Cork Creek Camp, four miles from Croydon in Queensland. Duhamel told police he was so drunk that he had no memory of killing her. 'I have killed my little wife, I will not survive her.' It is not known why Duhamel referred to Sarah as his wife. He swallowed half a teaspoon of strychnine (a poison) and then even more. The article continued: 'police are of the opinion that the woman's husband might have probably come in the same boat' as her murderer.[55]

The Australian Star, Sydney, reported that 'Duhamel is supposed to be a French escapee, one of four which landed at Bowen some 10 years ago' adding that Sarah had been 'a quiet, clean, and sober woman'. He was allegedly 'of mild demeanour, therefore his burst of ferocity is unaccountable'.

The reporters surmised that Walter and Duhamel were convicts who had left New Caledonia and arrived at the small town of Bowen on the north-east coast of Australia. The New Caledonia islands are a French 'unique collectivity', Nouvelle-Caledonie, in the Pacific Ocean some 900 miles east of Australia. Melanesians settled the islands about 3,000 BC and were mainly cut off from outside contact until 1774. James Cook, the British explorer and navigator, landed with his crew on the largest island and called it 'New Caledonia' in honour of his father's homeland, Scotland. Colonisation began.

In 1853, France took possession of most of the New Caledonian islands with the aim of using the territory as a penal colony. The Melanesians tried to resist this invasion and were brutally dealt with by the usurpers.

Between 1864 and 1897 almost 30,000 male and over 1,000 female convicts arrived from France and were held prisoner in New Caledonia, hence the Australian police thinking that the murdered Sarah's estranged husband and the alleged murderer Duhamel might have arrived in eastern Australia together, on a boat from the penal colony (and, remember, Rodolphe in his Will stated that Walter was in prison in France in 1870).

'THE GOLD-CRAZED POPULATION'
Questions as to whether Walter and Duhamel were one and the same man never went away. In 1933, the Australian newspaper *Truth* featured the murder of Sarah Ann, declaring that 'even among the gold-crazed population' the savage murder 'created an immense sensation'.

Walter's successor in Sarah's life, Duhamel, was said to have become jealous of the attention another Frenchman was paying to her. One night he drank fast and furiously, went home, slit her throat with a razor and fell down dead drunk.

'By a peculiar coincidence' said *Truth* 'it was the Frenchman who discovered the crime'. He ran to call the police. There was no suggestion that the deceased Sarah's estranged husband, Walter, was in the vicinity of the grim scene.

BOGGO ROAD JAIL

Oher newspapers described Duhamel as having been a sailor or a soldier, not a convict from New Caledonia. Whatever the truth, he was found guilty of Sarah's murder. Finding religion on death row, on the last morning of his life came his admission to the murder of Sarah. His last words: 'I hope for Heaven's pardon.'

Edmond Duhamel, thirty-six, was hanged at Boggo Road Jail, Brisbane in November 1888. A photograph on tacked-up posters showed Edmond's name and place of death.

Where was Walter?

Walter's photograph was taken by police in February 1891, in another country. Unfortunately the photo has disappeared. Although there are no public photographs of him, later descriptions of Walter do not match in any way the physical appearance of Monsieur Duhamel in the latter's final photograph. Duhamel was fair-skinned with light hair.

Duhamel and Walter were clearly not one and the same. Walter's tracks disappear until 1891, when spotted again – not in Australia.

'FORGERY AND UTTERING'

Walter must have travelled from Australia to New Zealand at some time between 1884 and 1891.

NEW ZEALAND POLICE GAZETTE 1891. TRIAL MARCH 1891. 'FORGERY AND UTTERING'; TWO YEARS' LABOUR.

CUTS, SCARS AND AMPUTATIONS
NEW ZEALAND POLICE GAZETTE 1892. RETURN OF PRISONERS REPORTED AS DISCHARGED etc. Native of: LONDON, Trade: LINGUIST, born: 1855; Complexion: SWARTHY; Hair: BLACK; Eyes: DARK BROWN; Nose: medium; photographed in February 1891. Remarks and previous convictions: Flags and anchor on right arm; three cuts on left arm; sabre-cut on left knee; scar on left calf; three large scars on right leg and knee. (Police Gazette, 1892, page 170).

So, Walter had served time in Wellington Gaol, on North Island, New Zealand. He is next heard of locked up in Lyttleton Gaol on South Island:

NEW ZEALAND POLICE GAZETTE 1893. WALTER HENRY D'ESCURY. Where tried: TIMARU; LARCENY; six months; Native of: FRANCE; born 1847; one previous conviction. THREE RIGHT FINGERS AMPUTATED; wreath and flower on left arm.[56]

Did Walter ever receive the 500 dollars left to him in his brother Rodolphe's Will in 1870? And, what life did he make for himself after that 1893 incarceration in New Zealand?

Chapter 11

HELEN D'ESCURY AND MODESTUS FELIX DE THOUARS D'ESCURY

Eleanor and Adolphus' third and fourth children: Helen and Modestus. The birth of Helen was registered in the last quarter of 1848 at Shoreditch, London, when her father (known to some people as 'Henry Desbury') was serving his first sentence in Gloucester prison.

A Protestant Church record in France gives her birth as being in September 1848 (no details). She was twelve when baptised at the Reformed Church in Paris in January 1861. If a correct record, her French baptism was the year after the death of her father, Adolphus.

Why would young Helen have been in Paris – and with whom?

In her brother Rodolphe's Will in 1870 she (his only full sister) was named as 'Helen Caroline de Thouars d'Escury', said to be in France. Perhaps with the tension of writing his Will he was mixing up family names, or perhaps she was in contact from France with Rodolphe in the USA.

Helen was 'Mary Ellen' in some early records in England, then in the Church Register as 'Marie Helen De Thouars' when she married a Frenchman in 1874. They were both living at 55 Bunhill Road – the

Hampton family home, the house where the Hampton family had lived for over thirty years.

Not forgetting Eleanor and Adolphus' last baby, Modestus. Born in 1851, he died at six months and was buried at St Luke's, Old Street, London.

PART TWO
CLARA AND ADOLPHE'S CHILDREN

Chapter 12

CLARA AND ADOLPHE'S FIRST CHILD

HENRY EDOUARD DE THOUARS D'ESCURY (KNOWN AS HENRY EDWARD DE THOUARS)

Henry Edouard de Thouars d'Escury (known as Henry Edward de Thouars) in adulthood always said that France was his birthplace. The first child of Clara and Adolphe, his baptism took place in September 1855 at St Pancras Old Church, London; birth 'March 1854'. The family lived in Chalcot Terrace, near to the impressive grassy summit of Primrose Hill, with its extensive views over London.[57]

By 1861 (his father having died the year before) Henry Edward, seven, was living with his mother, the three younger siblings and their aunt, Ellen Chamberlain, in the London Borough of Tower Hamlets.

Their dear mother Clara died in 1866 – and that terrible blow for her four offspring was followed by the death of Aunt Ellen just two years later.

By 1871, Henry Edward lived in the town of High Wycombe, Buckinghamshire, thirty miles outside London. Perhaps spotting an advertisement in a newspaper, he seized an orphan's opportunity and was apprenticed to Charles Pearse, 'hairdresser, perfumer, tobacconist' for work, bed and board.

Just a few years later Henry Edward was off again. To the very far side of the world.

Like his father, Adolphe, and his half-brothers, Rodolphe and Walter, he went to sea and came ashore as a foreigner. In November 1873, he was 'Henry de Thouars', a seventeen-year-old British crewman arriving at Sydney from Melbourne on the steamship *Wentworth*, probably having travelled to Australia from London.

On his 'Naturalization' application form in 1925 he wrote that he arrived in 1877 as a member of crew, disembarking from the SS *Lusitania* [not the RMS *Lusitania*, which was launched in 1906]. This may well have been the first voyage of the Pacific Steam Navigation Company steamship on the Orient Line from England to Melbourne, taking about forty days.[58]

ALL THINGS ADELAIDE

In 1836 the capital city of the state of South Australia was named Adelaide after Queen Adelaide, queen consort to William IV of the United Kingdom.[59]

As is commonly found in these stories, there was a name change. The Queen had begun life as 'Adelheid' (German).

Henry Edward declared he lived for 'ten years' at Brunswick, Victoria. Did he then choose to move to Adelaide because that was the name of his sister? There he married Henrietta Wagener; his names were recorded as 'Henry Edward De Thouars De La Tremoil d'Escury'. He gave his father's forename not as Adolphe but as 'Frederick George'; perhaps this son did not want to be traceable; disliked his father and did not want to disclose his late father's name?

Possibly, Henry Edward was still in contact with Freddy (Frederick

George) his younger brother (about whom more later). By 1882 – whether Henry Edward knew it or not – young Freddy was not in England and no longer known as Frederick or Freddy.

Former seaman Henry Edward turned his hands back to practising his hairdressing skills. He was in Gawler, a town now within the metropolitan area of Adelaide. The name 'Adelaide' was featuring centre stage in his life – and did so constantly until his death.

Henrietta and Henry Edward's daughter, Clara Amelia (named Clara after both his mother and his late sister – a sign of his feelings towards them) was born in Adelaide in May 1885.

Very sadly, baby Clara died less than a year later, in March 1886. That month, her aunt Adelaide Bartlett was in deep trouble, far away in London. Had Henry Edward kept in contact with his sister Adelaide for all those years since he left England? What a shock it must have been for him to learn of her circumstances in 1886, with the newspapers full of her name. How quickly did the bad news about her reach Australia? Terribly stressful – at the very stage that he and Henrietta were grieving, after the death of their only child.

What became of Henrietta? In 1893, Henry Edward married Ada Leah Barclay, née Wilkinson, and they had a child. In the 1900s the family lived in Victoria.

During the First World War, Henry Edward was a cook with the Australian Imperial Forces at Mitcham Army Camp near Adelaide. In 1922, he was a chef.

The official report in response to his application for 'Naturalization' stated he had not understood that, as 'a citizen of France', he should have been registered as 'an alien' in Australia during the war.[60] Any person making a false declaration was 'liable to a heavy penalty for doing so'. He could not produce any documentation as to his birthplace or nationality.

'A PERSON OF GOOD REPUTE'

Henry Edward was a widower when he submitted his application for a Certificate of Naturalization in 1925. He described himself thus: seventy-one, born in 'Orleans', France; lived in England for 'nineteen years' before coming to Australia; five feet six and a half inches tall with grey hair and brown eyes; 'Any Special Peculiarities': left blank. Retired, after employment at the River Murray Works.

Intriguingly, he wrote that his French father was 'Rudolphus' (rather than 'Adolphus' or 'Adolphe') – using almost the original spelling of his oldest half-brother's birth name (Rodolphus). Henry Edward's use of the name 'Rudolphus' in 1925 for his father strongly suggests that he knew (or knew of) his older half-brother. It is feasible that the young stepbrothers had spent time together in London – and that he knew of Rodolphe's death in 1870.

Either Henry Edward wanted to bury any links with his late father or by 1925 he was confused as to the facts. Having given a wrong name for Adolphe at his marriage in 1882, it seems that disassociation was his plan. And perhaps he had not wanted his name to be linked with Adelaide's when bad publicity about her was everywhere in 1886.

Henry Edward applied for an old age pension in Australia, renounced his French citizenship and allegiance to the Republic of France and took the Oath of Allegiance, to His Majesty King George the Fifth, his heirs and successors, before a special magistrate. As a resident of the state of South Australia he was swearing (as did all Australians in that era) his loyalty to the monarch of the United Kingdom. Result: he was granted a 'Certificate of Naturalization'.

DEATH IN ADELAIDE

Henry Edward de Thouars died in Adelaide in 1927. The words on his gravestone at West Terrace Cemetery are:

'A PATIENT SUFFERER AT REST'

Adelaide: with her active, restless spirit – a temperament strikingly different from that of her older brother – was she too by then 'a patient sufferer at rest'? Or was Henry Edward's mercurial sister still alive?

Chapter 13

CLARA AND ADOLPHE'S SECOND CHILD

ADELAIDE DE LA TREMOILLE DE THOUARS D'ESCURY

CENTRE STAGE: ADELAIDE FROM FRANCE

Adelaide, Clara and Adolphe's first daughter, is the person everyone has been waiting for in this story. From the evidence of the ink flourishes certifying her birth on 19 December 1855 in Orleans (some eighty miles south of Paris, France) to her baptism in England in 1856 and on to the 1871 Census, Adelaide had an unusual and disrupted childhood and became an unconventional woman. Her disappearance from the public gaze at the age of thirty has remained of interest to aficionados of true-life mystery stories ever since, the case famous/infamous in the annals of murder trials.[61]

Adélaïde: a name of French origin. Her name may have been chosen by her parents after happy times living in Primrose Hill, walking down the long Adelaide Road with her older brother, Henry Edward, when he was a baby. And, of course, the name Adelaide has the first two letters of her father's name.

Her birth surnames were an amalgam of illustrious ones from France.

This child of Adolphe's was the first one to have 'de la Tremoille' bestowed; whether his family was one of the so-called noble families of this name and the 'de Thouars d'Escury' names, who knows? Did Adolphe give himself the names? Whatever was true, these surnames were bestowed on Adelaide, the first of the two daughters of Clara.

At some stage the family returned from France to London and were living at 8 Mayfield Street in Dalston when Adelaide's baptism took place on 9 September 1856 at St Mary's, Haggerston, Hackney. Her father's occupation was given as 'professor of mathematics'.

In 1918, it was declared by Sir Edward Clarke QC, MP, that her 'true' father had been 'an Englishman of good social position'.[62]

This 'fact' – from one of the most famous and respected barristers of that era – was repeated in each story published about Adelaide; it was incorrect. That is, Clarke either did not know, or had not revealed, the correct nationality and social standing of Adelaide's father. Perhaps Clarke's was a deliberately indirect reference to a close relative of Adelaide's, her influential maternal uncle, William Chamberlain. William, 'an Englishman of good social position' – of excellent standing, successful and prosperous.

ADIEU ADOLPHE

Adelaide's father, Adolphe, an enigmatic, violent and persuasive man of many and some missing parts, died in March 1860 at 4 York Place, near Baker Street in central London.

His sister-in-law, Ellen, who was with him at the end, gave the details required for the registration of death. His age given as 'forty-three', Adolphus/Henry/Adolphe was felled and silenced by *morbus cardis* (heart disease) and gangrene in his feet.

'ADOLPHUS/HENRY/ADOLPHE
In the Revolution the cockade hats on the men
look like bats on cats,
like things they are not.
Adolphus evolves into Henry
into Adolphe,
each version of himself
clever, witty, a charlatan, a great pretender,
an educator, a professeur of linguistics
(with a sharp, yet to some, beguiling tongue).
Professor of mathematics
(with a head for figuring out
how to have
simultaneous intimate relationships).
Excitement, change, challenges for him;
violence, misery and humiliation
for the women.
And what for his children?'
(Rose Storkey)

By the end of September 1860, Adelaide's maternal grandfather, William Robinson Chamberlain of Loddiges Road, Hackney, had passed away.; his death and that of Adolphe disrupted the children's lives. By 1861, Adelaide, her two brothers, Henry Edward and Frederick George, her young sister Clara junior, and their mother were at 38 Havelock Road, South Hackney, with six other people in the house. Clara, carrying on as best she could, was still a teacher of French. Her mother, Head of her own school, died in 1862.

ADIEU CLARA

Clara's death in 1866 was a huge blow for her four children. When her sister, Ellen Chamberlain, died in 1868 the siblings were separated, Clara junior going to live with uncle William Chamberlain's family in Kent, Adelaide and her two brothers having to live elsewhere.

DEATH OF PRINCE ALBERT

Prince Albert, Queen Victoria's much-loved husband and consort, had died in December 1861 at the age of forty-two – Victoria was devastated. By 1863, the mood in the country among her subjects was that she should have returned to public life by then, as it was over twelve months since the death of her beloved. Only after ten years of virtual seclusion did she return to her public duties in 1871. Queen Victoria remained in mourning dress until her death, almost forty years after that of her beloved Prince Albert.

For Adelaide and her extended family – as for many families in many eras – illness and death were a constant fear and reality. Survivors had to face the losses, looking for ways to carry on as best they could, utilising whatever personal and practical resources they could muster. By 1871, Henry Edward had headed off, as we know, to become a hairdresser's apprentice in High Wycombe. After Aunt Ellen Chamberlain's death in 1868, Adelaide and her younger brother Frederick George, 'Freddy', were moved out to a Surrey village ten miles from central London. They lived with Ann and her husband William Wellbelove, a confectioner, at 25 High Street, Hampton Wick. Freddy attended the nearby English School (boys only). In 1871, Adelaide was listed as 'Adptd Daur' [Adopted Daughter] and Confectioner's Assistant; Freddy as a 'Boarder' and 'Scholar', which indicates that someone, probably William Chamberlain (Clara's brother) was paying the Wellbeloves for young Freddy's keep and towards his education.

Whether any of the arrangements were formal ones is not known. The development of a boarding-out system for children from workhouses, for instance, was taking place at that time in England. Adelaide and Freddy were orphans in need of support and stability when they arrived at the Wellbeloves and it is reasonable to think that Uncle William, or Emily, his wife, handled the arrangements for the niece and nephew. The Wellbeloves looked after other children at other times: John Macfarlane and Sidney Heath were two boys who were living with the Wellbeloves in 1861 and seem to have gone on to do well as adults.

Chapter 14

CLARA AND ADOLPHE'S THIRD CHILD

FREDERICK GEORGE DE THOUARS

Frederick George, presumably born 'Frederick George de la Tremoille de Thouars d'Escury', Clara and Adolphe's third child, was born in 1858. In England – or France? Recap: his father died in 1860, the following year Frederick George was living with Clara and her other three children in London; she died in 1866. 'Freddy' is next heard of at the age of eleven.

CLEVER FREDDY

End of term, everyone's excited on this Wednesday evening; 'tis Christmas entertainment time, 1869. 'Freddy' walks on to the stage at the boys-only English School in Hampton Wick. Pupils are performing in a room densely packed with the trustees, parents and friends. The *Surrey Comet* (25 December) highlighted this one boy. 'The two characters in the recitation King John and the Abbott [sic] of Canterbury were well-taken by F de Thouars'.

Looking out at all the faces, Freddy probably thinks about his parents not being there. Undoubtedly he can remember Clara but probably not his father, Adolphe. Hopefully one or both of the Wellbeloves are there to see Freddy. He is a 'boarder' with them and Adelaide lives with them too.

One of the trustees, T Nelson Esq, hands Freddy a prize of two shillings (twice the amount given to other pupils) for his 'admirable representation of the characters' of King John and the Abbot. Mrs May gives 'this boy an extra shilling' – thus he receives three shillings in total. The performing boys receive 'hearty bursts of applause'.

Fast forward to the following year. The *Surrey Comet* on 24 December 1870 singles out one youth (yes, dear Freddy again) who particularly distinguishes himself, 'not only by his excellent singing of the song, 'Massa's in de cold, cold ground' but [also] by his very considerable powers of mimmicry [sic] ... fully displayed in that comical recitation 'The Jackdaw of Rheims.[63]

'DROLLERY'

The audience laugh heartily at the drollery he infuses into the piece, and reward his efforts with 'hearty plaudits'.

WHY WAS FREDDY CHOSEN?

An interlude in this story: time to unpick the song and the poem chosen for Freddy to perform. Were they run of the mill pieces – or did something lie beneath the choices?

'Massa's in de cold ground' was called a 'minstrel' song. Apparently, Stephen Foster wrote the song about his father (white and poor) being sung about by black slaves. After the American Civil War the song was given an extra 'cold': 'Massa's in de cold, cold ground'. Did the music teacher decide this song fitted Freddy, in terms of his colour, his foreign name, his ability to mimic? Ironically his half-brother, Rodolphe, may have sung this song during a war far away, just a few years before Freddy's impressive performance. A question, as with Henry Edward and Rodolphe: had the half-siblings known of one another? Had they ever spent time together or lived in the same household?

The Ingoldsby Legends: a collection of poetry and ~~legends, supposedly~~ written by Thomas Ingoldsby (pen-name of Richard Harris Barham. The collection remained popular throughout the nineteenth century, with many editions published. *'The Jackdaw of Rheims'* is the best-known of the poems and is about a bird, a jackdaw, which stole a cardinal's ring; the bird is subsequently made a saint. The combination of rhythm, 'nonsense' – and a parody of certain excesses in established religion – forms a lengthy poem.[64]–

It refers to a bishop, abbot, prior, monk, friar, knight, squire and 'the Cardinal Lord Archbishop of Rheims' and it ends: 'So they canonised him by the name of Jim Crow!'

Why did Ingoldsby choose that name? Was it just a common name for a crow, or based on the use of the name 'Jim Crow' in shows?

'Jim Crow' was a minstrel-show character in America from the 1830s, portraying numerous negative stereotypes of African Americans. Jim Crow was supposed to be grateful to the white master for his lot in life. Perhaps not surprisingly Thomas Dartmouth Rice, aka Jim Crow, was a white man who painted his face and did a song and dance act, saying he copied it from a slave. Stereotyping and depicting a caricature of a black man, Rice, as Jim Crow, wore shabby clothes, shambling around as he sang.

FESTIVITIES OVER …

Back to 1870, Hampton Wick: the Christmas entertainment provided by the pupils has just ended. The Reverend FJ Champion de Crespigny, a trustee, declares to the large assembly that it is 'very creditable to the village to have such boys belonging to it.' He feels 'sure they must fill a respectable position in after life'.

'THE WAY THEY OUGHT TO GO'

How satisfying to read that Freddy was awarded a first-class prize for school work – the only pupil to be awarded the prize of 7/6 (seven shillings and sixpence) by Mr Nelson, who expressed a hope. This was that 'the Privy Council, when they send an inspector to this village' will be 'satisfied that they had done their duty here in training up the young in the way they ought to go.'

Compulsory education was about to begin in the village. Freddy had the benefit of an education which was paid for – not a large amount of money, but sufficient to set him up for the future. He was literate, articulate, extrovert, engaging, with a life full of potential.

Freddy, Frederick George de Thouars, would give himself a permanent role as 'George'.

Chapter 15

CLARA AND ADOLPHE'S FOURTH CHILD

CLARA DE LA TREMOUILLE

Clara junior, born in the autumn of 1859 in St Pancras, London, was Clara and Adolphe's last child, sister of Henry Edward, Adelaide and Frederick George. By 1871, she was living with her maternal uncle William and his family. They moved out to Beckenham, Kent. Clara junior's life was short; very sadly she died in 1873 of rheumatic fever.

By 1873, William Chamberlain was in his prime, with a highly successful career in a flourishing company: 'The Gas and Water Debenture Trust Company Limited, Secretary: William Chamberlain Esq. Capital: £2,000,200 in 100,000 shares of £20 each' (Lloyd's List, 22 November 1873).

Company Chairman was The Right Honourable Sir Seymour Fitzgerald, late Governor of Bombay (the city on the western side of India). William's role included entering into contracts on behalf of the company and being its public 'face'. Their offices were at 5 Lothbury, a short street and a stone's throw from the Bank of England.

SNATCH OFF THAT WRETCHED PINNY

Uncle William's situation was in sharp contrast to that of his niece, Adelaide. By the early 1870s, she may have reached the stage where a job behind the shop counter day after day felt restrictive and humdrum, such an existence beneath her. Given her subsequent approach to life, and coming as she did from a family in which teaching and related jobs for women were a reality, it seems reasonable for her to have yearned for challenging opportunities, getting resentful about not having been able to attend a school.

One can imagine Adelaide wanting to snatch off the wretched pinny, gather up her skirt and run freely – somewhere, anywhere – as long as it was exciting, be with people who valued her and where there was money. With an excellent brain and longing to use it, yes, over-ready and keen to embrace life and its fascinations. She knew her mother married at nineteen – and look what a short life and painful death Clara had …

Adelaide went on to take the principal part in a mystery that has never gone away. The search, poking for truths and lies amongst the stories, pulls us on. Now that you know something of her extended family's complexities, it is time to introduce a husband for young Adelaide. The simple part is that they both live in the county of Surrey.

PART THREE
THE HUSBAND, THOMAS EDWIN
BARTLETT (KNOWN AS EDWIN)

Chapter 16

HOME AND AWAY

Edwin was born on 8 October 1845 in Fulham, west London and probably educated in Kingston, Surrey. A schoolmistress there, Caroline Smith, was a relative and Edwin's two younger brothers, Charles Joseph and Frederick Oscar, attended her school. By his early teens Edwin was an assistant to a well-respected grocer, Charles Whittaker, in Croydon. Alongside Edwin was Edward Baxter, an older, ambitious, grocer's assistant who soon went on to run his own shop in south London.

A few years later, Baxter gave Edwin an ideal opportunity: by the age of seventeen, Edwin's numeracy skills and industrious nature were being put to good use in the provisions business at Baxter's shop in Herne Hill. When he had proved his worth, Edwin was accepted into partnership. Baxter & Bartlett worked hard and long, expanding their small chain of shops and large range of retail goods (including confectionery). Such was Edwin's situation in 1875.

Adelaide probably used the name 'Blanche' to emphasise her French roots and to try to shake off some of her past. It was the name she used when introduced on just one occasion to Edwin Bartlett senior, a short while before her wedding to his one of his sons, Edwin.

How long before the wedding had the couple first met? Edwin gave a clue on 30 December 1885 as to when it had been. He, Adelaide and a certain George Dyson were discussing the subject of 'trust' and Adelaide. According to Dyson, Edwin said:

'Oh, you can trust her. If you'd had twelve years' experience as I have had you'd know you could trust her.'

Dyson may have forgotten the real answer; Edwin may have met Adelaide in 1873 – when she was seventeen or eighteen – but Adelaide would have none of it, as a story. She maintained they married shortly after meeting in 1875. Edwin was said (by his father) to have met 'Blanche', as she was calling herself, in February 1875 at his brother Charles' home where she had been living 'for a short time'. It is very tempting to think that Edwin met her in the Wellbeloves' shop when he was buying sweets for personal consumption or for retail sales in the Baxter & Bartlett shops. But perhaps by that time Adelaide, well-nurtured by the Wellbeloves, had moved on to nearby Kingston. Was she at a school with Edwin's niece, Charles Bartlett's daughter?

Mysteries still surround Adelaide's pre-marriage years – and indeed most of her married life.

One story: they became engaged in late 1874 with a plan that the engagement would continue until Edwin had built up the business with Baxter and could provide a home for her and a steady income. For whatever reason, the 'long engagement' plan went out of the window. They applied to marry at St Paul's Church in Herne Hill but were refused as Adelaide was under twenty-one and did not have anyone's permission to marry, her parents having died.

On the morning of 6 April 1875, Adelaide, nineteen, walked down the aisle of Croydon Parish Church to wed Edwin. 6 April, the start of the tax year: was it advantageous for Edwin to marry on that date?

Her late father was noted as Adolphe, a 'professor of mathematics'. Edwin, twenty-nine, had until now prioritised his work and the opportunity to be in a business partnership. He was a steady Eddie – boring perhaps? Or was he enterprising, in love and taking a risk by marrying now rather than sticking with that unappetising 'long engagement' plan? It is easy to imagine that Adelaide's ways and intelligence were attractive to him, exciting, but perhaps on occasions disquieting and frustrating.

Much more to mull over about Adelaide's character and actions later; for now some observations about the largely maligned and drably portrayed Edwin. He may have been more unconventional and fun-loving than the man recalled by witnesses after his death. His father recalled his late son's 'merry disposition'; Edwin senior was biased, yes, but there was evidence of Edwin's cheerfulness and joking. Even, for example, his comments when looking forward to food and particular meals during his darkest days in December 1885.

Edwin was described as well-built, muscular, looking much younger than his years, with fair hair, blue eyes and a beard. After beginning to learn the grocery business as a youngster with Mr Whittaker, he spent his entire working life with food and enjoyed partaking of it in his spare time. Food was clearly his livelihood, a pleasure and a comfort.

Edwin had relatives in the area where he worked and 'was married from the house of Mr Russen, the well-known Croydon and London carrier'.[65]

Adelaide's parents, maternal grandparents and younger sister all having died (and her two brothers who knows where?) at least her maternal uncle William Chamberlain stood by her side for the wedding. Edwin's father, a cabinetmaker, was at work; Edwin had neither told him nor invited either parent to his wedding. Edwin senior and his wife were probably upset and angry afterwards that they were not involved. And a sense of unease and resentment did not go away, for Edwin senior at least. The two other Bartlett brothers were elsewhere on the wedding morning.

Deed done, the couple's signatures in the Register witnessed by Uncle William and Carolina Ann James (she was said to have later married a cousin of Edwin's) then off to a wedding breakfast. The sensible and steady bridegroom was given to understand by Adelaide that William would provide her with a dowry of £1,000 – or so it was said by some of Edwin's friends to a newspaper reporter in February 1886. (NB £1,000 in 1875 may be equivalent in purchasing power in 2022 to somewhere between £80,000 - £120,000).

Being a man of business, a partner in the small chain of grocery stores, Edwin would have been impressed by stories about successful William, the stockbroker – and presumably delighted by William's presence at the wedding. But Adelaide was an unusual prospect. One can picture Edwin being drawn in by the attractions of Adelaide: her quixotic looks, her unusual accent, her vivacity and youthful charms – and probably not the wife 'his sort' would normally choose.

Were Adelaide and Edwin ill-matched? Or did opposites attract, love blossom? Or was it a mutually expedient transaction? Business for him, escape for her? Did it soon become business for him, subjugation for her? The Married Women's Property Act 1870 was in force at the time. Its implementation allowed married women to keep any money they earned (Adelaide did not earn any money in marriage) but not to retain any personal property from before marriage (she did not have any, as far as is known). However, she would state in 1886 that she had money which went into Edwin's business.

There they were, a married couple, about to embark on a life of ... What was in the minds of these disparate characters?

Adelaide, who probably thought she was worth much more, escaped from what she may have regarded as a dull life behind the sweet counter in Hampton Wick High Street ... to what in Kingston ... and into what she said was an 'arranged' marriage. Edwin: happy? Or beginning to have doubts about Uncle William providing the £1,000 that Adelaide said he would?

'A TACIT UNDERSTANDING'

Wedding breakfast over, no one sat around for long. Time is money; there was work to return to. Uncle William went off to the Stock Exchange as usual.

Off go the couple, with news to convey. Edwin announces the done deal and deed to his parents. Sarah and Edwin senior naturally assume the newly-weds will live together. Not so. That is not going to happen – yet.

To his parents' surprise and puzzlement, Edwin tells them that Adelaide will begin her married life in Stoke Newington, at the school of a Miss Dodd.

Wait a minute, look at that again: Adelaide is taken off to school in north London by Edwin. He then goes home to south London. She is in yet another new 'home' for her; he returns to his parents' home – it's his home too – in Herne Hill.

Edwin gets on with his usual grocering and goes home most nights. Sometimes he visits Adelaide in north London and the newly-weds spend time together during school holidays. They meet away from Edwin's home, away from all the shop premises and from the eyes of his older business partner, Edward Baxter. Edwin had the 'tacit understanding' with Baxter that he would not marry for three years from the start of their recent business partnership. So perhaps Adelaide is hidden away? Or is there a compromise deal between Edwin and Baxter that Edwin will not yet spend money on a home away from his parents? Adelaide is using the educational opportunity she has probably always wanted – and her uncle William may be supporting. The upshot: Adelaide and Edwin are married but detached.

It seems plausible that Edwin got himself into a pickle by marrying instead of having a long engagement – and equally believable that Adelaide would not have agreed to the latter. She never seems to have been someone who would subscribe to deferred gratification. She would surely have baulked at living with the in-laws if it could be avoided. Thus Adelaide was away from the perplexed father-in-law, Edwin senior, who might have smelt a rat – even if he did not yet know what sort of one. He began what turned into ten years of angry and infuriating watchfulness.

THE MARRIAGE 'CONTRACT' OR 'COMPACT'

For Adelaide's side of the family, or maybe for just Uncle William, an 'understanding' would probably have been too loose. A marriage 'contract' was required; Adelaide later called it a 'compact'. Edwin may have had a similar imperative, anticipating that a dowry would be paid to him. Previous writers thought it unusual for there to be one, but dowries have been part of society for thousands of years, among all classes. In the Victorian era, dowries in the upper and middle classes were seen as early payment of a daughter's inheritance. Cleverly, the size of a dowry was expected to be in proportion to the status of the groom – not of the bride – as a way for him to acquire a bride of similar status. From a bridegroom's angle, this signified 'I'm this class, I'll cost you £ …'. From the bride's family's point of view: 'if you want to put a ring on it, we can pay you £ … to do so'.

Given that her father had died in 1860 and her mother in 1866, it is likely that a dowry for Adelaide was money 'earned' via the Stock Exchange by her maternal uncle, William Chamberlain. He was the most likely source of a dowry – and due to hand it over, according to Adelaide.

This and other really juicy pieces of information were 'leaked' about Edwin and Adelaide to the press almost eleven years later. *Lloyd's Weekly Newspaper* was the hugely popular paper that passed on a huge scoop of facts and opinions about the Bartletts to other newspapers.[66]

On 24 February 1886, below a column of the latest news about 'The Pimlico Poisoning Case', the *Wigan Observer and District Advertiser* had the 'intelligence' about Edwin from his friends (and probably from Edwin senior).

This sensational story seemingly escaped the notice of previous researchers and sat in the archives unused, until now. It will appear in full when Adelaide's story reaches February 1886. Here are the details pertinent at this stage of the couple's lives.

The marriage contract stipulations were firstly that Edwin would take responsibility for Adelaide, secondly that he would not refer to her origins – ever – and lastly that he would supervise an education for her. It is highly likely that those requirements (facilitating an escape with good prospects) suited young Adelaide too: not having to work as a confectioner's assistant; no tiresome, awkward and demeaning references to her past; belatedly receiving a good education (like her younger brother Freddy). Perhaps it suited Adelaide to spend most of her time away from her husband and in-laws – but into what traps might 'escape' through this oddly-matched marriage lead?

SECRETS AND SCHOOLS

Adelaide had lost her family and replaced it – not with a full-time husband (as was expected of her) – with an institutional life. The unconventionality of this, when publicised in 1886, impacted negatively; it was viewed as a distinctly odd thing to do. A woman was expected to live with her husband unless he was absent through work, for instance. In 1886 no light was shone on the question: when was the marriage consummated? Questions were asked about various sexual matters – but not *that* one.

She became a pupil or an assistant at a residential establishment, the historic Manor House School in Stoke Newington, north London, an area she knew as a child. Edgar Allan Poe, the American writer and literary critic, was fostered in London and attended the school from 1817 for three years.[67]

By 1871, it had become a large boarding school; two of the pupils were from Adelaide, Australia.

It may have been Adelaide's choice to be at that particular establishment, preparing to emulate her parents and her maternal grandmother in teaching, rather than her being told what to do by her husband. And told too by an absent 'father', as has been portrayed in some accounts (those which suggested that she was the daughter of a prominent Englishman).

During school holidays she stayed 'in apartments' with Edwin, according to his father. So perhaps Adelaide and Edwin had sex there – protected sex of some variety – unless it was sometimes unprotected sex. If it was unprotected, did she have a specific reason, a pregnancy, for her next unusual move? Nothing has ever been evidenced.

Now a short detour to events in another part of London in 1876, before returning to watch Adelaide's next step …

THE MYSTERIOUS DEATH OF CHARLES BRAVO

It is highly likely that in July and August 1876, Edwin, and possibly Adelaide, were reading shocking reports from the second Inquest (which lasted five weeks) into the death of barrister Charles Bravo in Balham. He died an excruciating death through poisoning by potassium antimony (referred to as tartar emetic in the Inquest). Who knows what was NOT published: the sensational details – including sex and certain unmentionable sexual practices – were considered to be too shocking for women to read about.

And women were controlled by the men who refused them attendance at this, the second Inquest. Parts of the material published after that Inquest were deliciously thrilling to some and filthy to others. Bravo's widow, Florence, was caught up in this mortifying scandal. Her life ruined, she never recovered from that Inquest and whatever trauma she felt around the death of her second husband. Her companion, Jane Cannon Cox, went through days of grilling at the Inquest; no one was ever charged with Charles Bravo's murder.[68]

Back to Adelaide's next move. She and Edwin always told friends and relatives that after being at school in Stoke Newington she spent about eighteen months at a convent school near Antwerp, Belgium. Perhaps that was the country of her father's birth, or where he lived after the Netherlands and before France. Whether Adelaide had to go there for a particular, personal reason (a pregnancy) or whether it was for a religious education (in a Protestant or Catholic convent) is not known. In 1886, some newspapers said it was a secular school. Dutch was the local language but many people would also have spoken other languages. Edwin visited Adelaide regularly in Belgium. Then at last he took his wife home.

'Home' to south London to live with him – but not at the Bartlett seniors' home. Edwin and Adelaide had a flat above the BAXTER & BARTLETT double-fronted shop at 1 & 2 Station Road, Herne Hill. The clue is in that street name: the shop attracted customers going to and from London and elsewhere by train. A convenient shop, handy for groceries and confectionery, among rows and rows of terraced houses built for those moving to this suburb, for those flocking into the Big Smoke for work.

Adelaide's interaction with her father-in-law was fraught, Edwin senior being suspicious of Adelaide's absence for those first few years after the wedding, and perhaps suspicious about her motives in marrying his son. He may not have questioned Edwin's reasons for the marriage.

The first and longest-lasting triangle in the married life of Adelaide and Edwin was that with Edwin senior; the second (real or imagined) was with Fred, Edwin's younger brother.

A young man named George Dyson would take a side in the last of the three known triangles. The shape of things to come.

Chapter 17

BED AND BORED

There they were, in their own home (rented) for the first time. Whether Adelaide had a plan to settle for and with Edwin (using him as a stepping-stone to a more fulfilling life) or had no plan, she had little or no contact with her birth family after marriage. And her interests were unconventional for that era, her personality perhaps too volatile to sustain friendships for long. Or did Edwin limit her social sphere? Visitors were mainly Edwin's male friends – and Adelaide was an intriguing prospect, a woman to be observed and questioned about her background. She felt put through her paces to show off her skills, objectified rather than valued for her whole self. Women were supposed to know their place and stay in it. Adelaide knew this – but neither wanted to be nor could be constrained for long.

'WE WERE AFTER HER'
According to Edwin senior it was not long before Frederick Oscar, known as Fred (youngest of the three brothers) became the next Bartlett to appreciate Adelaide's attractions. Whether or not she really did go 'to visit an aunt' or whether she spent time away with him, Adelaide and Fred were missing from their respective homes for a week and also for odd days at various points in early 1878. Edwin senior said in Court in 1886: 'Edwin

and I thought she had gone with my son Fred and we were after her.'

Hunting for Adelaide: it sounds very distasteful. They were on her track and that would never be forgotten by her, a hunted woman who would turn upon the men at a time of her choosing.

Fred, without going back to London to face the music, and probably having been told, 'Stay away!' by the Bartlett men, headed for the United States that June. Adelaide went back to her only home, chez Bartlett. Edwin senior told the Court in 1886 that Fred sent her letters. Whether or not Adelaide and Fred had been together, she probably felt annoyed that he went off to a new life while she was stuck in a place where she felt undervalued – and would be watched. Mrs Bartlett senior, Sarah, died in May 1878; Edwin and his father were understandably sad and rather lost afterwards. How they must have hated this crisis in their lives, the (allegedly) despicable behaviour of Adelaide and Fred!

'A HOME FOR LIFE'

Edwin senior (in 1886) asserted that after Sarah Bartlett's death, Edwin made this promise to him: 'Where I have a home you shall have one.' To Edwin senior this meant 'a home for life'.

Adelaide was neither consulted nor told about this significant offer until it was a fait accompli. In either case she would have been reluctant to continue to be under the same roof as her father-in-law – particularly after being hounded by him about Fred.

The suspicions of Mr Bartlett senior about Adelaide's behaviour and what she got up to with Fred soon led to a simmering family row, culminating in a public venting. Edwin hovered over a very uncomfortable chasm between the two of them. And to add to his pain, this was when his teeth began to play up. A Mr Bellin sawed off some of them right down to the gums; Edwin told people that the dentist had been unable to remove the teeth individually as they were 'stuck' together.

When her father-in-law repeated his derogatory comments about her during the autumn of 1878, Adelaide made a dramatic decision. She worked incessantly upon her husband until he felt forced to act to try to keep the peace. By doing her bidding, Edwin was caught up in her plan for revenge.

WHAT ADELAIDE DID NEXT

Adelaide's frustrations, perhaps guilt – and most definitely her anger – led to an extraordinary action and a dramatic outcome. Any concept of keeping family matters private, under wraps, was swept aside by Adelaide demanding that her husband go to a solicitor. The chosen man, Edward Negus Wood, didn't know it then but he would be in on this family's troubles for the long haul. And what a long and terrible haul it later became.

THE HUMILIATING APOLOGY

Edward Negus Wood, the solicitor whom Edwin senior had recommended to his son some years before, was required to produce a damning document against Edwin senior. Dated 31 December 1878 (a New Year's Eve … remember that) it was signed – extremely unwillingly – by the humiliated Edwin senior. Its words covered many bases but gave no detail; the emotions behind them must be guessed at.

'Having made statements reflecting on the character of Mrs Adelaide Bartlett, the wife of my son, Mr Edwin Bartlett Jr., which statements I have discovered to be unfounded and untrue, I hereby withdraw all such statements, and express my regret for having made them. I also apologise to the said Mrs Adelaide Bartlett and to Mr Edwin Bartlett Jr., and acknowledge that all such statements are altogether unfounded and untrue. I authorise Mr Edwin Bartlett Jr., to make what use he pleases of this apology.'

'MAKE PEACE'

Edwin senior had to stand and listen to this, and relive it in court in 1886 when cross-examined by Edward Clarke, who led Adelaide's defence as she looked on. Edwin senior insisted that what he called the 'suggestions' he had made against Adelaide were against his son, Fred, too. And that there were witnesses who could 'prove' it (meaning: others could say what went on between Fred and Adelaide). He also declared that Mr Negus Wood knew the suggestions were true and the apology 'false'. Edwin senior's dislike of this daughter-in-law was palpable.

The reason Edwin agreed to insist on the apology from his father was to try to placate Adelaide. In 1886, Edwin senior said he signed the apology document because his son 'begged' him to 'make peace'.

The signed document was distributed to Edwin's friends and family, showing anyone whom Adelaide insisted should know that she was the wronged party in this bitter, toxic family rift.

The hurts and alleged wrongs were on paper and went public. Edwin senior, through loyalty to his son, had signed what would these days be called a grovelling apology.

Widening cracks in the marriage facade: imagine Edwin in the shop, one foot on a floorboard, his other on another board, front door open and people going by, seeing him struggling to keep his balance as the floorboards move apart. The troubles from the upstairs flat have come down here, into his working life. The household's usual privacy is no more; Adelaide has seen to that.

New Year's Eve, the date on which Edwin senior signed the document, continued to be a deeply significant day of the year for the Bartletts, as will be seen later.

APRES THE APOLOGY

Adelaide had pulled off a coup against the menfolk. This was an act of retaliation, defiance, sheer brass neck. It must have been chilling for them, Adelaide asserting herself so emphatically in a male world. She tested her husband's loyalty, called the tune, demanded he submit to her and act against his father – insisted it went public. Thus she humiliated Edwin and her father-one-law simultaneously. Edwin was in this tricky triangle – his penultimate one. Brother Fred had absented himself from the scene. The Bartletts, Edwin junior and senior, plus Adelaide, were still under one roof.

Could civility and privacy return? Could the marriage, the rubbing along together, last?

Adelaide's insistence upon a signed apology, distributed publicly, must have been an extremely rare action by any woman in Victorian times. Adelaide and other women were not expected to act in such a way. And she had been decisive against not just one man, but two. Adelaide would brood on her situation for many years to come. Although Edwin had taken the action she demanded against his father, it became evident in later years that her husband's response had been nowhere near wholehearted enough for Adelaide's liking. Despite some relief obtained when throwing himself into work, Edwin probably felt tense at home. And miserable; his teeth getting him down so dreadfully put him increasingly under the weather.

Whatever dregs of true happiness were left in the marriage presumably began to seep out of them, whatever bright faces they showed to the world.

In stark terms, if Adelaide had had enough, things must change. And she did not forget or forgive. Her stoked-up rage burned on, despite outward appearances. How did it feel to be her?

'BORED
Adelaide, bored.
More bored than ever before.
Teeth-grinding, buttocks-clenched,
shrill-toned, tight-wired,
bolt upright piano,
banging on the keys,
bored.
Fingers, fists, knees
up hard
under the keyboard,
that sort
of
bored.
Angry too,
about money
that
she said
was hers.
When would there be more
to life?
She felt
she had a right to want
to see
an end to this tedium
in sight.'
(Rose Storkey)

Chapter 18

WHAT ADELAIDE DID

After her indignation and her humiliation of the Edwins, Adelaide's other behaviours were conventional, in practical matters at least. She embroidered, sewed, played the piano and sang, sometimes for Edwin's male friends, helped the servant with a little housework. And walked the dogs: they needed a great deal of exercise every day and probably she did too, to combat restlessness. One of her abiding passions was reading; she read voraciously, widely, deeply and for hours on end. In the absence of a job, a family, having few friends and a husband who was out working long hours for six days of each week, she gained comfort, stimulation and new ideas from books. Coming from families in which the positive results of reading, education and teaching were evident on both sides of the tree, Adelaide always felt a need to read. Learning and literacy were like food and drink to her and those families.

Edwin greatly admired learning in others; intelligence, study and debate would have been two of the numerous qualities attracting Edwin to Adelaide and they held his interest during their marriage. He was bright, applied himself and was adept with figures, but it is unlikely that he had any education after his mid teens, and little free time for reading after that. However, either he or Adelaide became interested in unconventional subjects and discussing books about such matters was one of the few satisfying things (other than the breeding of dogs) that they had in common.

MARY GOVE NICHOLS AND THOMAS LOW NICHOLS

Adelaide ordered copies of medical books and esoteric works, including those by the Americans Mary Gove Nichols and Thomas Low Nichols. The couple lived in London for over twenty years until Mary's death in 1884.[69] [70] [71]

The Nichols's are little known in the twenty-first century, but as influential writers and practitioners they were prominent individually in the 1840s and together from the 1850s. Mary's first husband, Hiram Gove, was abusive and she left him, taking their daughter with her. Mary was ill in childhood, had four miscarriages and suffered during childbirth. For many years she took her experiences to platforms and venues as a radical social reformer and feminist advocate for women's rights, speaking out on women's health and anatomy – taboo subjects for many.

From 1844, she studied water cures and eventually found a permanent place to practice in New York. She treated a huge range of acute and chronic diseases and conditions, achieving what was deemed a high success rate. All this was in the context of women being blocked from attending conventional medical colleges. There was no requirement at that time in the country to obtain a 'license to practise'. Mary's views and skills were much sought after; she emphasised the importance of happiness and discussed women's desires, as well as explaining bodily functions and possible problems.

Desires which women often felt unable, or not allowed, to express. Desires which Adelaide probably felt. Did she discuss them with Edwin after reading Mary's books? One can imagine Adelaide wanting to explore her responses to the words, and her feelings about her body ...

On Christmas Eve 1847, Mary met and later began to work and live with Thomas Low Nichols. Undeterred by criticisms of their unconventional behaviour, they inspired one another's work on health and marriage reform. Mary, an experienced hydrotherapist, founded (with Thomas) the first American Hydropathic Institute, based on using water cures as part of a healthy regime and for the treatment of diseases. In 1851, they opened a medical school, to which women were admitted – how could it have been otherwise, with the tenacious Mary involved? She became a spiritual medium in 1854.

Her book *Mary Lyndon, Or Revelations of a Life. An Autobiography* (under her full name, Mary Sargeant Gove Nichols) made public her childhood travails – and also the misery of her marriage to Hiram Gove, in which she was belittled and controlled. Despite their negativity about the institution of marriage, Mary and Thomas had wed in 1848, and founded what many described as a 'free love' colony, the Memnonia Institute. From 1856, their spiritual beliefs swung towards Catholicism.

Mary and Thomas left their homeland in 1861, being against the Union cause and the American Civil War. Heading over the Atlantic Ocean, they made for the Malvern Hills in western England. This range of ancient rocks (now designated an 'Area of Outstanding Natural Beauty') has long been known for its spring water. In the nineteenth century, the spa town of Malvern expanded rapidly. Dr James Manby Gully (who later featured prominently in the Charles Bravo case, of which yet more in this story in 1886) developed 'water cure' treatments there with a colleague. Hydrotherapy clinics, associated health services and the necessary infrastructure, including the railway link in 1859, changed the town of Malvern forever. Charles Darwin and Florence Nightingale were among the clients who visited the fast-growing inland resort.

Thomas and Mary Gove Nichols were valued by many open-minded individuals for their forthright and detailed broaching of health and sexual matters; most Victorian men and women were ignorant of such and uninformed, but usually did not say so. Thomas and Mary's work (promoting ideas such as specific foods for good health, also about spiritualism) was not to everyone's taste but attracted enthusiastic 'converts'.

To be within reach of the many people who sought their help, and to increase their clientele, the Nichols moved from Malvern to London. Their health ethos struck a chord with Adelaide, and Edwin read some of their work. His views on it? There are just two clues, one slight and one significant. Edwin had a cold bath every morning; secondly, Dyson saw the 'Esoteric' book at the Bartletts and initiated a discussion with Edwin about Dr Nichols' writing. Yet frustratingly few details of their conversation were revealed by Dyson in 1886.

And, apart from a couple of letters, Edwin the person is lost to us forever ...

Back to 'marriage'. A question allegedly put by Edwin to Dyson early in their friendship was about 'two wives': whether a man should have two at the same time. One wife for companionship and one for work. Or for something else? No mention of the unmentionable: sex. This 'two wives' issue was done to death in court in 1886, with enquiries as to what sort of marriage the Bartletts had. It was unanswered. Edwin was dead, Dyson vague and Adelaide was not saying. She gave no evidence, full stop.

The Nichols' book *Marriage: its History, Character, and Results; its Sanctities, and its Profanities; the Science and its Facts. Demonstrating its Influence, as a Civilized Institution, on the Happiness of the Individual and the Progress of the Race* had been published in 1854 (its lengthy title typical in that century).

Adelaide gave one of Thomas's books to a male friend of both Bartletts, George Matthews. *Esoteric Anthropology (the mysteries of man)* included details of the condition and treatment of the human reproductive system, gestation and childbirth. Chapters included 'Impregnation' and 'Evolution of the Foetus'. Matthews' outraged wife, Alice, rapidly returned the book – unread, according to Alice and George – to Adelaide.

More to come from the Matthews – and about *that* book – in 1886.

WOMEN IN THE VICTORIAN ERA

The concept of men and women occupying 'separate spheres' is applied to when, allegedly, men were hunters and women primarily child-rearers, minders and food preparers. And in western societies, role division has largely held sway.

In the middle classes during the Victorian era, the stereotypical view was that women belonged in the domestic sphere, and their rights were limited. In marriage, the husband controlled any property, earnings and other financial matters. The wife was the property of her husband; he had rights over her body in terms of sexual contact, over their children and her domestic labour. This was the context in which Edwin conducted his marriage with the young woman under a contract or compact. Adelaide was supposed to be under his control.

THE FIGURE OF THE 'NEW WOMAN'

In the UK, the Elementary Education Act 1880 built upon previous acts and made school attendance compulsory for children between the ages of five and ten. But many children still did not go to school; absentees included those whose parents could not afford for their children to be out of work. But many young people had already benefited from being able to attend school and had opportunities to seek employment beyond the sphere of their families. Education often leads to questioning the mores of previous generations and in Victorian England it led to demands from many women and men for radical change. Chafing at restrictions (physical, moral, familial, marital, personal and political) young women often wanted more than was previously permitted.

Debates about such subjects as reproduction, sexual activity without reproduction, sexual health, marriage, motherhood and rights arose alongside changes in sexual attitudes and behaviour. Of course, often the Establishment was in direct opposition to a discussion of the issues, resistant to any changes in attitudes and – perish the thought – practices. Repression and oppression went hand in hand with disgust and ignorance for many people, who were denied access to information and advice about sexual health, for instance. And what women might want as individuals did not feature a great deal.

Knowledgeable and 'alternative' practitioners, Mary and Thomas Nichols for example, were passionate in their work and valued by the people, particularly women, who flocked to their presentations and surgeries. As will be seen in 1886, opposition was harsh from many men in positions of authority towards women who wanted and needed to learn about their bodies.

'HOME DUTIES'

Census enumerators in 1881 often recorded women as having 'Home Duties'. Adelaide's were extremely light, because Edwin could afford a servant or two. So she had scope for other interests, such as developing expertise in the treatment of their beloved dogs' ailments, and plenty of time for exercising the big creatures. Adelaide was a young woman who was putting to use both her intelligence and whatever education she had as a young woman in London and Belgium. *Squires' Companion to the British Pharmacopoeia* was one of her tomes – and this fact, conjuring up images of a multitude of medications, loomed large in the sensational revelations of 1886.[72]

PART FOUR
ADELAIDE AND EDWIN ENDURE

Chapter 19

ILLNESS AND LOSS

'I ASSESSED HIM AS A FIRST-CLASS LIFE'
In November 1880, Edwin obtained life insurance to the tune of £400 – 'the usual premium'.

Dr William Clapton, assessing him for a suitable policy, examined him and gave a positive report. He assessed Edwin 'as a first-class life.' By the time the doctor repeated his words in 1886 they hung hollow in the air, drawing out a mixture of nervous and heartless laughter from around the Court.

It is understandable that a link might be made between Edwin's newly purchased life insurance and the deterioration in his health the following year. Understandable, that is, if one believes that Adelaide had a hand in his demise. Or perhaps there was no link between insurance and illness, no link between his tip-top condition in November 1880 and his breakdown in 1881?

Soon the mood up and down the land was glum. The First Anglo-Boer War between the South African/Transvaal Republic and the United Kingdom lasted from December 1880 until March 1881. It ended with the British agreeing to a truce (obviously they had expected to win) and led to the second independence of the South African Republic.

William Wellbelove, sugar boiler and ginger beer maker, died in May 1881. He and Ann had provided homes for at least four boarded-out children from London, and he had been a key figure in the early lives of Adelaide and her younger brother Freddy.

EDWIN BARTLETT'S FIRST ILLNESS

By the end of 1881 the Bartlett household had experienced mysteries and crises which culminated in a deep sadness. It had held a breakdown, a journey of convalescence, a pregnancy and a death.

Adelaide and Edwin still lived at 1 & 2 Station Road. Also at that address lived Edwin senior, three male grocery employees of Baxter & Bartlett and two female servants.

CONCEPTION

Adelaide conceived.

Up at Fopstone Road in Kensington, Thomas L Nichols, sixty-five, was recorded as 'Head' of the household, an 'Author, Journalist, Dr of Medicine'; Mary SG Nichols, seventy, as an 'Author & Physician'. They had a visitor, a 'Spirit Medium', an earthly being named Henry Bastian. He, like Mary and Thomas, was born in the United States. Mary had trained as a spiritual medium there.

'OVERWORK'

At some point in 1881, Edwin's nerves became strained. He broke down through 'overwork' (according to his father) after laying a floor in a newly acquired warehouse, part of the expanding business. Edwin senior spent his working life as a cabinetmaker/carpenter/builder and son Edwin was skilled in woodwork too; this made a change for him from the grocery business with its tea blending and tasting, ordering and organising.

'NOTHING BUT BUSINESS; HE WAS WRAPPED UP IN HIS BUSINESS'

So said the father about his son, always 'a very hard-working man'. Whatever the causes, physical and/or emotional, Edwin's energy failed him in early 1881. He roused himself sufficiently to go on a voyage to Scotland and continued overland to Balmoral. Some writers have posited that Edwin had been poisoned – either with lead acetate by Adelaide or through working with lead-lined tea chests. His partner Edward Baxter and the staff were not affected, so it seems unlikely that any poisoning came from the tea chests. Edwin's 'breakdown', as his father recalled in late 1885 when Edwin became ill again, raised the suspicion that Adelaide used lead acetate on Edwin in 1885, and that it caused a thin blue line to appear on his gums. And that she may have used it in 1881.

YSEULT BRIDGES

Crime writer Yseult Bridges' theory was that Adelaide used the substance on Edwin but stopped doing so when his doctor said tests should be done, to see if lead acetate was making Edwin ill.[73]

Yseult was born in Trinidad, a Caribbean island with a wide range of cultures, ethnic groups and religions; her mother was 'Creole French'. Yseult's book (edited and completed by Nicholas Guppy, her nephew) *Child of the Tropics: Victorian Memoirs* is an evocative story of her childhood in Trinidad. She travelled to England at the age of about fourteen to attend boarding school.[74]

Did Yseult Bridges know about or sense (at some level) Adelaide's heritage? If not, her fascination with the case is ironic, given she did not have knowledge of Adelaide's true birth father.

EXPECTING

In spring 1881, after his few weeks of convalescence, health restored by his rest and the change of scene, Edwin returned home. At some stage his wife's pregnancy was confirmed. Adelaide's story later: she and Edwin had only one 'connection' (sexual intercourse).

Perhaps Edwin's breakdown was linked in some way with Adelaide's pregnancy. There is no record of whether he was happy, sad or indifferent about the expected baby. Was Adelaide's baby Edwin's baby?

That autumn at Adelaide's request no less a personage than Mary Gove Nichols booked her a nurse, Annie Walker, who had fourteen years' experience as a midwife. Annie lived with the Bartletts for four weeks from October for Adelaide's 'lying-in' and the birth. In November, when the stage came that Adelaide was 'confined' (in labour, her baby's birth imminent) Annie's patient suffered great pain. There was a serious problem.

By April 1886, the story from Annie Walker was that Edwin would not agree to calling for a doctor to aid the birth because he did not want another man to interfere with his wife. The other factor, as stated in Court by Annie, was that Adelaide had planned to avoid having a doctor involved, as she hoped to give birth naturally, with just Nurse Walker's help. Annie eventually sent word to a Dr Woodward, but terribly sadly the baby girl died before his arrival.

'IT WAS A GREAT GRIEF TO HER WHEN HER LITTLE GIRL DIED'

In 1886, Adelaide's friend, Alice Matthews, said: 'Mrs Bartlett was very fond of children, and it was a great grief to her when her little girl died'.[75]

Adelaide's experiences around the birth and death of her baby girl felt so traumatic that she dreaded getting pregnant again (at least if that was by Edwin, it seems). If there was to be further sexual intercourse between

Edwin and Adelaide it seems highly likely that she would not want it to be without a 'French letter', a condom, a preventive being used.

The month after Adelaide's baby's death, Ann Wellbelove died at Hampton Wick on Christmas Day 1881. It is not known whether Adelaide had contact with either of the Wellbeloves, or with anyone else in the village, after her marriage in 1875.

CASTING OFF THE FATHER-IN-LAW

Leaving their annus horribilis behind them, Edwin and Adelaide made a fresh start in 1882. The sad couple moved into a flat above another of the Baxter & Bartlett shops, The Exchange. In busy Lordship Lane – not the north London lane of that name – on an ancient thoroughfare in East Dulwich, south-east London. This was yet another, still rapidly expanding suburb with an ever-increasing demand for the provisions which Baxter & Bartlett were so proficient at providing. The Bartlett's small flat had a huge compensatory feature - for Adelaide - no Edwin senior! No room for him; no space for the father-in-law whom, when it was a good day, Adelaide addressed as 'Father'.

However, this move did not result in a long stay. The couple wanted fresher air and congenial places to walk their dogs, a breed of very large Alpine cattle dogs called Saint Bernards (used in search and rescue work by monks during the 1700s at a hospice near the Great St Bernard Pass, Switzerland).

The Bartlett dogs and humans were off to fresh fields – yet not far from the suburbs.

The Married Women's Property Act 1882 came into effect on 1 January 1883. It enabled women to buy, own and sell property, also to keep their earnings. Adelaide was conversant with the effects of this and the previous Act, knew their potential impact on women's lives – but she had no property and no earnings. In 1886, it was said she had wanted Edwin to remove from his first Will a clause that she could not inherit his money if she remarried.

Having cast off Edwin's father, Adelaide must have relished the move that the couple made during 1883 to a rural property, The Cottage at Merton Abbey. It was two miles from Wimbledon and Edwin took on a three-year lease. Life there suited them – and the dogs of course. Few friends were ever invited to visit but George and Alice Matthews stayed there for a week, just once. Edwin senior, despite the humiliation and the negative feelings Adelaide had about him, visited frequently – or was in their garden, at least. He was building kennels for the dogs and so his presence was tolerated by his daughter-in-law; he was doing something useful for the couple. Edwin senior was also in the habit of visiting his son at his various shops and warehouses. They were close, on some levels, certainly after the death of Edwin's mother, but presumably the isolated Adelaide was still a wedge between father and son.

Edwin was considerate and kind; for one thing regularly putting money into his father's hands. But some of that money was being sent on (unbeknown to Edwin) by the wily Edwin senior to young Fred Bartlett in America. Fred wrote 'scores' of letters to his father – some of them begging letters, perhaps.

Edwin senior would definitely not have told his allegedly cuckolded son, Edwin, that the unmentionable Fred was getting his hard-working brother's money – for nothing. If Edwin senior truly believed that Adelaide and Fred had an affair back in 1878, presumably he saw Adelaide as the guilty party.

YOU MADE YOUR BED …

Inevitably, the more Adelaide educated herself, broadened her horizons, and the busier Edwin became, the more she yearned for changes in her lot. In that humdrum life, by 1885, her married state may have felt like making the best of a bad job, putting on a brave face, stuck with the security of Edwin. Trapped because she had no money of her own, no support from outside the marriage. Yet whatever different facets he saw in her by then, there is no evidence to suggest Edwin had tired of his wife's allure and personality. Ambivalence on his part? Finding his wife's looks highly attractive still, her personality a strong pull – but unnerved by her boredom? Adelaide may have felt or feigned an interest in Edwin's work, and they still had their joint interest in dog breeding. The true situation, the positives and negatives, will never be known. Outsiders don't know the half of what goes on behind closed doors.

... NOW LIE IN IT

From 1 January 1885 at their home in rural Merton Abbey, Adelaide had the services of Mary Ann Furlong indoors and Mr Furlong outside; he did the garden and looked after the St Bernard dogs. That February, the Bartletts began attending a Methodist church; some newspapers in 1886 suggested their attendance was due to the influence of Edwin's business partner, Edward Baxter, attending one in Brixton. A change of religious observance for Adelaide – or had she and Freddy gone to a Methodist church with the Wellbeloves when living with them at Hampton Wick?

The Bartletts' small action, attending the Methodist church in Merton High Street, led to devastating events. Take heed, this was the tipping point in the lives of three people, and of their families and friends.[76]

Chapter 20

DYSON FILLS THE VACUUM

BEING GEORGE DYSON

Ironically, as it turned out, in 1885 the Reverend George Dyson was working as a 'Preacher On Trial'. That title was given to those who after training had a foot on the ladder to becoming a minister in the Methodist Church. Dyson's job title preceded the romance and tribulations which led to his involvement in a court trial the following year: a still-notorious trial. Born in Northampton, central England in 1858, he was the son of a well-respected Minister whose peripatetic work resulted in his family, including young George, living in numerous parts of England and Wales.

Dyson boarded at the Methodist school at Kingswood, on the northern slopes of the beautiful city of Bath in the west of England. The original school was established in 1748 by the Methodist founder, John Wesley at King's Wood near Bristol (until 1851) to provide an education for the children of local colliers; the area had coalfields. Subsequently the sons – not the daughters – of itinerant Methodist clergymen were admitted to the school.

After Kingswood, Dyson spent four years studying at Headingley, Leeds in the north of England and did six years of preparatory courses for the Wesleyan ministry. So, like Adelaide, he spent time living in institutions; in his case a great deal of time.

In his first job, Dyson was given charge of a small church in the High Street, Merton. Having met Mr and Mrs Bartlett among his congregation that spring, by June 1885 he had accepted Edwin's request to tutor Adelaide in Latin, history, geography and mathematics. Whether it was actually Adelaide's idea to receive one-to-one tutoring will never be known.

There followed an intense period of interaction between these three disparate characters as they fashioned a puzzling, triangular relationship. Mesmerising influence, magnetic attraction and damaging subterfuge seemed to be involved – for some if not all three of them.

PLAYING BOTH SIDES AGAINST THE MIDDLE

From June to the dire end of December 1885, Dyson had an insider's view of the Bartlett marriage – whatever sort of marriage it was – and his frequent presence obviously changed its dynamics. In 1886 he voiced a selective, self-serving version of the three of them when, selfishly but understandably, saving his own neck was his pressing priority. He comes across as having been utterly besotted with Adelaide – and as a man playing both sides against the middle in relation to his trusting friend, Edwin.

Adelaide, and probably Edwin, felt the tensions at the hollow heart of their marriage – and Dyson seemed up for filling the gaps. With him on hand, and Edwin allegedly pushing them together, Adelaide recreated a scenario. A man handing her over to another man. As a teenager she had an arranged marriage, she alleged, and became the property of Edwin. Now she was being given, by her husband, to Dyson, she later claimed.

It is as though the real or feigned helplessness of the first event should be avenged by scheming against Edwin. For a crucial period she wielded control of both men, charming and wooing Dyson right under Edwin's nose. Perhaps as she had done with Fred Bartlett.

DYSON DRAWS NIGH

Dyson: eager, willing and probably 'wet behind the ears'. Adelaide: the one most likely to have made the running, bowling the novice over. He soon became a keen participant. In June 1885, he began to spend hours with Adelaide, rapidly becoming infatuated with her, going between his church work, his parishioners, and back to the Bartlett residence. And *quelle horreur!* She visited his lodgings at 12 Thornton Road, Wimbledon – unchaperoned – 'not the done thing' at all. He had to tear himself away to spend a week at Trinity College, Dublin in Ireland to sit the examinations for his BA degree; he was awarded a First. Most of his life had involved studying. Dyson was not a young man who had sowed his wild oats; thought about it probably – sex – but nowhere near doing anything with someone. Until he met Adelaide, that is.

The ancient, agrarian saying, 'wild oats', originally referred to the worse than useless activity of sowing grasses commonly known as 'wild oats', grasses which spread and had to be laboriously weeded out of a field crop. The 'wild oats' saying was applied to young men who behaved carelessly. Later, urban dwellers neither knew much nor cared about oats, wild or otherwise, and the term 'sowing wild oats' became associated with male indulgence in sexual activity before marriage.

Frustratingly, we do not know how far Dyson and Adelaide 'went' …

FORMERLY OF ROAD/RODE

In July 1885, Constance Kent was released from Millbank Prison in London, having served the full sentence of twenty years for murder of her half-brother. News of her imminent liberation on a 'ticket-of-leave' had hit the headlines in numerous national and local newspapers across England that month. Doubtless the Bartletts and Dyson were among the readers wondering where Constance would go, how she would try to escape the inevitable, unwanted intrusion – and what she might be yearning to do during the remaining years of her life. She was forty-one; there was no hint about where she would go.

No one would have envisaged her living as she did, incredibly – after such hardship and stress – for another fifty-nine years. (Her photograph and an article featured in newspapers, in recognition of her life and her hundredth birthday in 1944.)

THE MISUSE OF CHILDREN

WT Stead, crusading journalist and editor, went out and about on the seamiest streets of London in July 1885, collecting material for an exposé of 'child prostitution'.[77] (His interest in supernatural forces and psychic experiences would lead him to write stories, including a chilling one about a large ship and treacherous icebergs in the 1890s. Foreshadowing his own tragedy, Stead named his fictional captain 'Smith' – the same name as the real captain of the ill-fated RMS *Titanic*, on which Stead was to lose his life in 1912.)

His exposé came in four hugely controversial instalments published by the *Pall Mall Gazette* in a series called 'The Maiden Tribute of Modern Babylon'. Titles included 'The Violation of Virgins', 'The Confessions of a Brothel-Keeper' and most notably 'A Child of Thirteen Bought for £5': the story of 'Lily' a thirteen-year-old virgin sold into prostitution by her mother who was allegedly an alcoholic.

Stead's purpose, along with colleagues from the Social Purity movement and the Salvation Army, was to pressure the government into passing a bill raising the 'age of consent' (to sexual intercourse) from thirteen to sixteen.

Many Victorians were flooded with moral panic; outrage and sustained public reaction led in next to no time to the Criminal Law Amendment Act. Passed on 14 August 1885, it was an 'Act to make further provision for the Protection of Women and Girls, the suppression of brothels, and other purposes'.

Meanwhile, newspapers were 'on to' the background of the child – who was *not* named Lily – and were busily investigating the case. They would break the true story.

THE CASE OF ELIZA ARMSTRONG

On 25 August, the *Pall Mall Gazette* had a piece, 'a final word', by the self-designated 'Chief Director of the Secret Commission' (Stead) about the case of Eliza Armstrong. Eliza, who had been depicted as the thirteen-year-old virgin, 'Lily', was 'handed over' to her mother the day before – on his instructions. There was no intention originally to mention real names; it became necessary after incessant pressure from national newspapers.

'SMELT THE CHLOROFORM BOTTLE'

Stead told a complicated story, adding how the girl was taken to a brothel, 'smelt the chloroform bottle and dozed off into a gentle slumber' – then woke all of a sudden. He said she had been needed in order to prove what went on when children were procured, including how chloroform was being sold for the drugging of victims. This 'Chief Director' tried to justify his actions – including Eliza having been subjected to an intimate examination by a midwife (to see if she was intact) – by claiming that Eliza had 'been restored to her mother ... much improved in both appearance and condition.'

But Stead and the public had not heard the last of all this …

'THE CHILD WAS ASKED TO GIVE IT A GOOD SNIFF'

The *Liverpool Mercury* of 8 September had the story of a case at Bow Street Court, London the previous day. Mr Harry Poland was one of the prosecutors (he will reappear in Edwin and Adelaide's story). The accused included a Rebecca Jarrett and WT Stead, brought before the Court for extremely serious matters including assaults on the alleged victim, Eliza.

'IT SMELT VERY QUEER'

Part of the evidence against Stead was that the child, taken to a house and given a bottle, 'was asked to give it a good sniff'. Eliza gave evidence; a Mrs Jarrett had 'put something on a handkerchief, held [it] to her nose, saying it was scent, and she was to take a good sniff up. It smelt very queer, and she took it out of Mrs Jarrett's hand and threw it away'. Obviously it (the chloroform) had not time to take much effect and Eliza screamed when a man (Stead) entered the room. The situation had gone from bad to worse for all concerned. Eliza had to 'sniff up' some chloroform (a colourless, sweet-smelling dense liquid): a powerful anaesthetic; an anxiolytic (inhibitor of anxiety); a euphoriant; a sedative when inhaled or ingested. Chloroform was all over the London and national newspapers that summer.

Things were hotting up over at Merton Abbey during the last two weeks of August. The servant, Mary Ann Furlong, seemed to have the measure of Mrs Bartlett and the Reverend. She was to say later that the Reverend Dyson dined six times with Mrs Bartlett – just the two of them, alone – and only once with Mr Bartlett present, on 31 August. Mary Ann added that

Mrs Bartlett told her Mr Bartlett did not like women. The servant was not asked whether anything more was divulged. A pity.

'DEAR OLD DOVER'
Edwin rented a house that September on the English Channel coast, for time with Adelaide and their dogs, at 14 St James' Street, Dover in the county of Kent.

WHAT WAS EDWIN WORTH?
Something or someone prompted Edwin to write out a new (or first?) Will. It was brief. He signed and dated it 3 September 1885. 'I will and bequeath all my property and everything I am possessed of to my wife Adelaide for her sole use.' The two Executors were the man of religion, reliable Rev Dyson, and Edward Negus Wood, solicitor. But this Will of Edwin's was not sent to the ever-reliable Negus Wood for safekeeping. The solicitor first saw it after Edwin's death.

This Will contained a crucial change from the first one Adelaide said her husband had made: there was nothing in this fresh one that said she must not remarry. She presumably knew Edwin's worth: he took about £300 per year from the business. According to Edward Baxter, his business partner, Edwin owned no property.

MONEY MONEY MONEY
Money was always important to Adelaide; it featured in her mind and sometimes she voiced her preoccupation to others. Intrusive thoughts can come out as rehearsals or confessions; some of her uppermost thinking about money will reappear in the account of January 1886.

Money, important of course to Edwin too; he always wanted to get on in life, not just get by. Why a new Will – or was it his first one? Why now? In 1886, Edwin's solicitor said he had never seen another Will by his client.

Money in mind, what or who prompted this will-making? Was Edwin under tremendous pressure, even mesmeric influence, when deciding to write it? He took the Will with him to work on 3 September and had his signature witnessed by two employees. Not only was it Edwin's last Will and Testament, this was to be his last September.

Dover, September, 1885. Adelaide being seen around town and on top of the white cliffs with the huge dogs; in all likelihood she was never happier than when striding along enjoying the freedom and fresh air with the St Bernards. Her husband commuting to work, often alongside travellers from France, on the 'tidal train', the 'boat express' to London, into the city by 6 a.m.

A couple of day trips for Edwin senior and two or three staying visits for Dyson. By these Dover days, both Bartletts addressed Dyson as their gorgeous 'Georgius Rex'. He paid visits to them totalling between six and nine days – Georgius Rex could not remember how many exactly, when asked further down the line. Edwin took him for a day to Calais, France, paying for the trip and the cash-strapped curate's various train fares around London.

Edwin senior (who knew nothing of Dyson, never met the man) could have told Dyson about Edwin's kindness; paying the fares of this friend was probably typical of Edwin's behaviour towards someone he liked, admired and trusted.

Georgius Rex returned to London to a new address, 18 Parkfields in

Putney, to start a new job. Promoted, put in charge of a large church. Time to get his head down and do serious work.

Edwin paid for George Dyson's season ticket from Putney to Waterloo, so that he could continue visiting the couple.

On 20 September, Edwin travelled up from Dover for a visit to his trusted friend at Putney, to tell him about his new Will, the leaving of all his money to Adelaide. And that Dyson had been made an Executor.

HAVE FAITH

On oath, Dyson later claimed that he told Edwin he was 'growing very attached to her' – to Adelaide of course – and 'it was disturbing' him in his work. He asked Edwin whether he should discontinue his friendship with the Bartletts. Allegedly, Edwin replied with a question: why should he? No need to stop being great friends; Adelaide liked the Reverend's preaching and it 'had benefited her'.

Edwin appeared somewhat preoccupied by what he perceived as Adelaide's faltering faith. Both Dyson and Edwin were well aware that in Methodism, God's pardon is granted through faith alone; sinners can receive pardon through having faith, which suffices. Edwin showed his friend one of Adelaide's letters, written in the convent. A very 'devotional' letter: Dyson alleged that Edwin had wanted him to lead Adelaide 'back more closely to that frame of mind or disposition of heart'. He had confidence in Dyson. Edwin's aim had been reawakened devotion by Adelaide to her faith – not devotion to Dyson. The Reverend presumably took the husband's encouragement as: pray continue … carry on with my wife. Or, put bluntly, abused Edwin's trust in him.

Ponder four specifics about Edwin: he kept Adelaide's convent letter all those years; his faith mattered to him; he wanted faith to matter again to his wife; he conveyed to the Reverend his belief that the preacher guided Adelaide's spiritual development.

LETTER FROM EDWIN
And Dyson kept a fulsome letter received from Edwin:

'Dear George, permit me to say that I feel great pleasure in thus addressing you for the first time … I hope our friendship may ripen … without anything to mar its future brightness.'

Edwin expresses his thanks for the 'beautiful, loving' letter Dyson sent Adelaide that day:

'it would have done anyone good to see her overflowing with joy as she read it whilst walking along the street, and afterwards as she read it to me I felt my heart going out to you. I long to tell you how proud I felt at the thought I should soon be able to clasp the hand of the man who from his heart could pen such noble thoughts. Who can help loving you. I feel that I must say to you two words, "Thank you", and my desire to do so is my excuse for troubling you with this. Looking towards the future with joyfulness I am yours affectionately, EDWIN.'

And there we have Edwin first hand: humble, happy, forward-looking; generous of heart towards Adelaide as his wife and towards Dyson as a newfound friend.

'THE CONFIDENCE AND TRUST OF OTHERS'
On 23 September, Dyson replied, 'My dear Edwin, thank you very much for the brotherly letter you sent me yesterday.' Encouraged by Edwin's letter, Dyson's reply was all about their friendship, 'founded on a firm abiding basis, trust and esteem.' Read today that phrase rings very hollow, coming from Dyson.

'I have from a boy been ever longing for the confidence and trust of others. I have never been so perfectly happy as when in possession of this.'

He was talking about Edwin's 'trust' in him – but surely it was when with Adelaide that Dyson felt 'perfectly happy?'

'I ought to confess that I read your warm and generous letter with a kind of half fear, a fear lest you should ever be disappointed in me and find me a far more prosy, matter-of-fact creature than you expect.'

Sounds like a guilty conscience and the voice of (hidden) truth emanating from the Reverend towards the husband, who had already sent a telegram and money for his friend's next visit the following week to the Bartletts, still in their holiday abode. George gushed:

'Thus far I have been able to stave off any work, and trust to be able to keep it clear. Dear old Dover, it will ever possess a pleasant memory for me in my mind and a warm place in my heart. – With very kind regards, believe me yours affectionately, George.'

Little did Dyson know that he would soon be remembering Dover with deep regret, so deep that it probably stayed with him throughout his extraordinary life.

THE SECRET OF A SECRET
With time on their hands, delicious hours of privacy in Dover, Adelaide and Dyson shared not only their feelings for one another but also their

deepest thoughts – and more.

According to Dyson, Adelaide confided that her husband had a growth in his abdomen and that a Dr Nichols said Edwin had less than a year to live. Dyson told the court in 1886 that Adelaide told him, 'Annie Walker had brought her chloroform'. He spoke 'frequently' with Adelaide about Dr Nichols because he, Dyson, was 'interested in him'. So, Dyson initiated or encouraged their discussions about Dr Nichols; Dyson already knew about mesmerism and Dr Nichols' other interests.

Adelaide added that Edwin was in great pain, knew the seriousness of his condition – and swore her to secrecy about it. She claimed there had been a prolonged bout of dysentery a few years previously and that, through the necessity to nurse him, she had studied and now knew a great deal about treatments and medicines. Thus, it seems, she smoothed the way for certain softening-up conversations with Dyson over the coming months. Gliding into talk about the future: her future, his future, their future.

Feeding him bit by bit with these shocking morsels of information about Edwin's alleged ill health, Adelaide tested young Dyson's reactions and responses, giving a credible context for her husband's enthusiasm towards a deepening relationship between the new couple. Was this an explanation as to why Edwin made the new Will?

Adelaide, spinning a yarn about Edwin anticipating an early death … how much bait would Dyson swallow? Could her explanation bring him on board or would it be a stretch too far? Adelaide, confident in her ability to reel the Reverend in, told stories to elicit his sympathies and galvanise him into action.

For some, love is a foolish and truly dangerous thing.

PART FIVE
PIMLICO

Chapter 21

THE ACCOMMODATING MRS DOGGETT

Straight from Dover and intentionally homeless, Adelaide and Edwin spent two nights in a hotel on the Strand in central London. Then it was October: they made their planned move a short distance east, into yet another leasing arrangement. Like many people in the Victorian era, the couple were used to leases. Did this one feel different or is that just an outsider's view with hindsight? An advertisement for dog kennels in the vicinity may have attracted them. The Bartletts took two first-floor rooms at 85 Claverton Street, Pimlico ('Claverton' from the name of a village and parish, once part of the Hundred of Hampton, near the city of Bath).

Why choose Pimlico? What did Adelaide anticipate doing in and around that part of London? She probably chose Pimlico for its proximity to the Embankment for walking by the River Thames (not far from Millbank Prison) and taking the bridges across the river, to railway stations and omnibuses. Handy for journeys to and from Dyson at Putney, just the other side of the Thames. Edwin may not have been involved in the decision to move to Pimlico; it has 'Adelaide' written all over it. Or possibly not, if Edwin had precisely the public transport routes needed to go to and from his business locations.

ONE SINGLE BED

Their landlady, Mrs Caroline Doggett, turned out to be most accommodating. She acted on Adelaide's specific requirements; these included the provision of all meals and a request to order a single bed. Mrs Doggett agreed to provide the Bartletts with three square meals a day and, after a week of sharing a double bed with Edwin, it came about that Adelaide took delivery of one single bed – paid for by the Doggetts, surprisingly.

Dyson would visit, for hours on end; Edwin would arrive home, sometimes at 5 pm, other times at 10, very weary from his business (said Dyson). Sometimes Edwin put his hand to his left side, having a sharp pain in his abdomen (said Dyson).

Within their shrinking space, Adelaide had created distance between herself and her husband. There was no longer a marital bed and she had scope for further, profound changes.

OCTOBER–NOVEMBER 1885, LONDON

For Edwin, celebrating his fortieth birthday on 8 October, domestic adjustments were definitely not leading to changes for the better.

Public attention turned back to the abduction story in the newspapers; people all agog again over the disturbing court case involving WT Stead, still pioneer of investigative journalism and editor of the *Pall Mall Gazette*. The law 'for the Protection of Women and Girls' had been changed; the true story of the misused Eliza Armstrong and her mother had been told. The Judge's summing-up at the Old Bailey included his finding that the child, Eliza, had been 'subjected to chloroform' as part of the offences against her. On 10 November, Stead and two others were found guilty of abduction and procurement. His sentence: three months in prison.

Picture Adelaide, Edwin and Dyson, perhaps in pairs or a threesome, as they mull over the shocking revelations unfolding bit by bit, month by month in the newspapers about the exploitation of children in Victorian England. Stories including the use of chloroform to try to subdue Eliza Armstrong with 'a good sniff'.

A 'big sniff' – and obviously not a beneficial one for Eliza. Perhaps it provoked ideas at 85 Claverton Street, Pimlico.

Chapter 22

THE DESPERATE TIMES, DECEMBER 1885

'INDISPOSED'

On 8 December, for perhaps the first time in his life, Edwin could not complete the day's tasks and had to go home unwell from his beloved work. He wrote to his business partner Edward Baxter that he was 'indisposed'. Bartlett must have felt really ill to have left everyone in the lurch, being such a hard-working, conscientious chap. The next morning, oddly for a man off sick, Edwin went with Adelaide and their St Bernards to a dog show. It may have been one of those organised by Charles Cruft. And alongside them went Dyson.[78']

Edwin soon fell ill with vomiting and diarrhoea and had to rush home. He wrote to Edward: 'I have little hope of being with you tomorrow'.

ENTER DR LEACH

Alfred Leach, a young, inexperienced doctor living and working less than quarter of a mile from the Bartletts, was contacted for the first time by Adelaide on 10 December and he visited Edwin that morning. In court the following April, the doctor described Edwin's faeces: 'melena' – black, from bleeding in the intestine. Edwin was 'suffering from diarrhoea, some pain in the left side, foetid breath, and ... signs of indigestion, sub-acute gastritis – one might call it mercurialism', the 'effect of an ordinary dose of mercury, in a person with an idiosyncrasy for that drug.' By his last phrase Dr Leach meant: Edwin might have been a person 'more liable to the injurious effect of mercury than others'.

Edwin said he had swallowed a 'blue pill' (allegedly a sample left by a salesman) from his office desk drawer – but denied Dr Leach's enquiries as to whether he was treating himself for syphilis or had a syphilis phobia.

A 'blue pill' signifies nothing specific in modern times; in 1886 it was commonly understood to mean a tablet containing mercury. Many examples can be found concerning the varying compositions and uses of such pills throughout the period from the seventeenth to the nineteenth century. Piliula hydrargyri was a mercury-based medicine, a blue pill, also known as blue mass, used as a remedy for syphilis. Also used in cases of tuberculosis, constipation, toothache and 'hyponchondriasis' – thus for both physical and mental symptoms. A blue dye or chalk was used in such pills (hence the name); pharmacists used their own 'recipes' in terms of ingredients and quantities. All of these pills included mercury, often as mercury chloride, 'Calomel'.

When excessive amounts of mercury were present in the pills this led to heavy-metal poisoning, causing diarrhoea, vomiting and often violent emotions. Remember something of such doses from earlier: Lincoln and his blue pills. In Edwin's case, there is no evidence as to whether he took more than one blue pill and none as to its effect upon him. Dr Leach observed a thin blue line on the gums and decided that the blue pills had caused it. But was Edwin's line from mercury – or from lead?

Edwin, in dark December, lying in his narrow bed, felt absolutely terrible and knew not why. Over the first week of his new patient's treatment, Dr Leach prescribed a range of medicines and washes for various parts and problems. Morphia for injections and opium 'to procure sleep at night'.

Why did the doctor not keep a record of treatments he administered, and of the ones which Edwin took himself, and of any which were supposed to be given by Adelaide to her husband? Typical practice, or just Dr Leach's way?

When Edward Baxter visited on Sunday 12 December, Edwin was 'very ill indeed … scarcely able to speak.' Thereafter Adelaide sent Baxter a short note nearly every day, usually saying Edwin was not so well.

Far too ill to go to work and feeling depressed in their unhomely home, Edwin's routines disappeared and his world shrank into one room. And down to one narrow bed. Adelaide arranged for that little camp bed to be moved into the drawing room, overlooking the street. She became increasingly wakeful and watchful, lying each night on a small sofa or chair beside her husband. His debilitation revolved around the mouth, those dratted stumps left after many of his teeth were sawn off in 1878 by Mr Bellin. A mouth oh so painful after Mr Bellin's sawing that Edwin could never bear to wear false teeth. And now his own, few remaining teeth were rotting, his gums painful and foetid. All of that to contend with, and those wretched abdominal troubles. No wonder he felt so glum.

Edwin's world had become one of pain, depression and puzzlement as to why he felt so wretched; a sinking into increasing dependency on Adelaide for company, nursing and decision-making. She exerted control (did it feel like power?) over his situation. Yet she still had no money to call her own, was still financially dependant on him.

Sleeplessness became a major feature of Edwin's life and added to his vulnerability. Questions would arise in April as to whether he had been mesmerised by Adelaide, by Dyson or some other friend. Mesmerism[79] (referred to in the twenty-first century as hypnosis) was perceived by many medics at the time as a cranky practice.

Mesmerism definitely interested Dyson, who raised the subject with Edwin (not the other way round). Mesmerism may have been of interest to Adelaide too, perhaps used by her, yet Dyson was never asked if he talked with her about it.

Whatever methods and medicines were used, it appears that when Edwin showed signs of even a slight physical or mental recovery, he became subdued again. Or was being subdued by someone.

Unbeknown to him, his beloved business and provisioning days were behind him. Now he showed a labile, pitiful, loyal reliance on Adelaide and the enthusiastic yet puzzled Dr Leach.

On 16 December the doctor took a local dentist, Dr Thomas Roberts, to meet the Bartletts. Work began on Edwin's foetid mouth, including the removal of two loose teeth. And next day, the trauma of eleven more being yanked out.

On 19 December, Dr Dudley, selected by Dr Leach to give a second opinion as to the causes of the patient's condition and to recommend treatment, visited and wrote a report. No sign of disease, complains of sleeplessness, disinclined to raise his eyelids, no head pains, seems hypochondriacal; gums spongy (but no blue lines along them now). Edwin told the doctor he had overworked and needed rest and sleep.

A BIG BIRTHDAY

That same day, a milestone was reached. Adelaide's thirtieth birthday, yet no mention of it remains. Celebrated in some way by Adelaide alongside one or both of the men in her life, or was it quietly ignored?

Dyson must have had much conflicting food for thought. His hopes and dreams about Adelaide, his ministry; Edwin's condition. The revering Reverend wrote and illustrated a short yet revealing poem. He sent it to Adelaide. She kept it.

What illustration? A door, a heart, a queen, a throne, a bird? Adelaide's face? Oh, to see his drawing ... but no chance; it was destroyed or hidden away at some stage later.

'DYSON'S DITTY
Who is it that hath burst the door,
Unclosed the heart that shut before,
And set her queen-like on its throne,
And made its homage all her own?
My Birdie.'
(George Dyson).

So, she was his Queen Birdie and he was her Georgius Rex, her King George. He used the possessive, 'My Birdie'. Dyson obviously talked with Adelaide about marriage, about when he could marry 'someone' – and his intention to marry her. Apparently, one of the reasons he did so was because his Birdie told him that his firm and generous friend, her husband Edwin, was terminally ill. Adelaide and Dyson talked privately of a future together, without the Messrs Bartlett (Edwin and his dear father) in their lives.

What Dyson probably did not think about was that some birds sing and most birds fly. They need, want to fly free, and will do so, unless caged.

DOWN AND UP

By 19 December, Dr Leach thought Edwin was beginning to recover and Roberts the dentist thought him much better. On 20 December, Dr Leach gave Edwin chloral hydrate, along with the bromide and morphia he had been using (and leaving at 85 Claverton Street) since his visits began on 10 December. Edwin would not go on any outings and became agoraphobic. His life since 8 December had been bad but, 'by Jove', on 23 December it felt a damn sight worse.[80]

THE WORM 'THAT THREW EVERYTHING BACK AGAIN'

In court in April 1886, Dr Leach blamed a worm – the worm 'that threw everything back again'. Either Edwin or Adelaide found a lumbricoid worm in faeces in the chamber pot, and Edwin was 'much depressed by it; he thought certainly he had something wrong with him then.'

So, following a line of thought (not Dr Leach's) here:

Edwin may have had acid reflux – stomach acid causing an odd sensation of movement in the oesophagus. Some people describe this as a feeling of worms crawling up in the throat. He had dyspepsia and gastritis. Dyson said in court that Edwin got a sharp pain in his left side at various times, ever since the Bartlett lived at Merton Abbey.

Adelaide, on hearing Edwin complaining of worms, may have thought something like this: worms, you think you've got worms? I'll show you a worm …

There has been speculation that she placed a lumbricoid worm (Ascaris lumbricoides, intestinal roundworm) from one of their dogs into Edward's faeces, in his chamberpot or commode. And, as was described by Dr Leach, the finding of this worm greatly upset Edwin and set him back.

'THE PRESCRIPTION FOR THE IMAGINATION'

In that same court the Judge described Dr Leach's placebo of drops as 'the prescription for the imagination'. Ten drops 'to be given in wine' to Edwin on Christmas Eve, said Dr Leach. They seemed 'effectual' in aiding some much-needed sleep. And by then, convalescence for his patient was in Leach's mind – but not in Edwin's, whose Christmas time turned horrible.

LAST CHRISTMAS

Christmas Day 1885 heralded emptiness for Edwin, a man who always loved his grub. On doctor's orders, his annual special day of good cheer, feasting and making merry was replaced by fasting – not one bite to eat – and ghastly 'vermifuges' (worm medicines) on an empty stomach. After 23 December, Dr Leach had 'put off the treatment for a couple of days … partly to see if any more [worms] passed, and partly to let him gather up his pluck and spirit'.

Those worming powders had to be followed up with purgatives. The doctor explained in court that if the purgatives were not taken, his patient would have been made very miserable by the powders. Edwin would have 'seen everything green; he would have suffered from buzzing in the ears, and all sorts of troubles, which I did not wish to subject him to.' Dr Leach said he knew this 'from personal experience … I have tried the same drug on myself'. (He often wanted to experience what all his prescribing was doing to the person on the receiving end.) At least Edwin was spared from experiencing green lights and buzzing …

On Boxing Day the doctor decided to subject Edwin to 'severe' treatments in order to try to evacuate his bowels. One wonders whether the prescribed croton oil was for Adelaide to administer – and perhaps she deliberately did not do so? Dr Leach tried galvanism (the use of an electric current) on Edwin's abdomen. With no idea as to why there was not much effect, the diligent doctor gave up for that day. Flummoxed, perhaps he scratched his head as he walked the short distance home wondering about his perplexing patient and what on earth to try next.

Edwin received a visit from Dyson, returning to his flock (or rather, to Adelaide) after a brief spell at his relatives' home in Poole. Edwin allegedly confided about Adelaide: he 'was afraid she was breaking down with nursing'. And he told Dyson about the ghastly worms.

DYSON DOES

Next day, Dyson arrived at Claverton Street just as Adelaide was going out to post a letter, so he accompanied her. It was Sunday 27 December. She asked him to buy chloroform for her to use; allegedly her request came out of the blue to young Dyson.

In court, he described it in a seemingly casual manner – but did he really take her request in his stride on their Sunday 'stroll'? According to Dyson, Adelaide told him that the nurse Annie Walker bought chloroform for her in the past – 'but was gone to America'.

At the Trial, he maintained that Adelaide said the drug was needed to soothe Edwin to sleep, and she used it on a handkerchief in the past. Under pressure from her Defence, Dyson blustered; it was used to deter any recurrence of violence in Edwin, or to calm his paroxysms.

On their 'stroll' the Reverend, sensibly trying to wriggle out of the discussion about purchasing chloroform, asked Adelaide to get it through Dr Leach. Her response was that the doctor 'did not know she was skilled in drugs and medicines; and not knowing that, he would not entrust her with it'.

Presumably wanting to keep on the right side of his beloved, Dyson took the sovereign (one pound sterling) she held out to him for the planned purchase. Correction: it is likely that Adelaide knew he would have to make *several* purchases of the drug in order to get the relatively large quantity, unstated in court, which she was demanding. Dyson had clearly fallen for Adelaide in an all-consuming way; she must have known that now he had agreed to help her, she was pushing at an open door. The door to his 'unclosed' heart, as he described it in his precious little poem to her.

Chapter 23

THE POISON

OVER THE WORST?

Edward Baxter visited Edwin on the evening of 27 December for about two hours. His business partner seemed much better, except that he talked about worms, that he'd passed worms, that worms were wriggling up in his throat.

Adelaide said, matter-of-factly: 'We call them snakes.'

SEEKING ADVICE

Dyson, diligently eager to please, to be in Adelaide's good books, sent a letter and later a telegram to a medical student in Bristol: to Theodore Styles (whom he knew from Poole) enquiring about purchasing chloroform. Dyson received no reply. A later version of this story was that Adelaide told Dyson to send a telegram in order to withdraw the request contained in his letter.

She must have felt absolutely horrified, worried and angry that Dyson sought advice – particularly in writing – from a medical man. Whether

Dyson was trying to help Edwin, or to deter or harm him, or just help Adelaide, no one knows. Adelaide persuaded Dyson to buy chloroform saying Edwin's money would pay for it; she had no money of her own.

On 28 December, Edwin still not having had any significant bowel movements, Dr Leach prescribed a 'strong purgative'. No effect, so he again gave his patient some croton oil. That too failed to work, so the remedies of Christmas were repeated – this time administered by the doctor – again using galvanism.

Edwin's health and mood improved, noted Dr Leach, who thought it high time that his patient consider a spell of convalescence – and told him so.

PURCHASING POISON

On the same morning, Dyson ventured out to the first of three Dickensian-sounding chemists. To Mr John Bawtree Humble (late of Wales and India) at his shop just fifty yards from Dyson's church in Upper Richmond Road, Putney. Dyson asked for pure chloroform, ingenuously enquired if it would remove grease stains, paid, received a full ounce bottle. Secondly, with the remaining cash from the Bartlett sovereign, the Reverend went to Wimbledon's Mr Penrose, pallbearer (occasional) at his chapel; they knew one another well. Again, Dyson asked if the chloroform would remove stains he had found on his clothes when in Poole. (That question, a rehearsed embellishment, a lie – he had no stains on his clothing.) And Penrose sold him two ounces of the drug.

Then, being fortunate enough (although in this context, extremely unfortunate) to have in his congregation yet another friend working at a pharmacy, the crafty Reverend went lastly to Mr Mellin, chemist's assistant, at 36 High Street, Wimbledon. Dyson bought either two ounces or an ounce and a half of chloroform there – he couldn't remember which quantity.

But Mellin knew the amount – and stated it in his evidence the following year.

On the evening of 28th, Edwin senior went to see his son, despite a letter from Adelaide which almost put him off visiting. Her words must have hurt, infuriated and frustrated him. She told he was only welcome when invited by *her* – and at no other time.

'I HAVE NEITHER FORGOTTEN NOR FORGIVEN THE PAST'

'You seem to forget that I have not been in bed for thirteen days, and consequently am too tired to speak to visitors. I wish you to understand that I have neither forgotten nor forgiven the past. Edwin will be pleased to see you on Monday evening any time after six.'

She didn't need to make it any plainer for her father-in-law that their bitter history was still coming between them. However, his visit lasted for about two and a half hours.

SANS STUMPS

Edwin told his father that he would be 'alright now, for the stumps have been taken out' and he felt 'better'.

Adelaide concurred …. but, said Edwin, worms were crawling all up him – 'We call them snakes,' interjected Adelaide, just as she had with Dyson.

'Strange,' replied Edwin senior.

His weary, trusting son gave a simple reply. 'A good job she has doctored the dogs to clear away the worms, because she knew I had worms.'

NOT TO MENTION THE CHLOROFORM

Dyson took home the four bottles of poison and poured the contents into a large empty bottle obtained from his landlady. He wetted the CHLOROFORM label on one small bottle, removed it and patted it onto the big one. He took that to Adelaide the next day, 29 December. Again, they waited to talk about chloroform until well away from 85 Claverton Street. At the Trial, Dyson trying to sound casual, attempting to downplay the importance of the poison, said 'whilst we were out for a stroll on the Embankment I gave it to her' and 'I asked her if that would do, and she said that it would.'

So the quantity of chloroform Dyson managed to buy 'would do' the job which Adelaide wanted 'it' to do. Her young man had done her bidding – got back into her good books. She was in possession of a large quantity of chloroform to take back to the drawing room – now a bedroom – the sickroom.

'HER HUSBAND'S FRIENDS WERE SAYING UNKIND THINGS ABOUT HER'

Next day, Dyson called on the Bartletts yet again, this time to apologise to Adelaide. He knew he had caused offence by saying she should 'get in' a nurse to assist her with the patient. In court Dyson explained that his (unwelcome) suggestion was 'consequent upon her telling me that her husband's friends were saying unkind things about her'.

'IT WOULD BE BETTER IN THE EYES OF THE WORLD'

Dyson's opinion: 'It would be better in the eyes of the world' (meaning Edwin's friends and family) if Edwin had a nurse, partly so that Adelaide could get more rest, primarily to quell the friends' alleged criticisms. Adelaide, amateur nurse and wife, took offence at Dyson's bright idea, accusing him of suspecting her or distrusting her (as if daring him to admit it). Challenged, Dyson deferred to his beloved, replying that he thoroughly trusted her … Edwin overheard this part of the conversation, saw his friend's distress and (according to Dyson) agreed with Adelaide. 'Oh yes, you may trust her. If you had twelve years' experience of her as I have, you would know you could trust her.' So said the loyal husband …

'BUT HE FANCIES THEM'

Baxter received a written grocery order and cheery note from Adelaide:

'Dear Sir,
'With the other things will you please send a bottle of brandy called Lord's Extra, a bottle of Colonel Skinner's Mango Chutney, a bottle of walnuts, and a nice fruitcake? I know these things are not fit for Edwin to eat, but

he fancies them.

'You can see Edwin on Wednesday. A very happy New Year!

Yours truly, Adelaide Bartlett'

Baxter delivered her order on Wednesday 30 December and sat for about two hours with Edwin, the friend and much-respected business partner whom he had known for over twenty years. He found Edwin 'very much better' and intending to go to the seaside (Bournemouth or Torquay) just after Christmas, as it would 'prove beneficial'.

Time to buck up, get going again after that rotten business of feeling so wretchedly ill. Edwin intended to resume work in a week or two. He wanted to get back to business.

Dyson visited again on the afternoon of 30 December and, finding Edwin 'in great pain from his teeth', went straight back out to fetch Dr Leach. The doctor not being in, Dyson returned to Claverton Street and was relieved to find the doctor there with Edwin. Although Dr Leach had decided to reduce his visits, he arranged with Adelaide to accompany the Bartletts to the dentist that evening.

Dyson took his leave and said (unbeknown to him, his very last) goodbye to Edwin.

31 DECEMBER 1885
OYSTERS AND A JUGGED HARE

On the last day of the year, Edwin was making up for lost time in the eating department, after his emptiness over Christmas. The housemaid, Fulcher, served up half a dozen oysters for 'luncheon' at about noon, and then a delicious jugged hare for a very early 'dinner' between 2.30 and 3.30 pm.

'WE WISHED ALMOST WE WERE UNMARRIED'

Replete, Edwin went by cab with Adelaide and the doctor to the dentist that evening. On the way, according to Dr Leach 'the subject of recent marriages in the locality' came up.

Mrs Bartlett declaring: 'This morning Edwin and I, doctor, were talking about the number of our friends who are getting married, and we were saying we wished almost that we were unmarried, that we might have the pleasure of marrying each other again.'

The mufflered-up husband, prompted by Dr Leach, replied: 'Yes, we suit one another very well; we agree in our views [or 'in our ways'].' Dr Leach was not sure which.

Previous dental appointments had involved the use of a new drug, cocaine, as a local anaesthetic. Today, Roberts and Dr Leach felt that Edwin was better than they had ever seen him, and tried another drug, nitrous oxide, putting Edwin under its influence for some thirty seconds.

On this occasion the dentist found a small amount of necrosis (death of body tissue when too little blood flows to an area) in Edwin's jaw. He confirmed in court that Edwin was told about this new problem. It is not known whether the necrosis played on Edwin's mind, although it seems likely that it disturbed him, given the weeks of illness and low mood which he had suffered.

TALK OF CHLOROFORM AND FOOD

When the couple returned to Claverton Street, Adelaide asked Mrs Doggett if she had ever tried chloroform. In April, Mrs Doggett would try to remember the exchanged remarks …

The conversation moved on to food, yet again – eating being for Edwin such a great comfort. The anticipation of lovely food, then the look, the smell, the feel of it (even in his sore mouth) and the taste of it, some of his few pleasures left, given all his troubles. And after all, he had spent his working life surrounded by the stuff – good food.

Tea/supper at 9.30 pm was another half a dozen oysters, bread and butter, then slices of the 'nice fruitcake' ordered from Edward Baxter. Both Bartletts left traces of the deliciously spicy mango chutney on their plates. (With what had they eaten chutney?)

After partaking, Edwin felt better than he had done at all recently and dared to hope he was over the worst of whatever it was afflicting him. According to Mrs Doggett, Mr Bartlett told her, 'Dr Leach had said he ought to go away for a change'. The landlady would give evidence of Mrs Bartlett's retort that 'the journey would be too long' for Edwin.

'A LARGE HADDOCK'

Like many who enjoy food and have the luxury of feeling they 'live to eat' rather than just have to eat to live, Edwin moved on to thinking out loud about his next meal, looking forward to a big cooked breakfast. Fulcher was clearing away after the last meal, which was the aforementioned 'tea and supper both together.' Mr Bartlett was walking around the room, said Fulcher, and 'asked me to get him a large haddock' for his breakfast and 'he said he should get up an hour earlier at the thoughts of having it'.

Edwin was planning the start to a new year. Hopefully it would be a much better start to the year than its end. Feeling brighter than he had done for weeks, he aimed to be up for a big breakfast early tomorrow morning.

PART SIX
DEATH AND DENIAL

Chapter 24

ENTER THE REGISTRAR OF BIRTHS,
MARRIAGES AND DEATHS

NEW YEAR'S MORNING, 1886

Banging on their bedroom door, Adelaide woke the Doggetts.

'Come down, I think Mr Bartlett is dead,' she urged her landlord.

Deeply shocked, Fred Doggett dashed downstairs with her and saw Edwin lying on his back on the chair-bed. Fred had only ever spoken to Mr Bartlett once – and now this. He put his hand on the man's bare breast – 'perfectly cold' he said to Mrs Bartlett – 'he must have been dead for some two or three hours'.

It was '4.10 am by the clock on the drawing-room mantelpiece' stated Mr Frederick Horace Doggett, Registrar of Births, Marriages and Deaths for Belgravia, to a court that April. This was not part of his job: this terribly sudden death, such a tremendous shock, had happened overnight in his own home.

Mrs Bartlett told him she fell asleep with her hand around her husband's foot, awoke with a pain, a cramp in her hand, or arm, and found Mr Bartlett lying on his face. 'I put him in the position in which you saw him, and tried to pour brandy down his throat, nearly half a pint.' Mrs Doggett came in but soon ran right up to the top floor, woke the young servant Alice Fulcher and told her to be quick, fetch Dr Leach. Fred Doggett asked Mrs Bartlett if she had closed her husband's eyes. 'Yes,' and she remembered that Mr Bartlett's jaw had dropped.

Mrs Doggett returned to the scene and immediately asked Mrs Bartlett if she gave him 'those drops' they had talked about. Adelaide's reply was, 'I have given him nothing'. Suspicion mounted in the landlady's mind; she put two and two together because, before the previous night's supper, Mrs Bartlett asked her if she'd ever taken chloroform. Mrs Doggett replied that she took it years ago. Mrs Bartlett asked was it a nice or a pleasant feeling? Mrs Doggett hadn't known much about it either way.

Mrs Bartlett told her the previous evening, in Mr Bartlett's presence, about him being 'in the habit of taking some sleeping drops; ten was a strong dose but she should not, or did not, hesitate in giving him twelve'.

Fred Doggett thought the pungent smell in the room was of chloric ether (which in Britain at that time was chloroform mixed with about fifteen times as much strong alcohol; it was used as a sedative and mild anodyne).

He looked around him. On the end of the mantelboard (or was it on the table? – accounts differed later) stood two-thirds or three-quarters 'of a wineglassful … evidently brandy, with some other drug in it; it smelt like either ether or paregoric.' The smell from the glass was very like the smell pervading the room. He put the glass back down.

Whether Fred had ever smelt chloroform is not known, so as to whether said glass contained chloroform and brandy, rather than chloric ether and brandy, remains a frustrating, unanswerable question.

'I THINK SHE SAID HE WAS DEAD'

Meanwhile, just a few streets away, the housemaid sent by Mrs Doggett to fetch Dr Leach was having trouble with him. He had been roused by urgent knocking at the door, but then …

In court in April, the Attorney General questioned the doctor about this knocking-up, and the ghastly farce which ensued.

'I suppose you went as quickly as you could?'

Dr Leach: 'I did not.'

'When did you go?'

The tardy doctor felt sceptical.

'About half an hour later. I talked some time with the messenger to ask her whether it was merely one of his notions or whether he was really ill, and I think she said he was dead.'

'Did you delay after that, or did you go?'

THERE'S NO TELLING SOME PEOPLE …

Dr Leach: 'I scarcely accepted it as true and I asked, after that, what restoratives I could bring if he was really bad. She could only say, "I know nothing about it; Mrs Bartlett only tells me he is dead." I did get alarmed. Then we jumped into a hansom, and went.'

The Doggett's housemaid, Alice Fulcher, must have been trebly shocked: told that Mr Bartlett was dead; sent to fetch Dr Leach; jolted by his questioning of her. Incredibly, he took half an hour to be convinced; Fulcher must have been incredulous – and dreading her mistress's reaction to the delay. (Fulcher might well have wanted to shout at him: 'Don't shoot the messenger.')

Belatedly, Dr Leach arrived at the bedside of his (late) patient, briefly examined Mr Bartlett and confirmed the death. With Fred Doggett's help, he tied up the deceased's jaw and straightened the legs. They looked around the room. Dr Leach saw nothing that could account for his patient's death. But who knows what he and Fred Doggett saw – and what they overlooked in their shock?

'A NEW YEAR'S TOAST: OFF WITH THE OLD, ON WITH THE NEW
Into the New Year,
their room full of misery, a drear
tomb in the making.
Merriment upstairs and down,
shouts outside,
cries in the room
as a man dies.
A woman has changed her clothes,
then out of that
warm room she goes.
It is New Year's morning.
Soon she will be buying
her mourning clothes.'
(Rose Storkey)

On entering the room, Fred Doggett had noticed that the fire in the grate had been made up, attended to, just a short time before. That's odd, he must have thought, if Mrs B'd felt a sudden concern about Mr B (after supposedly she'd been fast asleep for hours) surely she wouldn't have stacked up new coals before banging on the bedroom door? He also did quick checks concerning Mr Bartlett's bed and yes: someone lying, leaning or sitting up could have reached up to the mantelpiece board where the wine glass was found.

For some reason, perhaps understandable in the stressful circumstances,

Fred Doggett did not think to, or forgot to lock away the glass and its contents. Later that morning a bottle of Condy's fluid[81] and a bottle containing a white powder were among forty-seven bottles removed by the Coroner's representative, Police Constable Thomas Ralph.

Ever the helpful landlady, Mrs Doggett went up to Mrs Bartlett's room to ask if she would have a little breakfast, and Mrs B replied with some such words as how strange it was that Mr Bartlett had not long made his Will. Mrs Doggett, like her husband had done, noticed the built-up fire and thought it very odd that Mrs B had attended to it for some reason, in such a situation in the night. People notice certain seemingly inconsequential details, look and listen for clues, even when shocked by major events.

'ARE YOU THINKING ABOUT MONEY?' –
Mrs Doggett had barked.

'It's necessary,' replied Mrs Bartlett, adding that her money was in the business – the money she'd had before marriage, before the Married Women's Property Act.

Mrs Doggett must have been incredulous about this sort of talk, what with Edwin just dead. No more was said about the money – but only because at that point in came Mrs Matthews, Adelaide's only known friend. Kind Alice Matthews had received a telegram from Adelaide, dropped everything she was about to do and rushed to her side.

'WASHED IT AWAY' –
Said the other Alice, the servant, having poured from a wine glass the liquid (which appeared to be brandy) down the sink. 'Washed it away'

after she had taken a trayful of glasses from the Bartlett's room to the kitchen that morning, said she in court, That might have been the glass previously seen on the mantelpiece; or perhaps one of the Bartletts used it for a midnight toast to the New Year. But, Alice did give a tumbler of fluid and a bottle upside down in it to PC Ralph.

Mrs Bartlett gave Alice Fulcher two letters to post, 'one to Mr Dyson, and one to Mr Wood'.

According to Dyson he received Adelaide's letter on New Year's Day. It was 'her grief' to tell him that Mr Bartlett had died, at 'about 2 o'clock as far as she could judge'. That evidence from Dyson was used to narrow down estimates of the true time at which Edwin expired.

Adelaide asked him to visit on 2 January. That New Year's morning, the young man must have begun feeling perplexed – guilty about his purchases and his feelings towards Adelaide? Above all, shock and worry. No one knows whether Adelaide said anything else in that letter, for instance about what Dyson should say or not say. He 'destroyed' her letter a few days later.

Edward Baxter, shocked to receive a death telegram from Adelaide, hurried off to fetch Edwin senior from his humble mews home in Berkeley Square. Baxter broke the news and took him to 85 Claverton Street. The devastated father bent over the body, deliberately to smell his son's mouth, suspecting that Edwin had been poisoned – with prussic acid. But Edwin senior realised the smell wasn't of that. Still, suspicious lurked …

LAYING OUT

Enter Ann Boulter, charwoman, a cleaner whose jobs included working for an undertaker.

She arrived between 7 and 8 a.m to lay out Edwin's body and while she worked, Adelaide talked to her. Because Edwin's legs had been tied (by Dr Leach) Ann asked if he'd had a fit and struggled. 'No, poor dear,' said Mrs Bartlett, 'he suffered very much with his head; also his teeth for some time.' When Ann turned the corpse over, some froth came out between his lips.

In court in April, asked by the Prosecution whether Mrs Bartlett said anything about her husband's Will, Ann replied:

'She remarked that it was curious, or funny, that he should make his Will a day or two previous to his death.'

'Did you say anything?'

Ann: 'I remarked how odd it was so, and asked if it was in her favour.'

'Yes,' Adelaide replied.

Question from the Prosecution: 'Are you quite sure it was not a month?'

Ann's hearing ability was doubted …

She was still in the room when Mrs Bartlett received a letter from her husband's brother (Charles or Fred?) wishing Edwin a Happy New Year. Mrs Bartlett exclaimed, 'Oh, how cruel!' or 'This is cruel'. Strange, thought Ann. But it is understandable that Adelaide mentioned the cruel irony in receiving greetings for a man who had not long died and had been washed for burial.

Back to Ann, pointing out that Mrs Bartlett talked about her husband's Will over his dead body. To Ann, someone whom Mrs Bartlett had never seen before – and thought she would never see again. Indecent haste comes to mind, in terms of the widow talking to a stranger about her late husband's Will at such a time, just hours after his sudden death. Adelaide in shock? And remember, reality was that as a married woman she'd had no money of her own.

Back went Edwin senior that evening to see his dead son. Surprised at what he saw, he grunted, 'You won't have him put in the coffin …'.

Adelaide: 'Dr Leach has to see to that, it has nothing to do with me or you.'

Edward senior: 'The undertaker had no business to put Edwin in the coffin.' The mortified father was thinking 'post-mortem'.

AN ALLOWANCE

Edwin senior had been due to start receiving a regular sum of money from Edwin as from this very day, 1 January. An allowance in lieu of a home at Edwin's; the father due to be paid to live away from the couple. 'Prior to that,' said Edwin senior, 'I have had from him what money I wanted. He was the kindest of sons'. The coincidence of the starting date and Edwin's death that morning would not be lost on those listening carefully in court that April.

There was no obvious reason for Edwin's sudden death. The Doggetts and their housemaid were shaken to the core. Did Adelaide know Fred Doggett's occupation when she made the arrangement for her and Edwin to live chez Doggett? Or was it a macabre twist of fate? Surely he would be the least likely man to agree to registering a death if he had any concerns whatsoever about its possible cause?

Chapter 25

THE POST-MORTEM EXAMINATION

AND THE FALL-OUT

SMELL

Edwin's corpse was subjected to a post-mortem undertaken promptly next day, 2 January 1886. In the Bartlett's back room at the Doggetts' home were five doctors, including eminent ones. Downstairs, the agonising wait for the findings was a tremendous strain on those in the smoking room at 85 Claverton Street – and for Edwin senior, pacing up and down the pavement.

At very short notice, five doctors (Green, Murray, Dudley, Cheyne and Leach) dropped everything, work and pleasure, to be there that Saturday. Time being of the essence after a sudden death and with the body being kept at home for the post-mortem (not unusual after deaths in that era) the doctors rolled up their sleeves and made a start. Each doctor had a specific role during the process: in lead role, Green, an eminent pathologist; he and Murray, who would perform the post-mortem, were from Charing Cross Hospital. Dudley was the doctor who made the second opinion visit to Edwin in December; Cheyne would observe on behalf of Edwin senior; Leach would take the notes.

As soon as the stomach was opened up they were assailed by a smell almost as strong as a freshly opened bottle of chloroform. This indicated the poison's quite recent entry to the stomach.

'THE SERIOUS AND REAL QUESTION'

To cut to the chase, 'the serious and real question in this case will be, how came the chloroform there?' as Sir Charles Russell, for the Prosecution, put it in April.

The doctors, not finding a cause of death but finding the smell of chloroform, told those anxiously waiting below that the matter would have to be referred to the Coroner and that tests would be needed. Foolishly, impulsively, perhaps arrogantly, Dr Leach suggested to those waiting that the suspicious, 'ethereal' smell from the stomach was probably chlorodyne. He did this despite knowing its identification as 'chloroform' by the lead doctor, Green.

'HE'S NO BUSINESS LYING THERE, A STRONG MAN LIKE THAT'

Dr Dudley, putting a hand on Edwin senior's shoulder, remarked, 'He's no business lying there, a strong man like that –' as though Edwin had a choice in the matter.

Or had Edwin chosen to do himself in? Dr Dudley must have been shocked to hear of the man's death, to watch the dissection of his body and to meet this grieving father.

Adelaide had to vacate the premises; the rooms would be sealed after more searches for evidence had been completed. She left with just her cloak. Edwin senior had surreptitiously checked the cloak pockets at some stage, presumably to see if she had a bottle of poison to spirit out of the house. He asked Mr Wood, the solicitor, to be in charge of said rooms; a sensible and appropriate request.

The widow made off in haste to the Matthews' home – an unplanned and unannounced move.

'THIS IS A VERY CRITICAL TIME FOR ME'

Here is Adelaide's alleged denial to Dyson on Saturday 2 January about using the chloroform: 'I have not had occasion to use it, the bottle lies there just as you gave it to me; this is a very critical time for me.' She spoke 'indignantly' stated Dyson in court, adding that she told him to put away from his mind two things: firstly the fact that she used a medicine chest and secondly that he purchased chloroform. She said he must not worry; worry upon worry piled into his addled head.

But, of course, the bottle did not lie 'there', it having been removed from the drawer by Adelaide around breakfast time on 1 January. And yes, she knew a pivotal, critical stage when she saw one.

On Sunday 3 January, Ann Boulter went back to Claverton Street with the undertakers' men and noticed a sticky froth on the late Mr Bartlett's pillowcase. She took that and his sheets to the local baths for washing. Also on 3 January, Dyson took fright and threw away the empty, small but offending chloroform bottles as he crossed Wandsworth Common at Tooting. The Reverend, on his way to lead the service at chapel. In April, he said he threw the bottles away because 'it was the horror that seized me when I imagined what might have happened … the sight of them was hateful to me, and in a panic I threw them away; it was not the motive of self-protection.' Panic – or actually self-protection? Desperate measures to rid himself of the poison bottles seem a natural reaction, clerical collar-wearer or not.

If Adelaide did say to Dyson that the big bottle was untouched, she was declaring that Edwin could NOT have used the chloroform from her. Yet he had swallowed chloroform from somewhere and from someone. She was acting suspiciously – and for once could not be in control of events. Would her denial of moving the bottle of chloroform convince anyone else?

Dyson scuttled off to Dr Leach on 4 January to ask about the post-mortem findings.

Afterwards, with increasing dread and suspicion, Dyson tackled Adelaide about what she had done with the chloroform ... and was met with a crescendo of anger. In April, Dyson would swear Adelaide shouted back at him:

'OH DAMN THE CHLOROFORM!'
The tale of ensuing events involving the pair that January day will be left over until the Trial in April; suffice it to say here that the respective heartbeats of Dyson and Adelaide must have shuddered with increasing dread. The delight which they had felt about one another during the previous year had gone for bad and forever.

ENTER MR BEAL
On 4 January, the two of them received their respective summonses to appear on 7 January before the local deputy coroner to give evidence. Adelaide's solicitor promptly engaged Mr Edward Beal, a young barrister-at-law, introducing him to Adelaide on 5 January. Beal would watch the

Inquest proceedings on her behalf because obviously she was - or could become -the prime suspect, in need of a lawyer if charged. Was Mr Negus Wood in an awkward, conflicted situation, having been the late Edwin's solicitor? No mention of that; for some reason Mr Negus Wood chose to go beyond the call of duty in relation to Adelaide and acted for her. But if she was pulled into deeper trouble there was the crucial need for a top-notch barrister to try to extricate her from trouble, from life-threatening danger.

Adelaide spent a long time questioning Dr Leach on 6 January, quizzing him as to whether Edwin could have died from chloroform. Rather than saying he could not comment at this stage, he behaved unprofessionally and reacted, informing her that chlorodyne appeared to be the cause of death. Chlorodyne, a patent medicine, the principal ingredients of which were usually laudanum (an alcoholic solution of opium) with cannabis and chloroform.

Adelaide later told Alice Matthews that, on 6 January, after fetching all her remaining belongings from 85 Claverton Street, on her train journey to Peckham she emptied the bottle of chloroform out of the carriage window onto the rails. And threw the empty bottle into the pond at Peckham Rye. Into, or onto? Alice knew that the pond was frozen over; perhaps it doesn't matter that a poison bottle was not found there by the police? The contents of Edwin's stomach definitely included chloroform, the poison bought by Dyson at his adored Adelaide's request for her to use on her husband. Chloroform, which Adelaide said she showed to Edwin on 31 December, handed to him and he'd put the bottle on the mantelpiece above his bed. She added that upon lying down Edwin turned away from her as if to sleep, or as though he was sulking.

Was any of Adelaide's story (via Dr Leach in court) true, or true in part? A memory from another night during their years together, of a different turning away, Edwin sulking – or not?

Chapter 26

TRYING TO GET TO THE BOTTOM OF IT ALL

INQUEST INTO THE DEATH OF THOMAS EDWIN BARTLETT
The Inquest began on Thursday 7 January 1886 at St George's District Board of Works in Hanover Square, Buckingham Palace Road, just a short walk from Edwin's last abode.

JUST THE MAN FOR THE JOB
Deputy Coroner (hereafter 'the Coroner' in this case) Mr Athelstan Braxton Hicks was the son of a renowned obstetrician. No less an obstetrician than Dr John Braxton Hicks, whose surnames live on in relation to the intermittent contractions experienced during some pregnancies, often months before the birth.

The son is less well known yet had a significant impact on vulnerable lives in his role as child coroner. Athelstan's particular interest lay in the perverse incentives and unintended consequences of child life insurance. In the worst instances, babies and children were done away with by adults wanting to make financial gains. He tackled the scandals and tragedies of 'baby-farming' and later in life wrote about infanticide.

THE INQUEST JURY

Formal procedures for trying to get to the bottom of deaths are age old; apparently the Gauls had inquiries after particular deaths and Julius Caesar is thought to have said about the practice:

'If a matter comes into suspicion about a death, they hold an inquiry (a *quaestio*) concerning the wives, in the method used for slaves, and if guilt is established, they kill their wives, who have been tortured, with fire and all torments.'[82]

Too close to home in this tragedy of 1886 ...

Jurors would have an important role in *this* Inquest, determining whether a person should be committed for trial in connection with the death.

Edwin's grieving father, first witness at the Inquest, gave vent to his bitterness at being kept away from Edwin, by Adelaide, for most of December.

Called as second witness, Adelaide did not wait for questions. She flung back the mourning veil, baring her face, and furiously accused her father-in-law of being vindictive and meddlesome, adding that he had always disliked her for being 'a foreigner and a Roman Catholic'. Almost overwhelming negativity had been stored up on both sides.

Many spectators must have been disappointed when the Coroner – rather than let this drama run to see what other choice words were thrown across the boardroom – intervened. These family matters would not be gone into at this Inquest.

Damn! He and everyone present did not know it, but this was Adelaide's *only* appearance *to give evidence, to be questioned* in a court – and now the opportunity to hear about the family from her perspective had gone forever. No chances to hear more of her views about Edwin senior, nor to learn about her origins, her religion, her feelings towards Edwin, his illness and death. Nothing. Damn!

INQUEST ADJOURNED

The Inquest had opened and adjourned on the same day. They would all need to come back when there were experts' responses to the numerous questions arising since Edwin's sudden death.

Mr Braxton Hicks had tamped Adelaide right down – undoubtedly much to her lawyer's relief – and adjourned the proceedings until 4 February. By that date the eminent Home Office analyst, Dr Stevenson, Professor of Medical Jurisprudence, would have submitted his crucial report.[83]

DINNER À DEUX

After the adjournment on 7 January, Adelaide and Dyson dined together in a small, private room behind Mrs Stuard's confectioner's shop, sizing one another up anew. Given their respective predicaments, foreboding was such that the gulf between them widened with each word and pause.

Dyson told her bluntly that he was not afraid to stand by the truth when it affected him. Adelaide made clear *her* ploy in a promise, or a threat: if Dyson did not incriminate himself, she would not incriminate him.

He had so much at stake. Had Adelaide felt sure, prior to this, that the Reverend George Dyson would not put himself, his life, reputation and career at risk by telling people that he bought the poison at her request? She must have felt she had him hook, line and sinker, but she had not thought of the possible consequences. What if he wriggled off her hook?

Dyson's whole upbringing, training and faith meant that confession came naturally to him. His mounting anger, despite a pervading fear, gave him backbone and resolve. Adelaide must have begun to realise that he might spill all, pour his heart out to fellow Methodists. And to realise that he may let it all out to law officials at some point, in a wary, self-protective manner. Whichever way the Reverend might tell them, it would be confessing.

On 9 January, Adelaide was at Mr Matthews' workplace when Dyson arrived. This was an accidental meeting, but the three of them went to join Mrs Matthews at home. According to Dyson he told Adelaide he was puzzled as to 'what really had become of the chloroform' and she asked him why he didn't 'charge her outright' with having given it to Edwin.

Then it was Edwin's funeral. Adelaide and Dyson stood together in silence at the graveside.

As far as is known, not another word ever passed between them.

NO VITAL ORGANS

PC Ralph delivered to Dr Stevenson on 11 January the four jars containing Edwin's intestines for analysis. The vital organs were not removed at the post-mortem and had been buried with his body so there could be no tests on, for instance, his liver. The opportunity for more thorough investigation, if anyone wanted it, had been lost at the post-mortem.

Dr Stevenson got to work on Edwin's limited remains and found in the deceased's stomach a marked presence of chloroform. It turned out to be a large quantity of the poison.

WHAT IS CHLOROFORM?

As noted earlier, in relation to the sad case of the child Eliza Armstrong in 1885, chloroform has a pleasant smell (similar to that of ether). A non-flammable, clear and colourless liquid which is denser than water; chloroform's downside is 'a relatively narrow margin of safety'. Hence it has been 'replaced by better inhalation anaesthetics'.[84]

Chloroform, $CHCl^3$, is also called trichloromethane. It was prepared for the first time in 1831, and from 1847 used as an anaesthetic by influential Sir James Simpson, a Scottish physician. Chloroform came more fully to public attention in Britain when Queen Victoria's physician administered it to her during the birth of her eighth child in 1853 and of her last baby in 1857.[85]

According to Linda Stratmann, author of *Chloroform: The Quest for Oblivion*, 'chloroform revolutionised surgery, but also caused hundreds of sudden deaths, the cause of which was a hotly debated mystery in which physicians took sides and hurled insults at each other in the medical press'.[86]

The flustered widow decamped from the Matthews's home and found lodgings in Weymouth Street, adjoining Portland Place in central London.

The day of 26 January was filled with Adelaide's confidential disclosures. She had gone to Dr Leach on at least four occasions in that month and (to use a modern, rather vulgar expression) 'got in his ear'. Persistence paid off and she extracted information about the test results on materials from Edwin's corpse – details to which the doctor was privy and which he should not have divulged to her. Unbelievably, he acted without restraint, telling her that chloroform was the identified cause of Edwin's death. Crassly, he said she was lucky it hadn't been prussic acid or a secret poison, because if so she would have been a suspect. Then, if Leach heard her correctly,

Adelaide's response was …

Well, wait until April to find out what Leach said about her response.

It is frustrating to know that Adelaide had written down notes about her husband's death – yet her notes were never seen. Damn!

'THE INFERENCE WHICH MAY BE DRAWN'

On 11 February, the Inquest resumed and Mr Beal stated that, as some suspicion was attached to the widow, he would prefer that she not give her evidence until after Professor Stevenson's. The Coroner could not force Mrs Bartlett to give evidence, but he declined to agree to Mr Beal's proposal, saying:

'If the widow does not give evidence it will weigh with the jury. I will not press it, but you must remember the inference which may be drawn.'[87]

Mr Beal replied that although there was no charge against his client, he could not take the responsibility of sanctioning any examination of her before they had heard from Dr Stevenson.

Thus Mr Beal had protected his client. And another key opportunity to hear words from Adelaide was lost.

'BRANDY WOULD ACT AS A SOLVENT FOR IT'

The toxicology findings were given by Dr Stevenson on behalf of the Home Office, conveying five key points. 'Everything pointed to the administration of a large and fatal dose of chloroform … Nothing would take away the hot and fiery taste of chloroform, but it would be greatly mitigated by mixing it with a bland liquid. He had never known chloroform used for homicidal purposes. Brandy would act as a solvent for it.'[88]

So, did chloroform mixed with brandy slither down Edwin's throat?

In the Pimlico Mystery, doctors, lawyers and court officials are in abundance; police hardly figure. Enter one police inspector, Henry Marshall, of the Metropolitan Police, holding a copy of Squires' *Companion to the British Pharmacopoeia*, found in the Bartlett's flat when searched on 11 January. Tome handed to the Coroner, Inspector Marshall drew the Jury's attention to two significant facts: it appeared to open naturally at the very page on which chloroform was described, and there was a note on that page. (However, Dr Leach had told the Inquest that both the Bartletts could read prescriptions – and no investigation had been made into who wrote on the 'chloroform' page.)

Coroner Braxton Hicks, after Dyson's evidence, offered Adelaide one last opportunity to speak, because he knew that if put on trial for murder she would not be allowed to give evidence of any sort. Her lawyer stood up and declined the offer. She would not be giving evidence to the Inquest. End of …

Beal and others were only too mindful of the horrendous probing of Florence Bravo in 1876 at two Inquests, following death by poisoning of her barrister husband, Charles.

The Jury at Edwin's Inquest made a second crucial decision – perhaps anticipated and inevitable, nevertheless dramatic. After the stark evidence from Dyson and the three chemists who sold him chloroform, the Foreman announced their opinion.

'MRS BARTLETT SHOULD NO LONGER BE LEFT AT LIBERTY'

The spectators in Court quietened, the Coroner accepted the pronouncement. Everyone present knew this would lead to Adelaide being taken into custody. He had wanted 'to give her one last chance' to speak – but of course she had declined. (And now just a couple more stages would be gone through before her being locked up, pending trial.)

The daunting day, almost over but not quite. As soon as the boardroom emptied, Adelaide (in the presence of her solicitor, Mr Wood) was formally cautioned by plain-clothed Inspector Marshall.

'After what… passed here today, I must take you into custody for the wilful murder of your husband by administering to him, about midnight on the 31 December last, a poisonous dose of chloroform.'

Adelaide: 'I have nothing to say.'

Off to nearby Rochester Row Police Station; locked in a cell until morning.

THE MAGISTRATE, MR PARTRIDGE

On to a different procedure: Adelaide put before the Magistrate, Mr William Partridge, at Westminster Police Court, on 12 February, stood charged with causing her husband's death 'by administering a poisonous dose of chloroform to him on or about midnight on 31 December, 1885'. Mr Wood's reply on her behalf: 'No sir' – nothing to say as to why she should not be remanded in custody. Off east, across London to Clerkenwell House of Detention. A lock-in place for prisoners like her, remanded and awaiting trial. That district held the haunts of the Chamberlain family – but now of course she was without the liberty enjoyed there as a child.

Apart from appearances in court, Adelaide would be behind bars until April, at the very least.

THE DUPED, DECEIVED DYSON – AND 'A FALSEHOOD'

On 15 February, back at the Inquest, Dyson under cross-examination admitted that before tutoring Adelaide he had never had another female member of his congregation as a 'pupil'. And hence the unvoiced inference made in court that not much of a 'tutoring' nature went on between Dyson and Adelaide, in terms of history lessons and suchlike.

Asked why he felt 'duped', Dyson replied that he felt 'deceived'. His use of the word 'duped' in relation to Mrs Bartlett 'had nothing to do with marriage. It referred to the matter of the chloroform purely. I believed that the chloroform was going to be used in an innocent way'. Mr Dennis, appearing for Edwin senior, asked the Reverend why, concerning the chloroform, he resorted to 'a falsehood in order to get it'. Dyson's lame reply:

'Simply because I knew I could not explain my relations with the family to a chemist.'[89]

Asked by Mr Dennis if he could explain why (when chloroform was found in Edwin's body) Dyson had said he was 'a ruined man', Dyson replied clearly, 'I can.' He must have welcomed the (temporary) relief of replying spontaneously in court; he could tell the truth about why he had felt 'ruined', could do that part without having to choose his words carefully. He had to be utterly careful throughout all of his other evidence in order to protect himself, as best he could, in such dreadful circumstances.

'AN IMPROPER PURPOSE – I MEAN A CRIMINAL PURPOSE'

Dyson proceeded with the story of how Mrs Bartlett confided to him that Edwin 'was suffering from a disease that would shortly prove fatal'. And that when, after Edwin's demise, she denied saying such a thing, he knew in a ghastly instant 'that the whole story of the sickness, and nursing, and skill in the use of medicine was false, and it flashed across my mind that she must have wanted the chloroform for an improper purpose – I mean a criminal purpose.'

'I AM AS MUCH ASTONISHED NOW AT HAVING DONE WHAT I DID AS YOU ARE'

The Coroner challenged the Reverend as to whether it did not occur to him that Mrs Bartlett – or Dyson himself – should have asked a doctor whether chloroform be given, unbeknown, to a recipient.

Dyson: 'I am as much astonished now at having done what I did as you are, but at that time I was without any doubt whatever.'

Thus implying implicit faith in Adelaide's knowledge of chloroform's use – and why he did exactly as she bade him.[90]

The *Alcester Chronicle* reported that Dyson, asked by the Coroner if he did not know that an overdose of chloroform was likely to prove fatal, replied yes, he 'knew that', adding that he told his friends 'about purchasing the chloroform, and at least half a dozen persons knew of it within a fortnight.' (Presumably meaning that he told them *after* Edwin's death about the purchases.)[91]

Dyson naïve, foolish, cunning, incurious? If friends were told, did one or more rub a chin and caution him: 'I wouldn't do that if I were you'?

On 16 February, the *Standard* had extensive news of the previous day's proceedings. Alice Matthews gave evidence about events after 1 January, including Dyson's questions to her about Edwin's former health and her answer that Edwin hadn't been an ill man in the past. She gave details of Adelaide's lies and outburst of anger. She described the distress slipping out of Dyson, the sudden departure of Mrs Bartlett from the Matthews' house on Monday 11 January. Mrs Matthews explained: 'I told my husband I did not feel comfortable with her when she told those lies. Mrs Bartlett said she could not stay with us unless she paid. We could not have that at all, and she left.'

RESULT

Alice Matthews had no longer wanted Adelaide to stay in the house – and Adelaide knew that the couple, as her friends (friends up until then) would not accept money from her. Result: out and off went Adelaide. Not banished by the Matthews, but not welcome as a non-paying or paying guest either.

Another lie fell from Adelaide's lips before she left their home.

'Mrs Bartlett knew that I was aware that she had got the chloroform, and she told me [it was] to soothe Edwin; and that she had never touched it, and that it was just as she had got it, until the Wednesday ...' said Mrs Matthews.

Mr Braxton Hicks' brilliant question: 'Did she mention anything about Edwin touching it?'

Mrs Matthews: 'No.'

Adelaide had told her about pouring the chloroform out of the train window and throwing away the bottle.

'At the time I did not attach much importance to the fact of her having chloroform, as she had studied medicine for the purpose of doctoring her dogs. They used to keep five or six dogs at a time.'

She added that Mrs Bartlett told her about the January visits to Dr Leach. Allegedly he told Mrs Bartlett she couldn't have given Edwin chloroform to drink 'because if she had done so, his screams would have roused the house.' Also, that if she gave chloroform by inhalation it would have shown up in his brain.

Immediately, Dr Leach piped up in the Inquest that the question to the witness should have been 'whether Mrs Bartlett said lung or brain, as he did not wish his name associated with a medical heresy.'

Mrs Matthews replied that it was 'brain', and Mrs Bartlett had 'also said that the doctor told her that there was a suspicion of digitalis or foxglove having been given.'

'DUPED BY A WICKED WOMAN'

George Matthews told the Inquest about being stopped in early January at Peckham Rye station by a panic-stricken Dyson declaring he had 'been duped by a wicked woman'. He told Matthews that during the second half of 1885 he became increasingly attached to Mrs Bartlett but had wanted to get away from her. She persuaded him to continue his visits – and Edwin had encouraged him. Matthews deposed that Dyson said, 'You will see that I was attacked on my weakest side.'

'SHALL I MAKE A CLEAN BREAST OF IT?'

Matthews said Dyson's next question was about having purchased the chloroform – 'Shall I make a clean breast of it?'

Matthews must have been extremely perturbed, but suggested Dyson wait, not do anything hasty. Chloroform might not be found – in other words, don't make a 'false issue' of it – decide after the results of the analyses. He added that Dyson 'seemed much relieved, and said I had made a new man of him, as if I had raised a load off his mind.'

The sum total of George Matthews' pragmatic advice to the young man: don't confess to anything – yet.

'MR BARTLETT'S PECULIAR FANCIES'

Dr Leach was put through his paces giving evidence. He deposed that 'more than twice' Mrs Bartlett told him – when her husband was in the room – 'Edwin says he will not live' or that 'he will not recover.' Dr Leach was not asked how his patient reacted.

The doctor said he laughed, as he 'thought it was one of Mr Bartlett's peculiar fancies' and that if he were to give evidence on these peculiar fancies and ideas, he should keep the Jury there 'for days'. (Please don't, they must have thought.)

'MR BARTLETT DID NOT DIE OF HIS IDEAS OR FANCIES'

The Coroner hurriedly said he did not think it necessary to receive such evidence, as it had nothing to do with the case (ah, but think upon it, when the week of 12 April arrives). He reprimanded Dr Leach, solemnly reminding all present that 'Mr Bartlett did not die of his ideas or fancies, but of a large dose of chloroform.'

Undeterred, Dr Leach countered: 'Mr Bartlett's peculiar fancies seemed to point to the idea that he was a man likely to do a very extraordinary thing.'

The Coroner admonished: 'That is very vague. I do not think it would have any bearing upon us. If more comes out before the Magistrate, I must say I shall have to condole with him.' (Laughter). Athelstan Braxton Hicks obviously thought that Dr Leach should have sorted the wheat from the chaff, not just been a windbag. And yet again an official had tamped down a person about to give crucial insights into the Bartletts as individuals and as a couple. Some or all of their doctor's unique utterances may have held relevance to the case.

This was an example of Dr Leach being ridiculed for taking Adelaide at face value. Edwin had said nothing peculiar, at least not on that occasion, but to hear about his 'peculiar fancies' could have been enlightening. The doctor's personality, the strain and the importance of the occasion were such that he ploughed on inexorably with certain other lines of thought, none of any help to the Jury.

SEIZED BY THE 'HORROR'

Dyson, recalled to the witness box, had to answer a question at the request of a Juryman (via the Coroner). 'Would you give us the reason why you threw those bottles away?'

'Yes sir,' replied Dyson. He did so, seized by the 'horror' of it all.

Court would adjourn until 18 February. The Coroner finished for the day by requesting a surety for Mr Dyson. 'Mr Riggall said he would have pleasure in becoming surety for him.'[92]

It cost Dyson's friend, Marmaduke Riggall, 100/- for that (dubious) 'pleasure'.

SPREAD THE WORD

On Thursday 18 February the Inquest resumed. Word had spread along corridors and streets, thousands of printed words aired domestic secrets and marital mysteries seeping out from the Pimlico 'house of death'. Worth queuing for, said many to their mates.

A reporter from the *Citizen* had plenty to note next day. A large crowd gathered and some were admitted, squashing in, to sit or stand. But then the Coroner ordered the clearing out of everyone, except for witnesses and those there for the case business: Mr Lockwood (instructed by Lewis and Lewis) for Dyson; Mr Beal (instructed by Edward Negus Wood) for Adelaide; Mr Dennis for Edwin senior and relatives. Nothing more was written about these other 'relatives'. Inspector Marshall would watch the proceedings on behalf of the police authorities.

The key players, Mrs Bartlett and Dyson, 'a pallor' about them, were brought in. The Coroner directed that he and the respective witnesses must now read over the whole of the evidence taken and witnesses would sign their statements. The Jury would then be handed all that material to read before the Coroner delivered his summing-up. Rueful reporters jotted down that the reading took a long time …

The *Standard* had it that a Juryman sent a note asking, 'that a servant of Mrs Joggell's [sic] where deceased lodged, be called'.[93] Perhaps that reporter had popped out for a drink and misheard the name on his return – or the correct surname, Doggett, may have got joggelled at the printing stage.

While the Jurors read their notes and everyone awaited the 'sent for' Alice Fulcher, the Coroner 'pointed out that Mrs Bartlett informed Dr Leach that she had told her husband about the chloroform because she never kept anything secret from him, but Dyson said Mrs Bartlett expressed her wish to keep the possession of the chloroform unknown to the deceased.'[94]

Mr Braxton Hicks must have felt pleased about putting this contradictory evidence to the Jury, following it up with the fact that 'nothing about chloroform was brought out until after the first sitting of the Inquest.'

Summing-up, he reminded everyone that 'the Jury were agreed that Mrs Bartlett should be committed for wilful murder by the action they advised a week ago.' He left it to them to decide whether they were satisfied with Dyson's explanation about buying chloroform, or whether he was an accessory before the fact.

The Jury 'retired at 5.10'. The reporter watched the clock. 'After forty minutes' consultation' the Jurymen confirmed the opinion that Adelaide administered the chloroform, and they deemed Dyson an accessory before the fact.

THE REVEREND 'TURNED DEATHLY PALE AND WEPT'

Now labelled an 'accessory before the fact' of Mr Bartlett's death, the Reverend 'turned deathly pale and wept' as he slumped down onto his chair. The Coroner made out a warrant; friends gathered around Dyson. Detective Inspector Marshall stepped in and took him into custody just next door, at Rochester Row Police Station. Accompanied by his brother and the Reverend Marmaduke Riggall, George Dyson was formally charged, given refreshments and locked in a cell.

'NOT VERY HOPEFUL'

Behind bars, the much-shaken Dyson wrote that day to his parents in Poole and to a friend, Bernard, who lived in the same town. To the former he declared before God that he was innocent.

Dyson continued to be an expressive writer; thoughts gushed out to his friend.

'My dearest Bernard – Just a line to say that I am feeling calm, not very hopeful – (dear, no one sees more clearly than I the frightful suggestions of the facts to which I have confessed) – but invincibly strong in the consciousness of perfect innocence. Nay, I can't but remember that the fatal New Year's Eve was spent by me in prayer for the sick man, and, as I thought, his faithful attendant. You must not worry for me. If you could look at my face and look into my heart you would see that I was perfectly free from distraction myself. I have told the facts. Now they must deal according to them, or disbelieve. I receive hosts of letters of confidence. Good bye, my dear fellow. Pray that justice may have sway. They had a special prayer meeting at Putney for me. Best love – GEORGE.'

Presumably Bernard saw fit to release this letter in support of Dyson and it was published in numerous newspapers.[95]

A RIDER

Unrelated to the fate of Mrs Bartlett and Reverend Dyson, on 18 February the Jury had added a rider, suggesting that application should be made to the proper authorities to include chloroform, and all such poisons, in the first part of Schedule A of the Sale of Poisons Act.

For some reason the authorities did not do so.

'WILFUL MURDER'

Admission for spectators was by ticket only when a large crowd clamoured outside Westminster Police Court on 19 February, wanting to see Mrs Bartlett and the Reverend Dyson brought up on remand by Inspector Marshall.

She was 'covered with crape [crepe]' and seemed in 'deep distress'; Dyson had 'a very ordinary type of physiognomy' and a 'sallow complexion'. He 'keenly felt his position'. After luncheon and back in the dock to appear before Mr William Partridge, Mrs Bartlett 'for the first time lifted up her heavy veil and disclosed her rather attractive young face of a Milesian cast with a profusion of dark hair.'[96]

Whether the reporter was referring to Milesian Irish mythology, or there was a misprint of 'Malaysian' (a person from Malaysia) or of 'Melanesian' (an area from New Guinea to Fiji) is not known. Whichever, this reporter was on to something … in terms of trying to pin down Adelaide's heritage.

Thomas Low Nichols no less, witness, swore that to the best of his belief he had never seen Mrs Bartlett before now. He described her face as 'peculiar' (presumably meaning it was unusual; unlike others) and thought he would remember her if she had called at his house.

Mr Moloney entered the scene, leading the Prosecution on behalf of the Treasury. Mr Beal was there for Mrs Bartlett and Mr Lickford for Dyson. More witnesses gave their evidence, then the case was adjourned until 26 February.

Dyson and Adelaide were remanded again and despatched back to their respective prisons.

THE CHOSEN ONE

The next day, 20 February, was a portentous occasion in the fight for the life of Adelaide Bartlett. Charged with murder, she would be put on trial – but not just yet. Ever-helpful Edward Negus Wood, her solicitor, had explained to her the urgent need to engage the services of an eminent barrister and Edward Clarke QC, MP was the chosen one. Wood may have talked with Adelaide's uncle, William Chamberlain, about this niece's predicament and about fees. What was Clarke's going rate?

ONE IN PRISON, ONE 'TO FREEDOM'

Adelaide, locked up in a London prison on remand; one of her brothers, on the far side of the world, released after years on the receiving end of a harsh prison regime. It was Saturday, 20 February 1886. On her mind, the wait for her murder trial; on his, the journal of his prison experiences. Bitter irony: these two siblings on opposite sides of the globe, one in a prison in England, one leaving a prison in Australia.

Chapter 27

'TO DISPROVE THE STRANGE STATEMENTS

PROMULGATED'

An illuminating attempt to promote a positive, rounded image of the late Edwin was published soon after Adelaide had been locked up, unnamed friends (and his father) making public their opinions and knowledge of him.

Numerous newspapers took up the original scoop. 'The latest enquiries (says *Lloyd's Weekly* newspaper) tend to disprove the strange statements promulgated.'[97]

Those who had known the real Edwin gave Lloyd's their counterviews about the 'alleged celebate [sic]' and they challenged depictions of 'the eccentric and hypochondriac peculiarities of the unfortunate deceased'.

For whatever reasons, those revelations neither redressed the balance nor set the record straight, despite his friends' hopes. And perhaps the article did not strike a chord with readers, the real Edwin being buried deeper under a pile of 'Pimlico Mystery' reporting. Unfortunately, the friends' revelations were not included in books about the Bartletts down the centuries. Was that because the friends portrayed Edwin as a person rather than as a strange being? It seems doubtful that the article was deliberately omitted by writers; more likely they did not uncover it.

For whatever reason, no part of the article appeared in any subsequent literature about the case, even though it had been printed in many newspapers around the country in 1886.[98] Almost every line throws new light on the Bartletts and unlocks many of the enduring Pimlico Poisoning mysteries. The article contributes a different narrative and can now act as a legacy to Edwin from his friends and father.

They wanted the public to know about the real person. 'He was ... an industrious, persevering man' who, being in a business partnership, 'did not desire to burthen [burden] himself with the responsibilities of a home. In February 1875, however, he went on a visit to his brother's residence at Hampton Wick.' There Edwin met 'Blanche Escury', living next door. 'She was very fascinating in her manners, and had a most romantic history to tell.' Adelaide had 'lost both her parents when very young, but she told Mr Bartlett that she was of good descent and had considerable expectations.'

GOLD DUST

Stories of Adelaide's possible heritage have come down through the years with more drama than information. From the article here is what counts, to date, as the highest quality gold dust, with little iron pyrite.

'A RATHER WARM, FIERY DISPOSITION'

Miss Chamberlain, a sister of Mr Chamberlain at Shortlands, Kent, 'a gentleman well known and respected on the Stock Exchange' was married 'abroad' to 'Count de la Tremoyle, a gentleman [and] from his exceedingly dark complexion supposed to have had African blood in his veins.

'It is said he was of a rather warm, fiery disposition, and his daughter, whose real name is Adelaide, to some extent took after him. It was owing in great measure to this, and as she could not live very comfortably with her friends, that a home away from them was found for her at Hampton Wick.

'She gave Mr Bartlett to understand that her wedding dowry would be £1,000, and as Mr Bartlett thought that would be useful in his business, a marriage was at once arranged, but on the mutual understanding that no home was to be provided for three years, till Mr Bartlett's business justified it.'

The friends gave details of the marriage and the wedding breakfast, attended by Adelaide's uncle William. As to 'her wedding dowry', they stated that 'it appears that it was from him' she expected to receive the money which never materialised. Although 'to some extent disappointed, Mr Bartlett did not allow this to make any difference in his conduct towards his wife, but treated her with great kindness, and desired that not only should she endeavour to become domesticated, but should also cultivate her education.'

She was 'sent' to Miss Dodd's school, then to the convent near Antwerp. When she returned to England, she 'lived in full marital relations' with her husband and later had the stillborn baby.

'The relations between them as man and wife are said to have been of the most affectionate character, which with little exception was maintained till within the last twelve months.'

The friends credited Edwin senior with 'persistency' in demanding and obtaining the independent post-mortem. Whatever feeling Edwin had in December of something crawling up inside his throat, the statement that he was 'afflicted with worms is discredited by the friends.'

There is consistency with other opinions about Edwin's essential trust of others, in that 'the deceased only encouraged the visits of Mr Dyson so far as he thought they would be beneficent to his wife in a pastoral sense, and it was owing to his implicit confidence in him as a gentleman and a minister that he allowed his visits to the house.' To repeat, Edwin had implicit confidence in his friend Dyson, whom he thought was a gentleman with the morals of a decent clergyman.

Edwin's friends were clearly suspicious of Dyson's keeping 'all Mr Bartlett's letters, while he has destroyed those received from Mrs Bartlett.'

And they finished by wondering 'what information it was that Mr Doggett … wished to give to the magistrate, but which by the strict rules of evidence he was prohibited from giving' at the Inquest. Doggett continued to ponder about that fire in the grate …

On 27 February, the released former convict Constance Kent stepped ashore from the *Carisbrooke Castle* in Sydney. Alone, into the summer heat of Australia. On licence, but free to try to live a quiet life, to earn a living. Some of her family members already resided there. Constance, institutionalised, intelligent, strong-minded and (ironically) fond of children, had interests, skills and experience which would stand her in good stead after twenty years of incarceration.

On 27 February, the remanded Bartlett and Dyson were put back into the packed Westminster Police Court before the Magistrate, Mr Partridge.

'The Court, long before the hour fixed for the resumption of the case – two o'clock – was crowded by a mixed assemblage, of whom a large number were females.'

'A SENSATION'

Soon 'a sensation' was created by the testimony of a servant, disclosing that 'whenever the clergyman called in cold weather, Mrs Bartlett warmed a pair of slippers at the fire for him, and that generally she carefully pinned the blinds of the room wherein she entertained him. The servant swore that she had seen Mrs Bartlett and the preacher sitting on the floor together, and had also seen Mr Dyson sitting in a low chair with Mrs Bartlett on the floor before him with her head in his lap.'[99]

Some people in court looked outraged about the pair's behaviour – 'her head in his lap' no less. And, for whatever reason, the pair had not moved apart when the servant entered the room. Did they freeze or were they defiant – defying convention and the girl's gaze?

In the United States, the *Philadelphia Times*' headline did not beat about the bush. Edwin had been …

'A HUSBAND IN THE WAY'[100]

The article did not go into detail, but when living in Claverton Street the previous December, husband Edwin may have been 'in the way' of a deepening relationship between Adelaide and George. Yes, the pair could remove themselves physically from Edwin by going into a different room or out for a walk. However, if they desired more privacy – and a life together – they or he had to go. The balance had tipped completely out of Edwin's favour. And he, or one of the three, did something about it.

LARGE QUANTITIES

When the Remand Hearing at the police court resumed, the small room was even more packed 'and there was a large crowd outside unable to gain admittance'. Mr Braxton Hicks, the Coroner, was recalled 'to read the deposition of Dyson [given] at the Inquest'.

The eyes of spectators 'were strained and necks craned … to get a glimpse of their faces'. Adelaide wore 'deepest mourning' clothes, and looked 'dull and heavy about the eyes'. Her long black hair hung down and the long black widow's veil hung down over her face for much of the Hearing. Sitting in the same box, just a constable's width between them, sat Dyson, pale and quiet, yet showing a 'lively interest' in the proceedings once they got going. He glanced at his friends and frequently wrote notes, passing them to his Counsel, Mr Lickfold.[101]

Mr Humble the chemist from Putney, examined by Mr Moloney, recalled how he sold chloroform to Dyson, whom he knew by sight. He had shown Dyson a two-dram bottle and asked if that would be enough. 'No, more than that!' Dyson had requested, and when shown a half ounce bottle he asked for a 'larger bottle than that', or words to that effect. 'That will do,' said Dyson, when an ounce bottle was produced.

'SIDE QUESTIONS'

Humble had tried 'by side questions' to find out why Dyson wanted the poison, but found the Reverend extremely evasive. Humble produced the book containing the record of sales and read from it the 'special entry' he made on the day in question. He continued:

'I HAD A PRESENTIMENT'

'PRAY DO NOT tell us your presentiments,' shouted Mr Lickfold, hurriedly silencing the Witness, so as to minimise any further damage to his client, Dyson. Mr Lickford had stopped Mr Humble's 'presentiment' (an intuitive feeling about the future; a foreboding).

Mr Moloney stood up. 'Was that the usual quantity for you to sell at one time to one person?'

Humble: 'It was an exceptionally large quantity for me to sell at one time.'

Mr Moloney next called upon Mr Penrose the chemist from the Ridgway, Wimbledon, to give his evidence. Penrose sold Dyson a 'most exceptionally large quantity' of chloroform – and now declared, 'I should not have sold it unless I had known Mr Dyson well.'

Mr Mellin, assistant to his father the chemist at 36 High Street, Wimbledon, was next up. He had known Dyson for about eighteen months; thought he sold him two ounces.

Mr Moloney: 'Have you, since you sold this chloroform to Mr Dyson, ever sold any such large quantity?'

Mellin: 'No.'[102]

There you have it, with Mr Moloney, prosecuting, extracting important facts about Dyson and the chloroform from three witnesses: the three purchases; taking advantage of knowing the vendor; three quantities far larger than usual.

Mr Beal, for Adelaide, was only able to pick up three small scraps about just one point: confirmation from each vendor that Dyson had been shopping on his own.

Dyson told lies and made the purchases. Edwin was presumably unaware that *his* money was spent on unusually large quantities of a volatile poison, to be used on *him* by Adelaide – according to Dyson.

DR LEACH

Dyson, doubtless very nervous, looks quite collected … until, that is, until that man Leach starts on about his, Dyson's, visit to the surgery on 4 January.

'I WON'T sit here and listen to such lies! Look at him, look at his face: he's lying and it's abominable,' shouts the usually subdued and cautious Dyson, rising to his feet in an excited manner.

'Sit down. Your solicitor is in court.' Rebuked by the Magistrate, the Reverend sinks back down, deflated.

'But is there no protection for me?' asks Dyson.

'In anything you wish to complain of, you must communicate with your solicitor.'

Dr Leach appeals: 'May I ask in what way I have lied?'

Magistrate: 'He had no right to interrupt you. His conduct was most improper.'[103]

Alas, there is no record of what words from Dr Leach inflame Dyson and result in this eruption in court – his one and only outburst in public during the whole sorry mess.

Dyson and Adelaide continue to ignore one another. Together in trouble, alone with their misery.

Dr Leach covered the record of his visits and prescriptions with the following:

18 December: 'Mrs Bartlett complained that the patient's absence from business was keeping a lot of employees out of work.'

How come? Did they have no tea to mix as Mr Bartlett had not tasted it, not decided on the exact blend? One would imagine there was *more* work for employees to do in the absence of a key person.

Back to business in court.

Dr Leach confirmed he had been at the post-mortem and 'imagined that the chest was opened first, or the abdomen.' Which had been done first he could not be certain, as he had sat 'in a corner writing hard. It was all guess work.'

Asked about the Inquest, he said his words about Adelaide's visits to him (in January) were divulged 'mostly under protest.' By this, Dr Leach was referring to her confiding in him, and to his distaste at having to disclose in court their confidential patient/doctor consultations. However, he did do so – and would have to repeat her disclosures at a later date.

Dr Leach had not known that Edwin used chlorodyne, until Mrs Bartlett told him in January that her husband had used it regularly as a mouthwash. A newspaper listed chlorodyne's ingredients as 'chloroform, ether, caloricus Indica, morphia, prussic acid, treacle, peppermint and rectified spirit'.[104]

TRIAL POSTPONED

Adelaide and Dyson were remanded again on 6 March, Mr Moloney, for the Prosecution, having applied at the Central Criminal Court for the charges to be postponed until the April Sessions. He did so because the prisoners had only been committed by a coroner and the case was still under investigation by a magistrate. The Recorder granted the application. The delay dragged the two prisoners further down.

Mr Beal 'asked that the female prisoner be taken in a cab to the House of Detention. She was in a very weak state. Mr Netherclift was called and deposed that he had examined her and considered that her removal in the prison van would be prejudicial to her health. She was sick and giddy after each journey and the van sergeant stated that the prisoner had been sick on her journeys to and from court. Dr George Pearce, divisional surgeon, said that Mrs Bartlett's heart and pulse were weak and he thought she should be conveyed in a private vehicle.'

Mr Partridge 'made an order on the medical evidence, the prisoner having been kept back until 6.30'. Adelaide would go by horse-drawn cab, not the prison van.[105]

'THERE WAS NOTHING WRONG UNTIL I STARTED LYING'

The remanded Reverend Dyson was locked up at Newgate Prison, on the corner of Newgate Street near the Old Bailey. Newgate, renowned for its terrible conditions and forbidding appearance had, despite numerous rebuilds, become extremely dilapidated. Since 1860 it had been used for short-term prisoners only; Dyson certainly hoped he would not be in there for a long stretch.[106]

Bernard Curtis, the Reverend's Wesleyan friend from Poole, visited him at Newgate. Goodness knows what the two of them thought of this grim place. And, pray, of what did their conversation consist? Probably a rueful and bitter denouncement of Adelaide by George. A little information emerged years later, a story via Bernard's daughter, Evelyn Curtis. George had been quite calm but realised 'it was touch and go' in terms of the pending court case and his future. Evelyn recounted how Dyson said to her father:

'Bernard, there was nothing wrong until I started lying. I lied to the chemists about the chloroform.'[107]

Yes, Dyson lied to the chemists about the use to which the chloroform would be put. But perhaps he did not admit to Bernard that he, Dyson, had been at best foolish and at worst a criminal for buying the drug on behalf of someone else (Adelaide, of course).

Bernard and his daughter, Evelyn, reappear near the end of this whole saga.

One can surmise from his rueful comment to Bernard that it had all 'got to' Dyson. He had erred and strayed onto a slippery slope, and fell into lying on behalf of a loved one. Telling lies is not what a religious person should do; telling lies to several chemists in sly stages, obtaining a large quantity of highly dangerous chloroform. He was a man of the church who gave a plausible reason for such purchases: to remove greasy marks. Dyson, when on the slippery slope, sinned by obtaining poison with a degree of deception. Its administration – by Adelaide or by Edwin – led to the latter's death.

Dyson's own actions would be on his, the young preacher's, conscience always - now that he knew chloroform's strengths and his own weaknesses.

Adelaide had not thought it through in December. This man, steeped in religion since babyhood, would put a confession, albeit calculated, ahead of any remnants of love he felt for her.

MR TOMBS AND THE 'YOUNG BARTLETT'

On 6 March, the *Thanet Advertiser* had news via the *Birmingham Times*. Someone in the know, a Mr Tombs (secretary of the South Birmingham Conservative Association) had disclosed particulars about the late Edwin.

Apparently they had been friends for many years. Mr Bartlett 'went to Birmingham about twenty-and-three years ago as assistant counterman to Messrs Philpott and Sons, of High-street.' This had been 'the largest grocery establishment in the town, and during the five years ... young Bartlett made the best use of the opportunity' to learn the business. 'His immediate superior, the chief counterman, was named Baxter.' They had earned about £35 and £75 per annum respectively. Upon the death of Mr Philpott and the consequent breaking-up of the business, Baxter and Bartlett returned to London and opened up in Herne Hill.

'A DOWRY'

The Kent newspaper had more information from Birmingham. 'It has been said that Mrs Bartlett brought her husband a dowry of £1,000, but Mr Tombs believes that it was not more than £200, and that Mr Bartlett was indebted for his commercial success entirely to his own energy and shrewdness.'

Mr Tombs clearly did not believe Adelaide contributed much financially to the marriage.

'A REMARKABLY MASSIVE HEAD'

Tombs' description of Edwin's personal appearance and manner carry weight, so to speak: 'below middle height, of fair complexion, and with a remarkably massive head. He was of cheerful and general disposition, ever ready for fun, and implicitly trustful of his friends.'

'GIVEN AWAY'

As to the wedding, Edwin was apparently 'very reticent as to the antecedents of his wife; all that he told his most intimate friends of the matter being that she was "given away" at the wedding day by an uncle with whom she resided in London'.

'FLASHES OF RHETORIC'

At the police court on 7 March, Dr Leach made a request to the Magistrate: 'May I ask that I should be protected from the flashes of rhetoric to which I was subjected yesterday. It is most unfair.' Presumably the doctor was referring to Dyson; one rhetorical person criticising another.

The Magistrate: 'You are in the hands of the learned counsel for the prosecution, and he will protect you. I cannot interfere.'[108]

Dr Leach confirmed to Mr Moloney that Dyson saw the post-mortem notes in early January; also that Mr Bartlett had shown NO tendency to suicide.

On various dates in March, Mrs Bartlett and Dyson were brought before Mr Partridge at Westminster Police Court. Dr John Gardner Dudley gave his account of examining Edwin on 19 December, having been called in after Edwin senior's concerns as to why his son was so ill. Father and some of Edwin's friends had expressed their worries to Edwin.

Dr Dudley found no disease – but yes, an unwell, sleepless patient. The doctor was at Edwin's post-mortem and smelt chloroform in the corpse.

Reynolds's Newspaper, London, 21 March 1886, contained huge chunks about the post-mortem, revealed the previous day in court.

BODY PARTS AND FLUIDS ALERT!

'It having leaked out that Dr Stevenson, the government analyst … was to be called on this occasion, and as this will probably be the most important evidence in the whole case, it is needless to say that the court was as crowded as ever.' Those present included 'two Indian qualified doctors'.

Edwin's dissected corpse had yielded few findings. Even so, Dr Stevenson, professor of medical jurisprudence at Guy's Hospital, described the contents of all the bottles removed from 85 Claverton Street, among which were the 'official' bottles from the post-mortem.

'No.1 bottle contained an entire lower jaw and the soft part, No.2 about a quarter of a pint of fluid taken from the bowels, No.3 a stomach which had been cut open, No.4 some mango relish, No.5 half an ounce of thick semi-fluid, No.6 a glass jar containing decomposed Condy's fluid, No.7 was a brandy bottle containing the same liquid, No.8 was a hamper containing thirty-six bottles of various kinds. On the 16th of January he received a further lot of bottles from the Coroner's officer.

'On the 12th of January he commenced his examination of the contents of the bottles, beginning with No.5. He smelt the contents [the half an ounce of thick semi-fluid] which resembled strong chloroform.

'He at once telegraphed to Dr Leach, and also wrote to him. He received a telegram in reply, and the next day proceeded with an analysis of all the bottles. No.5 had a good deal of mango in it; it was slightly acid, and by various tests he determined it contained eleven and a half grains, or nine drops, of chloroform. He also found a trace of alcohol in the fluid, but it was quite minute.

'There were no signs of prussic acid or morphia, bismuth, or chloral. The fluid did not contain any poisonous matter except chloroform.'

The intestines and bowels had a good deal of chutney and contained some chloroform; the stomach had recent and acute inflammation at the gullet end, 'such as might be produced from swallowing chloroform'.

Stevenson reported that only minute traces of lead and copper were found in Edwin's jaw; those metals were not the key to his death. He could not say whether mercury was present or absent. Everything pointed to a large, fatal dose of chloroform, which had acted on Edwin's stomach during his life and shortly after death. Stevenson repeated the main points he made at the Inquest: chloroform has a hot and fiery taste, perhaps very similar to that of the mango chutney and which might be slightly masked by a liquid, and brandy could be used to act as a solvent for it. Professionally, he had no knowledge of chloroform used in a homicide.

Yet again committed for trial and remanded, Adelaide and Dyson were returned to their respective cells until April. Strikingly different personalities with contrasting backgrounds, both equally worried – and rightly so. They would be at the mercy of the men of the jury, then judgement would come. They feared it would lead to the hanging of one or both of them. It must have been a long, lonely, almost unbearable wait.

PART SEVEN
THE OLD BAILEY, LONDON

Chapter 28

TWO THEN ONE

REGINA V BARTLETT AND DYSON[109]

The Old Bailey, in the street of that name, London's Central Criminal Court since 1673, was situated next to Newgate Prison. A major fire in 1877 forced a decision to pull down the courts and prison, but re-building was *still* in fits and starts.

The courtrooms were cramped and conditions unsatisfactory – not what one would expect of the most important criminal courts in the country.[110]

DAY ONE

On 12 April 1886, the first murder trial in Britain for alleged misuse of the drug chloroform was about to get underway. 'Three-fourths of the audience, other than bar and press, were ladies.'[111]

Eleven years and six days after she and Edwin married, Adelaide was on trial, charged with the wilful murder of her husband. And Dyson, the 'Preacher On Trial', on trial with her, quaking. As far away from her as possible – but the distance only be a matter of feet in the small dock. Both looked prison-pale and very ill.

To the surprise and amazement of many spectators (the news had already leaked out to those men at the solicitors' tables and in the barristers' seats) the Attorney General, Sir Charles Russell, proclaimed that after 'anxious and careful consideration' he and his learned friends offered no evidence from the Prosecution against the Reverend. In response, the Judge directed the Jury that they should find Dyson 'not guilty'. The Foreman, perhaps puzzled, duly rose and formally stated that Dyson was 'Not Guilty'. The shocked – not yet relieved – Dyson left the dock. The Attorney General proffered nothing against him, having decided on this approach precisely so that information about Adelaide and Edwin could be elicited from Dyson under oath. The Reverend must return to the court as a witness for the Prosecution.

'THE GREAT SHOCK'

So now, only Adelaide faced trial, 'a small figure, without hat or bonnet, shawl or mantle, but wearing a well-fitting black silk dress, relieved by something white at the neck, and conspicuous by the great shock of short black hair surmounting a somewhat broad and sallow face.'[112]

Gone, the long black hair of her Inquest appearances. Shorn, small and unadorned, she appeared vulnerable.

ADELAIDE ON TRIAL – ALONE

The Trial, compared with most held in those days for alleged murders, was to be very short. Even shorter than many of its era because Edward Clarke produced not a single witness for Adelaide's Defence. And the law until 1898 was that defendants could not give their own testimony – on the basis that they could not be relied upon to tell the truth! Thus, trials were without the defendants' voices.

Yet so much of this Trial went on to be taken up with what Adelaide, the Defendant, was said to have said and done during her life. And many words were put into the mouth of the deceased, so to speak. Russell would say later in the Trial, describing Adelaide at the Coroner's inquiry: she 'was there, but did not tender herself to give evidence or any explanation.' He said he was not suggesting any inference, it was just a fact. And as Defendant in this trial she could not 'tender' herself, even if she wanted to speak out.

The scene was set for Adelaide's Trial to commence in a few minutes. Everyone knew that her very life was at stake. If found guilty, she might hang at Newgate Prison.

Chapter 29

PROSECUTION, DEFENCE, JUDGE AND JURY

FOR THE PROSECUTION

Sir Charles Russell QC, MP, an Irishman, a Roman Catholic, the Attorney General (chief legal adviser to the Crown). Assisted principally by Harry Poland QC (who had been one of the prosecutors in the Eliza Armstrong case the previous autumn); also Mr Wright and Mr Moloney.

Russell, appointed as Attorney General only two months before the Trial, was being pulled in several directions at this challenging stage of his life, primarily by the demands of government and the First Home Rule Bill concerning Ireland. Pressure upon him was extremely high.[113]

It is reasonable to think that Russell was not totally on top of his Brief for court. Renowned for his dedication to work and his persistent, industrious nature, pressures from events at the highest level in the land trumped the case he was about to prosecute – even though Adelaide's neck was at stake.

DEFENDING ADELAIDE

Edward Clarke QC, MP, a Freemason, a devout Anglican, a man with lower middle-class roots. His father had not been wealthy (he managed a shop) and thus the nest was sparsely feathered. Clarke grew up working hard and continued to do so, building an illustrious career. Unlike Russell, for Mrs Bartlett's case Clarke allotted many hours for meticulous preparation. He took time away from the House of Commons, having been retained by Mr Wood as early as 20 February and his focus was thus wholeheartedly on Adelaide's defence.[114]

Also on the team were the highly competent Mr Mead and Mr Beal.

DEFENDING DYSON

Mr Lockwood, with Mr Mathews (not Mr Matthews, a witness).

THE JUDGE

Mr Justice Wills, Sir Alfred Wills, a new judge, in the High Court since 1884. He was scholarly, with a refreshing hinterland: the Alps. Wills made 'mountain-climbing' something fashionable for the wealthy British and was the third president of the Alpine Club in London. Surprisingly, it was the first mountaineering club in the world.[115]

THE JURY

Twelve men would give their verdict at the end of the Trial; they asked some very pertinent questions during the process. (The Sex Disqualification (Removal) Act 1919 which permitted women to be jury members in trials did not come into effect at the Old Bailey until 1922. Indeed, even then few women were eligible as they did not meet the property qualifications until those were abolished in the 1970s.)

The following is a (long) summary of the six days of the Trial.

RUSSELL'S OPENING STATEMENT

For the Prosecution, Russell explained that although there were 'circumstances of some suspicion' in the case against Dyson, he had not felt it justified the man being long in the dock 'upon the question of guilt.'

And so Russell turned the attention of all towards Adelaide. With regard to the prisoner at the bar, concerning the 'murder having taken place – if it were a murder – either on the night of 31 December or on the morning of 1 January', he had plenty to recount from her alleged history and life with her late husband. When Russell reached 19 December 1885 in the story, he told how Dr Leach called for a second opinion from Dr Dudley on Edwin's condition. And how Edwin thought it advisable, lest his friends 'should suspect, if anything happened to him, that Mrs Bartlett, his wife, was poisoning him – a very extraordinary suggestion ... which Dr Leach attributes to the deceased man.'

Obviously Russell had chosen to highlight this stark information early on in the case, to lodge it in the Jurymen's minds. It was clear too, that much would ride on the quality of Dr Leach's evidence when he gave it. Next, Russell wanted to highlight the chloroform stories Adelaide was said to have told Dyson. These were that Edwin had 'an internal ailment, an affliction of long-standing; that this had upon previous occasions given him paroxysms'; that 'he might die suddenly in one of those paroxysms'. Imagine the prisoner at the bar having to sit in the dock and listen to this in silence and without reacting. Perhaps 'Oh, damn the chloroform' came into her mind again ...

Unsurprisingly, Russell had not finished with the subject of chloroform, nor with Edwin's alleged ailments. He summarised allegations made by Dyson earlier in the year that Adelaide used chloroform obtained 'through the instrumentality of one Annie Walker' whom Adelaide said had then gone to America. Russell added that on one occasion when Edwin was suffering, 'a Dr Nichols, of Fopstone Road, Earl's Court, had said to her that her husband, Mr Bartlett, would die soon.' Russell was quick to add that there was 'no ground' for saying Edwin had a malignant growth, that there was no ground for claiming chloroform was obtained from Annie Walker, nor that Dr Nichols had been called in.

These were sensational challenges against the case which the Defence would present; challenges thrown down by the Attorney General to one and all in the court, primarily to try to convince the Jurymen, early on in the proceedings, of Adelaide's lies and guilt.

TRUTHS, HALF-TRUTHS AND LIES

The Reverend, says Russell, made a lengthy statement before the Coroner's Jury and now will be 'in the witness box on his oath, face to face with the prisoner, before you and my Lord.' A solemn reminder to Dyson of his situation's gravity and of the fact that very shortly the Reverend would take the Holy Bible into his hand and swear to tell the truth. Hopefully, the Jurymen's ears are pricked.

Dyson's priority, naturally, will be to try to save his reputation and credibility by walking a tight rope: distancing himself from Adelaide (now that he is out of the dock) and aligning himself with the late Edwin. He needs to convince the Jury that he had been a good friend of the husband: this is essential if he is to head off suggestions of a motive for murder. Dyson's exceedingly guilty conscience (around purchasing chloroform, at least) is unnerving him and he needs all the brain power in his bonce to manage the balancing act. Most questions he dare not, must not, answer spontaneously, because his story is a careful construct to cope with the hazardous road towards his goal: the survival of his reputation.

'Everyone seems guilty because everyone has something to hide. For most of them, though, the secret is not murder. This is the trick on which detective fiction turns,' wrote Kate Summerscale, about the evolution of crime fiction after the Constance Kent case.[116']

Secrets so often need to be covered over during the course of daily life. The trick is to remember what the secret something is and why hidden. Dyson has plenty to hide if he can. His aim, deadly serious: to save himself and his career in the Methodist Church.

As Russell put it, Adelaide 'had somehow or other obtained considerable influence over Mr Dyson.' This young man has to grow up instantly – and stand up for himself in court – watched by all; occasionally stared at and always listened to intently by the silent Adelaide.

WHAT IS WITHIN …

As in all poisoning cases, the preoccupation with inner things. Questioning, probing: what was in the mind of the alleged murderer; what was where in the home, the alleged crime scene (a model of their rooms was used in court to aid understanding). What was found in Dyson's searched room; in the bottles, glasses, prescribed medicines, drawers at 85 Claverton Street? What was in pockets? Adelaide's cape had been searched by Edwin senior, in case she had secreted a bottle to take out, but he found that it had no pockets. Edwin's pocket contained four or five French letters (condoms) – or had it been Dyson's pocket that had those French letters? What was in the numerous bottles removed by PC Ralph? What was found in parts of the deceased and where? What had been on Edwin's mind in December and just before he died? What was in his wife's mind? Why was there a large quantity of poison inside him?

… AND 'HOW DID IT GET THERE?'

Russell now chose to pose 'the real question in this case': how 'chloroform found its way' into Edwin's stomach.

'How did it get there? So far as I know, there are only three ways in which it could have got there.'

First, that the deceased took it intentionally 'with the view of destroying his life.' Russell told the court, dismissively: they would find nothing 'to support, or even lend an air of plausibility to, that suggestion.'

The second possible way: that Edwin took chloroform accidentally. But it was highly improbable that after pouring it, a man would not realise the mistake before it even reached his lips. Russell added that if chloroform was 'taken by the throat into the stomach' – whether taken to commit suicide or accidentally – so acute would be the pain that it would be followed 'by contortion and by outcry and by exclamation, which could not have failed to attract attention.' Russell did not say whose attention would have been attracted but obviously he meant Adelaide's attention primarily: someone would have heard the 'moan and pain and agony.' And of course, he knew Adelaide had mentioned no such thing to anyone since Edwin's death.

Russell's third hypothesis featured an unnamed person, given that 'there remains in the opinion of the medical men only one other mode.' Administration by that person would probably have caused the victim to cry out – unless 'preceded by some external application of chloroform which might lull into a stupor or a semi-stupor.' He didn't name a person, but everyone's thoughts inevitably turned to Mrs Bartlett. And their eyes too?

Russell kept on highlighting Edwin's positive frame of mind on the last day of his life; there was nothing 'to lend an air of plausibility' to any suggestion that the man took chloroform intentionally. The Prosecutor knew that when Clarke took to the floor, he would want to convince the Jury that Edwin was depressed enough to kill himself. Russell posited what Adelaide had in mind – and why – in order to pacify her husband. He explained how Dyson bought the chloroform and how the Reverend told Adelaide's story of events surrounding Edwin's death.

It had been on 26 January that Dr Leach (intrigued by Adelaide's disclosures and acting unprofessionally) told her that chloroform was the assigned cause of Edwin's death. Russell emphasised that Dr Leach told 'the prisoner at the bar' about chloroform being 'the cause of death [and said] that it was lucky for her it was not prussic acid, or secret poison.' Russell said Dr Leach was amazed by Adelaide's answer: she wished it were 'anything other than chloroform'.

She was in a tight spot. Out of Russell came Adelaide's story about Edwin, of there having been … 'no sexual intercourse between them for a considerable period of time; that he [Edwin] had … spoken to her as if contemplating his own death, and in that case making her over to Dyson; that when, after his illness … with returning to health he seemed to have manifested some desire to renew sexual intercourse with her' she planned to wave the chloroform in Edwin's face. To use the drug with the aim of 'lulling him into a kind of stupor, and so prevent him giving effect to his sexual passion. That is the story she tells.'

'MOTIVE AND OBJECT'

Russell had set out his stall, at the front of which he put Adelaide's 'motive and object.' She who had the means – but at this stage he did not mention any method.

The essence of the evidence to be delivered against her had been outlined. It was deeply personal, sexual and sensational. Ensuing questions would delve into sexual feelings, conduct and all manner of intimacies between those closely involved with Edwin Bartlett. The Prosecution, and later the Defence, would want to keep on highlighting motives. No wonder the spectators and reporters were on the edge of their seats or on tiptoe in the packed-tight Old Bailey.

Russell emphasised the shock the landlord felt upon finding Mr Bartlett dead, adding that 'Mr Doggett, the landlord, is registrar of births and deaths, and he promptly and, as I have no doubt you will believe, most properly declined to register the death until there was a post-mortem examination.'

One reporter noted an opinion and a fact. 'The Attorney General's speech was quiet, bald, and even tame, and the honourable and learned gentleman left the court when he had delivered it. Mr Poland thereafter taking charge of the prosecution.'[117]

Russell, the Attorney General, had matters of State requiring his full attention be somewhere other than here at the Old Bailey .

Prior to her Trial, Adelaide's stories of her life and of Edwin's death seemed made up of truths, half-truths and lies – but which was which and what was what?

The deceased's story and his widow's story would be told in the Trial through the witnesses – particularly Dyson and Leach. Of course some of the witnesses had vested interests – particularly Dyson – and were not impartial. Despite probing and lengthy cross-examinations, the witnesses could choose, to some extent, what they did and did not disclose. And they were asked to put words into the mouths of the deceased Edwin and the silent Adelaide.

What came out, fact or fiction? What came out was partly careful construct, partly on the hoof responses to probes.

Chapter 30

BEARING WITNESS

Time for questions, and for answers, from witnesses called by the Prosecution. No witnesses were called by Adelaide's Defence. Least said, soonest mended?

That summer, the Trial done and dusted, Edward Beal produced a complete and revised report of it: thousands of words, noted down throughout the proceedings.

A welter of words from which now to pluck salient points, building a coherent account. Those bearing witness included the set-free Reverend, the grieving, puzzled friends, and Baxter, Edwin senior, servants, doctors, pharmacists, a dentist caught up in events, and esteemed expert witnesses, proffering innumerable examples of deaths and survivals.

Throughout all this, the extractors: prosecutors and defenders; the interjecting Judge and the questioning Jury.

All utterances were painstakingly handwritten and turned in print for the official record. However, some of the disclosures were considered 'too rich a food' (to quote Dr Leach, writing after the Trial) to be laid out for newspaper readers. Protection from sex …

DR GREEN'S DEPOSITION

Dr Green, who headed the post-mortem, was now extremely ill and unable to attend court. Instead, his signed deposition from the Inquest was submitted.

Prosecuting, Russell went straight to Dr Green's note about 'the overpowering smell of chloroform in the stomach' – 'almost as strong as a freshly opened bottle of chloroform, showing that [it] had somehow or other got into the stomach at a comparatively recent time.'

Russell continued with the chloroform theme. Dr Leach had maintained that after he read out his post-mortem notes to Adelaide on 6 January, she asked him a question, 'Can he have died from chloroform?' Dr Leach told her that the cause of death seemed to be from a different substance, chlorodyne. Russell added that on 26 January, when Adelaide was told by the doctor that chloroform was the cause of Edwin's death, she confided in Dr Leach – who was now *her* doctor – about problems in her marriage.

Now it was time for the procession of witnesses to face rigorous questioning and to tell their stories under the scrutiny of professionals, men, and keen amateurs, many of them women. More about those women later.

MR BARTLETT SENIOR

Edwin Bartlett's father, who resided at the time of his son's death at 1 St David's Mews (at that time a very basic dwelling) in Oxford Street, was the first key witness. A carpenter and builder, he now lived at 44 Chancellor Road, Herne Hill.

Edwin senior's physical appearance was a surprise to several reporters:

they described it as that of a man scarcely older than Edwin at the time of his death!

The father-in-law, aware of Adelaide just across the courtroom, was put through his paces by a huge numbers of questions from Mr Harry Poland for the Prosecution. Many of them were designed to elicit facts from the one person who thought he knew Edwin inside out. And had known Adelaide since the marriage – or rather, since she and Edwin lived together. Many of these questions tested Edwin senior's memory and so it was a slow process. He struggled with sadness, nerves and anger, but out came a story nevertheless.

Edwin senior repeated his objection to Edwin being put in the coffin, adding fresh evidence about Adelaide's words on 1 January. She said: 'what a generous man [Edwin] was … a kind-hearted man' and how he 'died with my arm around his foot; he always liked to have my hand on his foot.' She 'supposed she had been asleep, for she awoke with a cramp in her arm, and then she went and called Mr Doggett.'

Asked about Edwin's Will, the father replied that to the best of his belief the signature on it was not his son's signature.

WITNESSES TO THE WILL

The two young men who were 'first and second hands' at the Herne Hill shop, witnesses to the signature by Edwin on his Will the previous September, were clear: it was Edwin's signature. End of.

MR BARTLETT SENIOR – RECALLED

Edwin senior on the receiving end of yet more questions: Mr Clarke put question after question to the bereaved man about his son. And prompted him: 'He used to chaff and joke, you said …'. Edwin senior: 'Yes, he was a very merry man' and added that his son spoke only once to him about married life in general. Edwin's remark: a man 'ought to have two wives, one to take out and one to do the work.' Edwin senior insisted that Edwin 'only said it once – them words.' Only this little word 'them' shows Edwin senior as the working-class Londoner he was; no other similar indicators appear in the official record.

Edwin senior added that the remark about 'two wives' was in Adelaide's presence; it was 'only a passing observation' by Edwin.

Asked by Clarke about the apology he had to write to Adelaide and Edwin, the beleaguered Edwin senior gave 'energetic answers'. Many women in the court 'were easily provoked to a state of titter and laughed outright' at him. 'The abrupt sentences in which he explained, in re-examination by Mr Poland, the cause of the apology … were productive of a more general sensation, and necks were craned in unison in the galleries to stare upon the prisoner.'[118]

All eyes on Adelaide. She sat throughout this first day of her trial with eyes closed, head bowed, an expression of pain on her face; 'no observable expression upon the countenance to indicate what her feelings might be, save once or twice when, with gloved hand, she used a smelling bottle'.[119]

Edwin senior had to stand there, facing hostility from some of the spectators and a grilling from the professionals. Question after question and his answers, who in the family had lived where and when; what Edwin's insurance policy of November 1881 was worth; how wrapped up Edwin was in the grocery business; how ill or well he seemed during visits last December; when had Adelaide written to her father-in-law, telling him not to visit Edwin. Overall, when he was permitted to see him, Edwin was 'not so sharp and impressive as he usually was.'

Mr Poland asked Mr Bartlett senior about wanting a second opinion, the worried and suspicious father-in-law having said to Adelaide that he would send a doctor down from London.

'No, we cannot afford it' was Adelaide's untrue reply, allegedly. 'You had better' was Edwin senior's caution or threat. 'No, we cannot afford it, and he is going on very well' was Adelaide's retort. Of course they had money – or rather, Edwin had money – and Edwin senior knew that Adelaide had talked nonsense in that conversation with him. Mr Poland had elicited that damning allegation from Edwin's father against the daughter-in-law.

People must have been wondering why Adelaide had been so reluctant for a second opinion. Because it was her father-in-law's wish? Did she have something to hide; had she given Edwin a drug?

And the Prosecution must have been confident that the full story would come out later in the Trial from Dr Leach, about Edwin being very willing for a second doctor to examine him.

EDWARD BAXTER, BUSINESS PARTNER

Baxter confirmed that he had known Edwin for over twenty years, in their partnership for thirteen. Edwin drew about £300 a year from the business. Like Edwin's father, whom he had supported since the death, Baxter was terribly shaken by the loss of his friend and business partner. But he was clear in his recollection of Edwin's good health over the years – apart from when ill for just a matter of weeks in 1881 – until last December. Baxter also went through the various letters Adelaide wrote to him in December about her husband's health and the visits he could make to Edwin.

Not forgetting her cheery letter with its order for brandy, cake and mango chutney – because Edwin fancied them. And a 'Happy New Year! Yours truly, Adelaide Bartlett'.

MR DOGGETT, LANDLORD

Frederick Horace Doggett was next up, his evidence much the same as given at the Inquest.

MRS DOGGETT, LANDLADY

Mr Wright, for the Prosecution, asked whether Mrs Bartlett asked her a question on 31 December about chloroform: had she ever taken it? 'Yes' And Mr Bartlett was there throughout their conversation. The Judge sought clarity. 'What did you say … when she said is it nice or pleasant?' Mrs Doggett: 'I said I did not think I knew much about it … Mrs Bartlett said that Mr Bartlett was in the habit of taking some sleeping drops; ten was a strong dose, but she should not, or did not, hesitate in giving him twelve.'

Adelaide chose the quantity of drops and Edwin swallowed them. By initiating that conversation, had Adelaide been 'softening up' Edwin, by her chatting with Mrs Doggett about chloroform and the sleeping drops dose?

(Was Adelaide rehearsing out loud what she might try? Or, unable to help herself, telling both Edwin and Mrs D what the plan was in her head? Or are those unfair questions?)

Mr Wright asked the landlady if Mrs Bartlett told her what the drops were, but Mrs Doggett could not remember the name.

Mr Wright: 'Then, I think, Mr Bartlett thanked you for his dinner, and said he enjoyed it.'

There endeth evidence about the brief chat on 31 December between the two women concerning chloroform, in front of Edwin. Later that night, everything changed for everyone in that house.

And at the Old Bailey, night fell at the end of Day One.

DAY TWO

Enter Adelaide, back to the dock.

'While the formalities of opening the Court … were gone through she read, with evident leisure and mastery, certain sheets of blue foolscap left with her' by a legal adviser, 'arresting her temporary occupation to bestow a passing glance upon the servant girl who gave evidence on Mr Dyson's visits to the Claverton Street apartments. She soon resumed her perusal of the papers, however.'[120]

ALICE FULCHER

Fulcher 'the servant girl' is first up into the witness box. Employee of the Doggetts, she also waited upon the wants of the Bartletts, from their arrival until Edwin's death. Oh the irony of the importance of servants' roles in their employers' private lives – and their often key evidence in courts – in contrast to their lowly status …

Fulcher was kept in the witness box for the long haul, because the legal people wanted her to tell all, about the comings and goings of Mr Dyson, the ins and outs of what was occurring between him and Mrs Bartlett, the old coat and slippers that he used to put on, the curtains pinned together.

And 'them sitting on the sofa … and the floor together'. Mr Poland wanted to know their position: Fulcher saw Mrs Bartlett sitting on the floor with her head on Mr Dyson's knee on one occasion.

On and on Fulcher was taken, through the terrible events of New Year's Day. And no, she heard nothing of what passed between Mrs Bartlett and the Reverend on Saturday 2 January. She told of the food she took up to the couple on New Year's Eve; about the water and the coals. The poor young woman had eventually got to bed well after midnight on New Year's Day … and blow me down was knocked up at four in the morning to run to fetch Dr Leach.

She answered Mr Poland's questions about glasses and bottles removed from the Bartlett's room. Mr Clarke cross-examined her about those pinned curtains – nothing significant emerged – more fruitless questions about coals and water and basins, whether Mrs Bartlett washed that evening before bed; did she have on a walking-dress and later a looser dress?

To tidy things but also to try to extract something vital, Mr Poland finished on Fulcher helping to pack Mrs Bartlett's boxes when she went away. Disappointment for the Prosecution: Fulcher didn't see a medicine chest.

ANN BOULTER
In addition to being a charwoman, Ann was your woman if you wanted someone laid out.

She recounted how she worked on Edwin's body and recalled Adelaide's words while she did so. Edwin's legs were tied earlier (by Dr Leach) and Ann asked if he'd had a fit and struggled. 'No, poor dear,' said Adelaide, 'he suffered very much with his head; also his teeth for some time.'

Mr Moloney, for the Prosecution, enquired whether Mrs Bartlett said anything about her husband's Will.

Ann: 'She remarked that it was curious, or funny, that he should make his Will a day or two previous to his death' and she'd commented to Adelaide about 'how odd it was so, and asked if it was in her favour.'

Yes it was, Adelaide had replied.

Mr Moloney to Ann about when Mr Bartlett's Will was made: 'Are you quite sure it was not a month?'

Ann: 'I am slightly deaf, sir' …

People, particularly women, in Court tittered and actually laughed (according to numerous newspapers). Ann was sure that Adelaide said days rather than months, but she presumably misheard and the Judge told the Jury to ignore this part of Ann's evidence.

But both Mrs Doggett and Ann Boulter had been shocked and disgusted by Mrs Bartlett's unseemly mentioning of her barely-cold husband's money.

WILLIAM CLAPTON

A Fellow of the Royal College of Surgeons and a medical officer for the British Equitable Insurance Company, Clapton gave details of his examination of Edwin, who had 'no ailment whatever' in November 1880. The tests were for an insurance policy: £400, the usual premium. 'I passed him as a first-class life.'

Some people laughed, a mixture of nervous and bitter laughter, at the judgement on a fit man and the January death of him.

'JUST AS 'GEORGE DYSON!' WAS CALLED …'

'Mrs Bartlett handed down a second note [to her legal adviser] … and for perhaps the space of a minute looked straight, steadily, and with a mournfully wistful expression at her former companion and teacher … She had gazed at him calmly and searchingly, but that done, betrayed no anxiety to hear what he should say … Mr Dyson did not observe this, since now, and throughout a long day, he was never observed to look towards the dock.'[121]

Huge anticipatory rumblings filled the Court when Dyson entered the witness box, then dead quiet descended. Like all the mere mortals, the Reverend was on oath and must have known he would be in the box for hour upon hellish hour of questions. He would have prepared many answers to have ready, yet for much of the time he would be drawn into unknown terrain, literally thinking on his feet for answers.

For the Prosecution, Mr Poland began with a series of questions about Dyson's work and how he met the Bartletts early in 1885. That June, Dyson explained, Mr Bartlett said 'he would like Mrs Bartlett to take up her studies again, and requested me to undertake the supervision of them.' (Had Adelaide been passive in that arrangement, or had she initiated it?) Dyson volunteered the information that he took Mrs Bartlett to his apartment in Wimbledon 'with her husband's knowledge'.

Answers about their time at Dover, about Edwin's Will, about Edwin's and Dyson's letters with their effusive expressions of love and thanks (not that unusual in Victorian letter-writing, as the Judge pointed out later).

Dyson said that when visiting Adelaide at Claverton Street he remarked that her husband seemed 'to throw' them (Dyson and Adelaide) together and he'd asked her why. Allegedly, Adelaide replied that Edwin's life 'was not likely to be a long one, and that he knew it.' Mutterings around the courtroom.

Much that followed was around the subject of Adelaide mentioning Edwin's 'internal complaint', some sort of 'growth'. Dyson claimed that ever since the couple lived at Merton Abbey he had noticed Edwin hold his side in pain. The Reverend readily agreed to a (leading) question, yes Edwin did so after he had 'taken wine'. Adelaide told him in confidence that Edwin was 'very sensitive to this affliction' he'd had for five or six years. At Claverton Street in December, she allegedly told Dyson that Edwin's disease 'caused him very great pain, and to soothe him she had been accustomed to use chloroform.'

'THE RAPID SCRATCHING OF THE JUDGE'S QUILL PEN'

Dyson alleged Adelaide's story was that she went to Dr Nichols for advice and the doctor told her Edwin had not long to live; 'he might die within twelve months'. Also that she had obtained chloroform for Edwin from Annie Walker. At the mention of those two, Nichols and Walker, the 'rapid scratching of the Judge's quill pen sounded almost startlingly loud in the hush'.[122]

Dyson answered questions about Edwin's condition: in December he suffered from 'sleeplessness'; seemed 'very depressed' on 27 December – talking of worms. That was the evening Mrs Bartlett asked Dyson, on their way to the postbox, to buy chloroform. Adelaide 'wanted it for external application'.

Here comes that word 'soothe' again. Alice Matthews and Dyson both alleged Adelaide used it. Edwin to be soothed (and subdued?) by chloroform.

'She wanted it to soothe her husband, to give him sleep, and asked me if I could get some for her. I told her I would, and I did.'

(Someone says jump … the other asks how high? That seems it in a nutshell: she asked, he wanted to impress her, do her bidding, keep his promise. He got it for her to use. It sounds as though he's crowing about it, but keeping promises was part of his moral life.)

Dyson: 'No one else could get it for her but me.'

The Judge sounded incredulous. 'Did it not occur to you that there was a doctor in attendance?'

Dyson: 'Oh yes, and I asked her to get it through the doctor.'

Mr Poland: 'Yes?'

Dyson: 'She told me that he [Dr Leach] didn't know that she was skilled in drugs and medicines, and, not knowing that, he would not entrust her with it.'

(*If* Adelaide did say that, perhaps it was an admission of some kind? A confession that she could not be trusted – and did not trust herself?)

Dyson said he agreed to get chloroform for her.

The Judge: 'Did she tell you in what way or what kind of external use was to be made of it?'

Dyson: 'She said to soothe him – to get him to sleep.'

The Judge: 'That is not what we usually mean by external use. Did she give any explanation?'

Dyson: 'Yes, that she used it with a handkerchief.'

The Judge: 'You mean by inhalation.' (He was telling, not asking.)

Mr Poland asked Dyson how much he was to get. 'A medicine draught bottle.'

Dyson recounted how he wrote a letter to a friend called Theodore Styles, a medical student, to try to obtain the chloroform, and telegraphed the next day. Unfortunately, Dyson was not asked what response his friend Styles sent. As said earlier, it is likely Adelaide was more than irritated by his trying to get chloroform from Styles and told her Georgius Rex to stop any such arrangement.

'I DID NOT GIVE THE RIGHT REASON'

'Something like a sensation arose while, in a low, uneasy voice, [Dyson] confessed the subterfuge by which he obtained the supply' of chloroform from the three chemists.

Mr Poland: 'Did you say what you wanted it for?'

Dyson: 'I did not give the right reason.'[123]

He recounted how he gave the bottle of poison into Adelaide's hands on 29 December.

On and on it went (similar to the questioning in February and March) about his relationship with Mr and Mrs Bartlett. Dyson said that all three of them had been 'on very intimate terms' but he denied any impropriety with Adelaide. But, only when pressed, he did confess to kissing her when her husband was not present.

Eddowes's Shrewsbury Journal was among many to report on 21 April that Dyson's voice was 'musical, but the trouble he gives to judge, counsel and hearers at large was generally caused by his half inaudible tones, hesitant manner, and a marked slowness, which might have been accidental, in meeting the question put'.

This inferred that the lack of speed in Dyson's replies might be a deliberate tactic, a ploy to give him time to think of answers that would show him in as good a light as possible. Responses that would not sound too damning of Adelaide nor too unchivalrous. Steering a course through obstacles thrown down by the Defence, the men who were there to save Adelaide from the gallows.

Dyson explained how he apologised to Mrs Bartlett for advising her 'to get a nurse to assist her' – advice against which she had taken indignant exception.

He confirmed seeing Edwin on 31 December. He did not remember whether Edwin was in the room when Adelaide told him that some necrosis of the jaw had set in. And he left before the couple went to the dentist in the early evening.

On New Year's Day, Dyson had received the letter from Adelaide informing him of Edwin's death. Now Mr Poland and the Judge became like dogs with a bone, but pulling in the same direction, evidence-extracting. An example: the intervention by Judge Wills when he and Mr Poland wanted to know where that letter from Mrs Bartlett went.

'I destroyed it,' said Dyson.

The Judge pounced: 'When?'

Dyson: 'Within a few days.'

How had Mrs Bartlett addressed him in the letter? Eventually Dyson answered the Judge's question. She had put, 'Dear George'.

Stirrings among spectators in court. Mrs Bartlett's addressing of Dyson in letters as 'Dear George' was 'sufficient to move the women in court to a lively interchange of mirthful comment'.[124]

Dyson gave Adelaide's account of finding Edwin dead; then it was time to satisfy rumbling stomachs: 'The luncheon half-hour became, thanks to the abounding presence of the fairer sex, a merry pic-nic'.

'A UNIVERSAL EXPRESSION OF HONEST PITY' FOR HER

People stretched and conversed freely, 'knitting was cast aside, and meat and drink were produced'. Adelaide, the 'ladylike little figure' had retired and 'knew nothing of the pleasure her trial was yielding to so many sisters'. And there was vehemence, some insisting that she was innocent, others that she was guilty – but 'there was a universal expression of honest pity' for her.

'After luncheon there was a new irruption [sic] of gay ladies, some of them asking whether the verdict would be given at this sitting' – but there was a long way still to go with the evidence. 'On reappearing in the dock Mrs Bartlett looked deliberately at one of the galleries, as if she recognised a face or was struck with some of the huge ornithological head-dresses overpowering there. She exchanged a word or two with the female warder, and then quietly but thoroughly scrutinised the jury' and 'taking one more steady look at Mr Dyson' she sat down.[125]

After the diverting comment on the huge feathered hats of some female spectators, back to the afternoon's ghastly events for young Dyson. He had gone to Claverton Street on 2 January and met with Adelaide in the front room upstairs. Edwin was dead in the back room. Allegedly the first thing she said to Dyson about the death was whether he did not consider it 'sudden' – yes, 'very sudden' he replied. He asked what Edwin died from and she told him that Dr Leach, who had ordered a post-mortem on the body, 'thought some small blood vessel must have broken near the heart, or on the heart'.

After the post-mortem the Bartlett's rooms were 'locked, sealed, and handed over to the Coroner.'

The penny dropped: that same day, Dyson asked Adelaide about the chloroform.

She made three quick-fire retorts.

'I have not used it.

'I have not had occasion to use it.

'The bottle is there just as you gave it to me.'

Mr Poland to Dyson: 'Yes, and then?'

Dyson: 'She said, "this is a very critical time for me." She told him to put away from his mind that she had a medicine chest and that he gave her the chloroform … she told him he "must not worry about it".'

Dyson told her he would visit Dr Leach on Monday (4 January).

Having visited the doctor and having notes from the post-mortem read to him, Dyson went straight to Adelaide and asked 'what she had done with the chloroform … she was very angry with me for troubling her about that.' (Of course, he was extremely anxious and felt justified in asking her for answers about the chloroform he purchased at her request – and which was, almost certainly, the chloroform that killed Edwin.)

Mr Poland asked Dyson what Adelaide said.

'OH, DAMN THE CHLOROFORM!' ... and she stamped her foot upon getting up from her chair. More stamping by her had brought Mrs Matthews back into the room. When she left again, Dyson told Adelaide that he had been to see Dr Leach, who told him that either chlorodyne or chloroform was found in Edwin's stomach.

Dyson said he reminded Mrs Bartlett that she had told him her 'husband was suffering from this internal affliction'. He said he probably spoke then 'of the fact that nothing was said about this affliction in the post-mortem' and 'asked her if she did not tell me that her husband's life would be a short one. I said: "You did tell me that Edwin was going to die shortly."' Now he hesitated ...

The Judge: 'Well?'

Dyson: 'She said she did not.'

Mr Poland asked him how he responded.

Dyson: 'I said I was a ruined man.'

Poland: 'Speak louder please.'

'I SAID I WAS A RUINED MAN' ...

Oh dear, the agony and ignominy! Having to relive it and repeat it yet again in a court. The ignominy of having to repeat what he'd said to Adelaide that day back in January, overheard by Mrs Matthews as she re-entered the room. It was Alice Matthews who said Dyson had better leave. 'Then I left.' Ah, but not so fast.

Mr Poland: 'Before you left was anything said about a piece of paper?'

Dyson resorted to 'I do not remember it ...' .... but when jogged by the word 'poetry' it was dragged out of him bit by bit, by Mr Poland and by the Judge, that it was the 'My Birdie' poem written by George about Adelaide. Now things became even more difficult. They hadn't finished pulling pieces out of him concerning that Monday night, 4 January.

Mr Poland: 'What more took place between you?'

Dyson: 'She spoke about the chloroform.'

Obvious next question: 'What did she say?'

No answer came from Dyson; perhaps he had switched off. The question was repeated.

Dyson: '... Oh, I told her I was going to make a clean breast of the affair.' (Do not think he meant to say 'affair' in the modern sense of the word.) 'She did not want me to mention the chloroform.' But he had repeated to her his intention to do so, and had to keep on telling all and sundry in this court about the deadly chloroform.

And even after that, here he was, still in court, the nightmare continuing. Mr Poland was pressing him to talk of anything else he said that day, 4 January. Dyson maintained he told Mrs Bartlett that he was puzzled, perplexed and alarmed; that he would tell what he knew about the chloroform. What more? (He must have felt some slight relief in moving on to the next question.) Edwin's watch. Adelaide gave it to Dyson before the post-mortem. (Indecent haste to give it so soon? Is that unfair to say?) Then he told how he returned Edwin's money to her, money given to Dyson for his travel expenses.

Dyson was led back to another of those terrible days in January, after his life had changed forever. On 8 January, he and Adelaide dined in the private room behind Mrs Stuard's shop. He told the court Adelaide said 'that if I did not incriminate myself she would not incriminate me. And I told her I was aware of my perilous position.'

When it was Mr Clarke's time for questioning Dyson, he went back through much of the evidence the man had been dragged through at the Inquest (in order to show Dyson in as poor a light as possible).

Had Dyson discussed with Adelaide as to when he could marry? 'Yes'.

Concerning Edwin, Mr Clarke asked Dyson if he (Dyson) had said, 'If ever she comes under my care, I shall have to teach her differently'?

'Yes' replied Dyson.

Clarke: 'Well, go on.'

Dyson recalled, about Edwin: 'He smiled and said … he had no doubt I should take good care of her.'

One can imagine Clarke leaving a significant silence, to let that response sink in to the Jury.

'WE HAVE LONG OUTSTEPPED THE BOUNDS OF DELICACY'

The Judge had stayed out of Clarke's questioning about the Bartletts. In the next stretch his Lordship's patience ran out temporarily.

Clarke to Dyson: 'Now, I have reminded you that letter is dated September 23, and was written by you while they were at Dover.' He read out the letter, which began:

'My dear Edwin,

'Thank you very much for the brotherly letter you sent me yesterday. I am sure I respond from my heart to your wish that our friendship may ripen with the lapse of time.'

Dyson said the letter was after the conversation between him and Edwin about the Will.

Clarke: 'What was the conversation?'

Dyson: 'This is a very delicate matter for me.'

The Judge: 'NO, NO, we have long outstepped the bounds of delicacy.'

Clarke wrung out from Dyson that the conversation took place when Edwin went to see Dyson at Putney and told him he had made a Will. He was leaving his money to Adelaide – 'and leaving you as his executor?'– as Clarke put it. 'Yes' replied Dyson.

Then back to what might have been a 'delicate matter' for Dyson.

'Now then, what did he tell you at that time about you and his wife?' demanded Clarke.

Edwin had not told Dyson anything, apparently. Dyson told *him* that there was no denying the fact that he was growing very attached to Adelaide and he wished to let Edwin know that it was disturbing him (Dyson of course) in his work. Dyson added that he asked Edwin whether it would not be better for him to discontinue the friendship with them.

'Why should you discontinue it?' Edwin had enquired.

'Well …?' said Clarke, wanting to know Dyson's reply to Edwin.

'He told me I had been a benefit to her; she liked my preaching … he showed me one of her convent letters … which was a very devotional letter; and he said he should like me to endeavour to lead her back more closely to that frame of mind or disposition of heart. He said he had confidence in me, and that he should be pleased if I would continue as friendly as I had been with them.'

As to Edwin's Will, Dyson said that, 'as a proof of confidence in me, he had selected me, with his legal man, to act as executor.'

Clarke saw and heard a reaction to Dyson's words from the spectators and Clarke, this consummate defender, was not going to risk his incredulity being missed by the jury. If he could get Dyson to show himself in a poor light, it might reflect better on Adelaide. Clarke (picture him, scornful yet polite) spelling it out. Hear his clipped, cold enunciation:

'Just let me remind you, Mr Dyson,

you were telling … the husband

that you had become attached to his wife and you say that the husband expected you, did you not, to continue the intimacy?

Dyson: 'Precisely.'

(Did Dyson not see how he had misused Edwin's confidence in him?)
A rapid row-back was attempted by Dyson.

'If anything happens to me, you two may come together.' Dyson claimed that Edwin said something like that in the Claverton Street house (perhaps when Edwin was feeling so ill in December that he thought he would soon die).

OWNING UP

Some of those listening probably considered Dyson a cad or worse. Some may have thought that Edwin 'passed on' his wife to his male friend; perhaps others were nonplussed. Clarke continued – knowing that Dyson's answer would contradict his question and expose Dyson's ungentlemanly conduct: 'I need scarcely ask you, as a gentleman, you had at that time said nothing to Mrs Bartlett about your feelings independent of Mr Bartlett?'

Dyson: 'I regret to say I had.'

Clarke: 'Did you tell him that you had?'

Dyson: 'Yes.'

For some reason, Clarke did not pursue that line of questioning. Perhaps he decided not to over-emphasise the point, feeling he had already shown up Dyson's caddish behaviour sufficiently.

Clarke took Dyson through the days of Edwin's illness and led him into talk about mesmerism. 'Now, you see, Mr Dyson, that Mr Bartlett told you morphia would not give him sleep, and he used to get up and walk about. Did you have any conversation with him about mesmerism?' Dyson thought it 'likely.' Clarke: 'You alone can tell us whether you did or not – did you?' Dyson remembered. Yes, at Merton. (And yes, remember, Edwin told Dr Leach they discussed the subject that summer when the Bartletts were living at Merton Abbey briefly). Clarke got out of Dyson that he was the one who initiated that conversation with Edwin about mesmerism.

Clarke pressed him as to whether Edwin told him about the night he 'stood for two hours waving his hands about over his sleeping wife?' Dyson denied being told that – and the subject of mesmerism was not pursued further by Clarke with Dyson.

Instead, he took Dyson's mind back to when he told the court about Mrs Bartlett mentioning to him the way the chloroform was to be used. She said she'd sprinkle it on a handkerchief to soothe Edwin and give him sleep, because, according to her, Edwin had been violent in a 'previous sickness'.

Dyson must have hated it when even more challenges flew at him about his most suspicious act.

Mr Poland, re-examining, asked Dyson which people he had told about purchasing chloroform. They were Mrs Matthews and his Wesleyan minister friend, Mr Riggall, at Poole.

Mr Poland asked him how Edwin described Dyson's impact on Adelaide. Dyson: 'in a spiritual way' – the Judge stopped that line of enquiry by insisting:

'I want to know, Mr Dyson, why you went to three different shops to buy the chloroform.'

Dyson: 'Because I did not get as much as I wanted in one shop.' The Judge wanted to know why he said the chloroform was for taking grease spots out of clothes. Dyson's reply was disingenuous. 'He asked me what I wanted it for.' The Judge jumped on 'it' – perhaps angrily.

'Do not let us have any nice distinction between telling a falsehood and acting on it!'

Dyson: 'I do not defend that my Lord, it was simply that I wanted to avoid an explanation.' This led, eventually, to an answer that Dyson wanted a large quantity because: '... it was used very quickly in the way Mrs Bartlett mentioned. I knew it was volatile. I had an idea that a very few applications would exhaust the amount.'

The Judge: 'Did you think the whole handkerchief was to be saturated with it?'

Dyson: 'Not saturated, but well moistened in it. I had never heard how it was done, and knew nothing of how it was done.'

So, he knew something about chloroform – 'it was volatile' – and yet claimed he knew nothing – 'I had never heard how it was done.' He wanted it both ways. If he had read about chloroform in the newspapers, in the Eliza Armstrong case for example, then he would know something about the use and misuse of the poison. And the word 'poison' must have been a stark clue, a danger warning.

His evidence ended in anticlimax. A visitor, Mr Hackett or Hacker, was with Edwin when Dyson arrived at Claverton Street to deliver the chloroform to Adelaide, so she joined Dyson and off they went, walking about.

He handed the poison over to her, his job done.

Here in court Dyson had been put through the mangle, words and embarrassing explanations wrung out of him. Dyson done, Day Two ended.

DAY THREE

The three Dickensian chemists, Humble, Penrose and Mellin told their stories of Dyson purchasing the chloroform. They must have thought it was a very rum do, being lied to by a preacher, one they had known and trusted, and all ending up at the Old Bailey no less, giving key evidence about their parts in this tragedy.

ALICE MATTHEWS

Alice Jane Selby Matthews' turn in the witness box, describing Adelaide's going to stay with her and her family on 3 January because the Bartlett's rooms at Claverton Street were being sealed off. On 4 January when Dyson visited her home, Mrs Matthews left him and Adelaide to talk. Hearing a noise, Mrs Matthews went back in. Adelaide 'was stamping round the room'. Apparently, Dyson was 'bothering her about a piece of paper'. Mrs Matthews said she left the room again and on re-entering heard Dyson saying to Adelaide: '"You *did* tell me that Edwin was going to die soon," and Adelaide's retorting, "No, I did not."'

Mrs Matthews continued. 'Then Mr Dyson bowed his head on the piano and said "Oh my God!" and 'as he left the room he said "I am a ruined man."' Dyson's ruin was thus being repeated out loud yet again.

When he had gone, Alice Matthews asked Adelaide what Dyson meant by the 'paper' and Adelaide told her 'it was a piece of poetry.' This was the 'Birdie' poem written and illustrated by Dyson for Adelaide.

Alice Matthews sounded a polite, assertive witness in this imposing setting, just unclear as to precisely when in early January she had tackled her friend.

'ALL THOSE LIES'

However, tackle Adelaide she had done, as a friend (and as someone becoming even more worried about Edwin's death).

She asked Adelaide why she 'told Mr Dyson all those lies'. The answer back from Adelaide: because he had bothered her so and he didn't believe her when she told him the truth. Mr Wright asked Mrs Matthews if Mrs Bartlett said what the truth was. Yes, that Edwin was going to die and she told him [Dyson] the lie … this must have been terribly confusing. Sensibly yet perhaps sharply, the Judge intervened and ordered Mrs Matthews:

'JUST LISTEN TO ME'

She was not daunted by the Judge's demand, nor by him immediately asking if she could remember what she and Mrs Bartlett had been talking about. Mrs Matthews took the opportunity to continue her account. 'No, my Lord … but I should like to say this, that I said to her then I didn't know that Edwin thought he was going to die soon, and she said he did think so latterly.' (Did Adelaide revise her story to fit her lie? Allegedly she had told Dyson, that September in dear old Dover, that Dr Nichols said Edwin had less than a year to live.)

GEORGE MATTHEWS

Mr Matthews, husband of Alice, told the court about asking Mrs Bartlett if it was possible that Edwin 'might have taken some poison himself?' and her reply was that 'she did not think there were any poisons in the house' (a blatant lie).

Mr Matthews described a conversation on 9 January when, in Adelaide's presence, Dyson told him 'that he was ruined so far as his prospects in the ministry were concerned' and Dyson had turned to Adelaide and said: 'Suppose it should be proved that you—'

'DON'T MINCE MATTERS'

'… don't mince matters; say it, if you wish to say, I gave him chloroform,' snapped Adelaide, allegedly. (Imagine her likely tone and how Dyson must have hated it, after the love he felt they had shared.) 'What would be the opinion of the world? How should I come out in such a case?' Dyson asked her.

Mr Matthews added that after Adelaide had been to see Dr Leach on 20 January she visited the Matthews. She said she had been informed that 'it would be impossible for her to have given him chloroform by inhalation without it showing in his brain; and she could not have given it to him as a drink, because it would have burnt his throat all down, and he would have aroused the house with his cries.'

On the subject of Dr Nichols' books, Mr Matthews said Mrs Bartlett lent him one – but he didn't read it, as it was not in his line of business; it was a 'queer' book (not his cup of tea at all).

ANNIE WALKER

Up stepped Annie Walker, a trained nurse with fourteen years' experience. She was attached to the London Association of Nurses, based in New Bond Street. Examined by Mr Poland for the Prosecution, she confirmed that in 1881 Mrs Nichols contacted her and hence she arranged to visit Mrs Bartlett at Station Road. Apparently Adelaide had read the 'Esoteric' book and it was through reading it that she'd applied to Mrs Nichols.

Annie gave a 'decided negative' in court against any suggestions that the book contained anything immoral or improper. The Judge asked for some details from it – and when Mr Clarke read extracts aloud, an 'old lady hurriedly scrambled out of court; all the rest remained'.[126]

Annie lived with the Bartletts for four weeks before Adelaide's confinement in November 1881. When Adelaide went into labour and began to suffer great pain, the nurse asked Edwin to let her have some medicine via a doctor. When he asked if his wife's life would be 'all right' Annie replied she 'did not fear for her' – but 'feared, if she did not have help at once, the child would be stillborn.' Allegedly and for whatever reason, Edwin replied that he would rather she 'took the case through; he would much rather not have any man interfering' with his wife.

So Annie agreed to go on alone with Adelaide, but when the woman suffered great pain, the nurse 'sent for a doctor at last.' Then at midnight, the great sadness: the child was stillborn, before the doctor arrived. For three weeks afterwards, Annie attended to Adelaide.

They became close (with that intensity of shared feelings around birth and death) and she continued to visit the couple. The first time she stayed was when they lived at Lordship Lane, then at their home at Merton Abbey, a total of four occasions until October 1884. She thought the couple had lived on 'very affectionate terms' and as far as she knew they shared a bed. On one or on several occasions Adelaide told her that she meant never to have more children – 'women often said that' commented Annie.

She was emphatic that she never used chloroform at the Bartletts and had never ever been to America. Two conversations Annie remembered from her last times with Adelaide were about Edwin not appreciating what she did – and also about his Will: that the property would come to Adelaide, provided that she did not marry again.

THOMAS NICHOLS

Annie Walker was soon out of the witness box and in went Thomas Nichols, described in some newspapers as a venerable gentleman with white hair and beard.

No, he had never met Adelaide, never seen nor knew of Edwin, thus had never said anything about Edwin's health nor about a 'brief' life. (The inference and impact in court would have been that either Dyson lied to them or misheard Adelaide about those key issues, or Adelaide told lies to Dyson about Annie Walker and about Thomas Nichols.)

THOMAS ROBERTS

The dental surgeon said that early on in his contact with Edwin, he thought his patient had 'mercurial' poisoning. At the end, Edwin had an area of necrosis, with fungoid growth a problem throughout his mouth.

DEPOSITION OF DR GREEN

As we know, Dr Green was too ill to attend, hence his evidence from the post-mortem was submitted in writing and gone through.

DR LEACH

Dr Alfred Leach was Edwin's doctor from 10 December until Edwin's death. The *Kilburn Times And Western Post* on 30 April (after the Trial) described how Dr Leach's 'sonorously rolled-out sentences, well-charged with technical terms, could be heard in the remotest corners of the court' and how the Judge 'completely destroyed one learned and touching exposition' from the doctor, by asking if it meant 'in plain English' that Mr Bartlett had taken 'too much blue pill?'

The Jury Foreman requested via the Judge that Dr Leach give them 'as few Latin terms as he possibly can.' (The doctor's reference to mercury pills (sometimes used in the treatment of syphilis) could be seen as significant in terms of how Edwin may have conducted his private life. Equally, he could have taken such a pill, or pills, for a completely different ailment.)

Dr Leach's generalisations, full of flair but of little use in a murder trial.

However, one section of his evidence was specific – and startling. Russell asked him why he brought in Dr Dudley to see Edwin. Dr Leach said Adelaide broke into a conversation one day early on in his series of visits:

'Mr Bartlett is very contented with your treatment, but his friends have on more than one occasion requested him to let them send a doctor of their own choosing' to assess Edwin. Allegedly Adelaide added, 'Mr Bartlett's friends are no friends to me.'

'MR BARTLETT'S FRIENDS WILL ACCUSE ME OF POISONING HIM IF …'

Dr Leach said Edwin added: 'We intend in future to manage our own affairs' (meaning their own matters). He agreed to see, just once, any doctor of Dr Leach's choosing. 'I am getting better than I was. I will not submit to any other treatment, but I will see any gentleman once. I do this for the protection of my wife.'

Mrs Bartlett threw three extraordinary points into this dramatic conversation. 'Doctor, Mr Bartlett's friends will accuse me of poisoning him if he does not get out soon – if he gets worse – if he does not get better.'

Dr Leach added something that at first sounds like a throw-away comment, but looked at a second time seems logical. 'Extraordinary as it was, it made little effect on me, as I hear many strange things, and I thought it referred to the mercurialism I had found on my first visits.'

When that conversation took place it was not a portentous occasion for the doctor because, to state the obvious, Edwin was alive – not very well, but a living person who had been unwell for less than a week. Of course the conversation took on a sinister edge after Edwin's death and hindsight kicked in for his doctor.

MESMERISED?

Dr Leach was asked about his various visits to the deceased and about the notes he made at the post-mortem the following day. And, about later 'swallowing chloroform' to test its effect upon himself.

Then the doctor quoted Adelaide's protestation to him (about why she sat for hours holding on to her husband's foot) that Edwin sometimes walked 'about the room like a ghost; he will not sleep unless I sit and hold his toe.' Did Edwin walk about like a ghost? Did he ask her to hold his toe? Did she do that? If so, was it a simple comfort – or was he mesmerised? Edwin also described to his doctor how one night he couldn't sleep, got up and stood over his sleeping wife with his hands up 'for two hours, and I felt the vital force being drawn from her to me.' Then, said Edwin, he went to sleep.

One can imagine Dr Leach standing there in court, meticulously mimicking Adelaide: 'That's a nice story. Imagine him standing for two hours and doing anything.' She was dismissive, partly because Edwin was in such a weak state and she considered he would have been incapable of standing like that. Perhaps also she was wanting to head off any further mention of mesmerism.

Dr Leach told the court that the 'vital force' conversation (two days before, or after, a discussion about mesmerism) was Edwin telling him, animatedly, about being mesmerised by 'a friend'. Dr Leach's evidence was that on the evening of 26 December Edwin raised the subject of mesmerism, speaking 'with an unaccustomed vigour and excitement'; Adelaide was present. That 26 December must have been quite a day.

Edwin: 'Last summer a friend, who could mesmerise, visited us and I asked him on several occasions to mesmerise me, but he always refused. Now, why do you think he refused?'

Dr Leach had no idea why.

Edwin: 'Well, I think he must have done it then or on some subsequent occasion—'

'Oh Edwin, how absurd you are!' broke in Mrs Bartlett. 'He does get such strange ideas into his head nowadays, Doctor.'

Edwin persisted: 'I think he mesmerised me through my wife. Is that a possibility?'

(Presumably almost everyone in court began thinking that, odds-on, Edwin meant Dyson was the 'friend who could mesmerise'. Everyone in court heard Dr Leach say it was Edwin's idea that the mesmeric influence upon him came from Adelaide. And here in court, what was Adelaide thinking as she listened?)

For some reason, Dr Leach had found Edwin's words about this mesmerism 'very amusing' – which seems a strange response, given that the doctor had already told Edwin that he 'frequently watched the effects of skilled mesmerists and applied scientific tests.' Many people in that era thought such talk was a sign of insanity.

Edwin had continued by saying he was 'doing such absurd things' and both he and his wife were doing things 'against common sense' but he gave no examples. Dr Leach took him on, thinking it was one of his 'phases of insanity' or 'a key to his particular nervous temperament.' But all he could get out of Edwin was that he liked the man who was doing it, the mesmerising. Adelaide jumped in, said Dr Leach, and she added, 'Edwin and he are the best of friends, and he is a true friend to both of us.'

(Cue everyone in court again picturing Dyson as the mesmerist – reason being that, according to Edwin and Adelaide, none of Edwin's friends liked Adelaide. Probably those in court discounted any ideas of Mr Matthews being the 'mesmerist': Matthews seems a regular chap – so it must be Dyson, they might reason. Nothing is said in court as to who the mesmerist might be, yet the spectators must be muttering and whispering. Who was it that allegedly made Edwin feel impelled to do queer things?)

The question whether 'any dominant idea could be made to possess a man in Mr Bartlett's state' had been put by Dr Leach to a colleague, 'a distinguished student of things mystical.' Whatever answer this 'occult acquaintance' gave Dr Leach, the doctor returned to his patient and said Edwin must have had 'delusions' – with which conclusion Edwin subsequently agreed.

This was a curious episode which went nowhere when Dr Leach questioned Edwin – and went nowhere in court. No more light was thrown upon it. Was Edwin delusional after many days of prescription drugs and then the vermifuges – or had he been mesmerised/hypnotised by Adelaide and/or a visitor?

Yet no one asked in court whether Adelaide might have mesmerised Edwin before he drank chloroform.

Dr Leach said that in January, not only did he try the powerful worming powders on himself (being conscientious and curious about what unpleasant effects his patients might suffer) but a couple of days after the revelations about the chloroform in late January, he did an experiment on himself with that highly volatile and dangerous substance. Dr Leach said he took a mouthful of chloroform, 'swallowed twenty or thirty drops of it, then ejected the remainder, and was surprised … to find my tongue looking very white. The interpretation of what I had then seen on the dead body [Edwin] came to me.' He admitted that as a doctor he had no experience of the drug, and had never seen another body with chloroform in the stomach.

He said perhaps tartly of Dyson that the Minister was around 'a good deal' of the time at the Bartletts. Edwin spoke of him 'in terms of the highest admiration and affection, so far as he would be likely to talk on the subject of affection'. And Edwin told him how highly-educated Dyson was. 'Oh yes, they were very proud of Mr Dyson, I know. They had his photograph in the room,' added Dr Leach in evidence.

Was it the original of the portrait of Dyson seen all over the city, together with the photos of Adelaide, being sold outside the Old Bailey all that week? One newspaper reporter surmised that the portraits were taken by a Wimbledon photographer.[127]

Two photographs had stood on the mantelpiece by Edwin's bed and were probably of Dyson and of Annie Walker, as she had given Adelaide a photograph.

'A DUTY TO HER WOMANHOOD AND TO THE MAN TO WHOM SHE WAS PRACTICALLY AFFIANCED'

Dr Leach continued by taking everyone back to 26 January, a very important day about which he was asked many questions. That was when Adelaide went to see him and he announced, 'I have some good news for you. There is a report flying about.' Allegedly the government analyst would 'give acetate of lead as the cause of death, which is nonsense' and 'a verdict of chloroform as the cause of death, which is very improbable,' said Dr Leach. Continuing: 'She then very much surprised me by saying, "I am afraid, doctor, it is too true. I wish anything but chloroform had been found" … and she then proceeded to a long statement', giving him her version of life with Edwin.

'A BREACH OF THE TERMS'

Her story included a marriage compact 'that the marital relations of the pair were, in deference to certain peculiar views held by her husband, to be of an entirely platonic nature; sexual intercourse was not to occur.' She maintained that the compact was 'adhered to, with a solitary exception, when a breach of the terms was permitted … in consequence of her anxiety to become a mother.'

Adelaide allegedly asked Dr Leach numerous questions, extracted confidential information and gave him what he considered to be her private stories (patient to doctor). The court was dependant on – depending on – Dr Leach for confidences and clarity. What happened when Adelaide got to know Dyson? She alleged her husband threw them together, then along the way Edwin's nature seemed to change and he wished to assume 'those marital rights which he had never before claimed – you understand my meaning …'

Prompting a question from the Prosecution, wanting more than that euphemism: 'You mean desiring to have sexual intercourse with his wife?' Dr Leach had to say more. 'Yes, she put it in as delicate a manner as she could, and that is the meaning.'

Allegedly Adelaide told Dr Leach about saying in December: 'Edwin, you know you have given me to Mr Dyson; it is not right that you should do now what during all the married years of our life you have not done.'

Dr Leach maintained she went on to Edwin that 'it was a duty to her womanhood and to the man to whom she was practically affianced at his wish, and he agreed that she was right.'

(So, allegedly Adelaide said she was 'practically affianced' to their dear

Dyson in accordance with Edwin's wishes – under his nose. Surely many in Court sucked their teeth or frowned at this juncture?)

Dr Leach's story was that as Edwin got progressively better he wanted sexual connection and 'these manifestations of his became very urgent, and she sought for means the more thoroughly ... to prevent his putting his impulses into effect.'

Following on from this idea of Adelaide looking for ways to prevent Edwin's impulses, Dr Leach added the inevitable subject: one of the means to prevent her husband's impulses 'unfortunately, was the possessing herself of a quantity of chloroform.'

After the understatement of 'unfortunately', the doctor alleged that Adelaide said, '...the presence of that chloroform in my drawer troubled my mind.' And that with regard to her husband, 'her object was to sprinkle some upon a handkerchief and wave it in his face every time it was necessary' (whenever Edwin had the alleged 'impulses') as she thought he would then go peacefully to sleep.

Dr Leach was fleshing out this climatic part of the summary which Russell had delivered in his Opening. The doctor recounted Adelaide telling him on 26 January about Edwin: '...on the last night of the year, when he was in bed, I brought the chloroform to him and gave it to him.'

(Her ambiguous phrase: 'gave it to him.')

She claimed that Edwin was not cross. They 'talked amicably and seriously, and he turned on his side and pretended to go to sleep' or 'to sulk' or something. Then she fell asleep in the chair with her arm around Edwin's foot, 'awoke and heard him snoring, and then woke again and found he was dead.'

That was Adelaide's alleged story to Dr Leach, as best (or worst) he could recall it. One wonders what the course of their lives would have been if, on hearing her account during January, Dr Leach had gone straight to the police. But of course he had not. He kept his patient's confidings confidential; that was what he did as a doctor. And subsequently he thought Adelaide would give evidence at court in February. He had held on until the legal process brought him to this climax.

His evidence would spill over into the fourth day of the trial. Slippery as an eel, but probably not deliberately that way. It was how Dr Leach's brain worked.

DAY FOUR
DR LEACH – RECALLED

Mr Clarke probed the doctor further with questions about the various potions and treatments he used on his patient, then led the doctor on to Edwin's 'crying fits'. Presumably Clarke was aiming to persuade the Jury of Edwin's instability of mind in December by quoting what Dr Leach told the Coroner. 'Mrs Bartlett said Edwin sits in his armchair and cries an hour at a time; and when I ask him about it, he says it was because he was so happy.' And Edwin agreed he had said that. Asked if Edwin was talkative, Dr Leach (returning to the topic of mesmerism) gave a clear reply, on this occasion, to Clarke. 'The only time I saw him what might be called talkative, was the time that he told me about his being mesmerised; then he fired up with quite unwonted eloquence.'

DR DUDLEY

He made the 'second opinion' visit to Edwin in December and was also present for the post-mortem.

DR MURRAY

He performed the post-mortem. (His name came to national attention in 1900, in relation to the ill-effects of asbestos.)[128]

POLICE CONSTABLE RALPH

An officer of the Metropolitan Police force, and Coroner's Officer in this case, PC Ralph took the various medicine bottles to the mortuary at 20 Millbank Street on 4 January, and was responsible for the removal of other items from the Bartletts' rooms at the Claverton Street address on 9 and 11 January.[129]

DR STEVENSON

Professor of Medical Jurisprudence, Dr Stevenson was appearing on behalf of the Home Office, giving analyses and professional opinions as per his previous court contributions. Questions extracted even more technical detail from him; he was in demand, kept there until the end of Day Four. The Jury, officials and spectators surely were at various points attentive, bored, puzzled; tired by it all and weary? Chloroform this, chloroform that, chloroform the other. Dr Stevenson quoted and detailed numerous deaths, including suicides, plus some survivors. Yet not one of them seemed to resemble the circumstances in *this* case. And so the esteemed doctor would be brought back in to start the next day, in case a new dawn could throw fresh light on his patient's end.

DAY FIVE
DR STEVENSON – RECALLED

Dr Stevenson and the subject of chloroform were back in the witness box.

To-ing and fro-ing, questions from the Defence, Prosecution, Judge and also the Foreman of the Jury. Answers from the doctor about the possible effects of the drugs; everyone desperately hoping that this expert witness had the answer as to what happened in the early hours of New Year's Day to Thomas Edwin Bartlett Esq. But now no one was enlightened. They did not know whether Edwin (when the drug was being given or used) was awake, asleep, given some to inhale – or just drank it down in liquid form.

And, even if Adelaide knew the truth, she had to remain silent.

DR TIDY

The authoritative Tidy, Professor of Chemistry and Forensic Medicine, called as an expert witness was, like Dr Stevenson, taken at mind-numbing lengths through different cases of death and survival in relation to chloroform: cases where administered by professionals, others in which self-administered (by desperate or curious people).

Tidy was another doctor who for this case had tested the drug on himself, in his laboratory taking some liquid chloroform into his mouth before spitting it out.[130]

Neither Stevenson nor Tidy, despite their efforts, kept as they were for many hours in the witness box by the innumerable enquiries from the Prosecution and Defence, could pull out of the hat much evidence relevant to key individuals' actions in this mystery,

MARY ANN FURLONG

The Bartletts' servant from Merton Abbey described the couple's routines when she had worked there. Also, the visits of Dyson and how, when she finished her day's work, she often left him and Mrs Bartlett to it.

Whatever it was …

Police had very minor roles in the Bartlett case.

INSPECTOR MARSHALL

Marshall gave an account of the arrests and also of his search for the chloroform bottles on Wimbledon Common with Dyson.

INSPECTOR BLAKE

Blake was present to explain the models and plans he had made for the court to view, to aid understanding of the layout inside 85 Claverton Street.

All witnesses having been heard, soon it would be time for summaries. Brains would be taxed, heart strings plucked. But, a way to go before Clarke could ask the Jury for a 'Not Guilty' verdict, and Russell ask them for a 'Guilty' one.

Chapter 31

FINISHING OFF

EDWARD CLARKE – CLOSING STATEMENT

The marathon Day Five of the Trial did not end when the witnesses' evidence finished. Clarke took over four hours to deliver his final endeavour in the case, his Statement, a work of art and science.

After asking the Jury to find Mrs Bartlett not guilty (when the requirement of a verdict was upon them) he criticised the fact that Russell, in his role as leader of the English Bar, the Attorney General, would be able to speak last and react to his (Clarke's) Statement. This was an understandable yet fruitless criticism, tradition being that when Counsel for the Prosecution was the Attorney General, he had the advantage of his Statement being the final words against the Defendant.

Perceived unfairness presented, Clarke shifted onto the matter in hand. 'Gentlemen, whatever the history of our medical jurisprudence may be, this case will long be remembered.' (Yes, true.)

Warmed up by making this lofty point, he added his next: '… those remarkable relations which appear to have existed between Mr Bartlett and his wife – relations which would be almost inconceivable if they had not been, as here they are, proved to be true.'

(No, not 'true'. In the absence of the couple, one being dead; the other silent because, as stated earlier, being the Defendant in a murder trial in that era, Adelaide was not allowed to state her case. No one else knew what intimacies did or did not go on in their relationship.)

On to the subject of the unnamed man (Dyson) who was

'declared by your verdict to be free from any imputation of crime' and 'having passed from the dock to the witness box, it is in great measure upon the evidence that he has given that you are asked to rely, in support of the charge against Mrs Bartlett.'

(In other words: as Dyson had been a prisoner, take his evidence, a great deal of the sum total of evidence, with a pinch of salt.)

Clarke emphasised things Adelaide did for her husband, during years of friendship and affection, how she had then 'striven to tend him, to nurse him', called doctors and 'taken all the pains that the most tender and affectionate nurse possibly could.' So why, he asked, was the Prosecution thinking the Jury would imagine 'that woman on New Year's Eve was suddenly transformed into a murderess?' and to believe that somehow 'she succeeds in committing that crime by the execution of a delicate and difficult operation.' By the latter, Clarke meant getting chloroform into Edwin's stomach, an 'operation' which would have been difficult for 'the highest trained doctor.' (If Adelaide did it, perhaps she had beginner's luck.)

'This is the first case that the world has ever heard of in which it has been suggested that a person has been murdered by the administration of liquid chloroform.' It seems incredible – a parade of doctors describing numerous cases of poisoning, yet never a known murder by chloroform and never such a trial. Clarke cited some uses of the drug since its 'discovery' forty years before and the fact that the Jury 'had the good fortune to see in the witness box two of the greatest living authorities' on the subject (Stevenson and Tidy). He repeated their specific evidence that the great majority of deaths from swallowing chloroform were recorded as 'death by suicide; in all the others, they have been death by accidental taking or administration of that drug' (by the latter phrase, meaning cases in which chloroform was given by another person, by accident).

Clarke emphasised that 'medical science can only say that [chloroform's] effects are so uncertain that its administration cannot be undertaken without great care and study.' (Surely there must be instances when given *carelessly* it finished someone off?) 'No one can define what a fatal dose is.'

He launched into a lengthy phase about the inhalation of chloroform – a speech that was irrelevant and possibly designed to befuddle the Jury – surfacing with a reference to the late Edwin: '...in the air passages of that body, no trace of inhalation was found.'

'SORDID AND VENGEFUL MALICE'

Clarke's harsh words against Edwin senior's evidence: 'sordid and vengeful malice'. Clarke's point was 'received with incipient applause which was promptly hushed. An hour later a similar demonstration, caused by an outburst of eloquence against the same witness, had to be suppressed'.[131]

(Clarke thus did a hatchet job on Edwin's father, presumably to garner sympathy for Adelaide. Some people obviously had it in for the man and perhaps too there was some class prejudice among spectators against Mr Bartlett senior.)

'HIS OWN RASH, UNJUSTIFIED CONDUCT'

Returning to the subject of Dyson, in the context of what he allegedly heard from Adelaide about Annie Walker ('chloroform') and Dr Nichols (Edwin had an 'internal complaint') Clarke cautioned against believing the man:

'I think Mr Dyson will never in his life read the account of a trial for murder without thinking how heavily his own rash, unjustified conduct would have told against him if he had been put upon his trial.'

'ANXIOUS TO PROTECT HIMSELF'

Clarke, cautioned the Jury against Dyson's evidence on the 'very strong ground for the suspicion that he has been anxious to protect himself without much regard to the actual truth in his relation to Mr and Mrs Bartlett.'

Clarke claimed that Edwin was 'cold, was desiring to assert his marital rights; that he had in effect given her to Dyson, had recognised the marriage which after his death might come to pass between them.' (This seems outrageous – try reading it again. The court had earlier been told Adelaide's alleged words to Dr Leach about Edwin, and Dyson's about Edwin – and of course Edwin was not there to fight his own corner.)

Having told the court Dyson did not have much regard for 'the actual truth', Clarke suggested that the truth was told by the Reverend (and by strong inference, Adelaide also) when Dyson claimed in court that she wanted chloroform to sprinkle and soothe her husband, if he had violent paroxysms. Edwin allegedly had such paroxysms in his 'previous' illness.

Clarke moved on to Adelaide not being able to raise the delicate subject of sex, her wanting no sex (yet she managed to talk to both her Georgius Rex and Dr Leach about it). Clarke's objective was to take attention away from the fact that Adelaide lied, in that Edwin never had any 'paroxysms'.

Clarke was resting much on the assumed lies from Dyson and on alleging that the latter changed dates to suit his own reputation, one example being Dyson saying Adelaide told him in the autumn that Edwin had a growth and would not live long.

Clarke's anti-Dyson and anti-Edwin approach may have planted plenty of doubts in the Jury's minds as to whether Adelaide was guilty.

Clarke, the supreme Defender, mixing the science of medicine with the art of emotion.

And now he turned to 'the book'. He did not need to name it, everyone knew by now of the book *Esoteric Anthropology (the mysteries of man)*.

Most people would not know the meaning of that title, let alone have read the book or heard anything about it. Clarke gave it an owner (no mention of Adelaide): 'Mr Bartlett had in his possession this book of Dr Nichols'.' Clarke pondered whether Edwin had been to see the 'unregistered medical practitioner' for treatment, without giving his own name.

Clarke thus made sure the Jury knew that 'Dr Nichols' was 'unregistered' – doing him down, perhaps to suggest he was a quack who might see people in secret, and not keep records. Clarke was implying that Edwin had worried he may have syphilis (yet there was no evidence that Edwin had that worry, apart from his telling Dr Leach about one blue pill – mercury? – and the post-mortem which found that Edwin did not have syphilis. And of course Edwin had neither contacted nor seen Dr Nichols.)

On went Clarke to the subject of Adelaide and her confiding in Dr Leach, Clarke pointing out that in this country, doctors were 'called on to reveal what has taken place in consultation.' When in a court of law, they could not keep a patient's disclosures confidential. He maintained that Leach had not expected to be called upon to give evidence to the Inquest, standing before the Coroner (Deputy Coroner) Braxton Hicks.

Adelaide's Defender claimed there were strange 'moral relations' between her and Edwin, which she told Dr Leach something about: '... once and once only I was admitted to my husband's love' and the child died. The 'hope and wish for a child went, and we resumed our old relations', by which Adelaide meant mere companionship, according to Clarke.

He raised the sticky issue of why she did not give evidence at the Inquest, prefacing it by praising one from his side: how 'indebted' he and Adelaide were 'to the judgement and ability with which Mr Beal discharged the anxious and onerous duties' before the Coroner and then in front of Magistrate, Mr Partridge. Clarke linked this issue to Dr Leach who 'had given at the Inquest a kind of statement' from the words Adelaide spoke to him in January. Clarke of course omitted to say she had not spoken with her doctor under any form of oath.

His line of defence continued.

'There was nothing for her to add; no reason for her to have gone into the witness box and exposed herself to cross-examination … I was going to use an epithet, but I refrain' … cross-examination by 'the solicitor whom Mr Bartlett senior had employed at the Inquest. It would have been to expose herself to a trial as severe and terrible as any woman could ever have undergone.'

Clarke was probably correct in saying that Adelaide would have experienced a 'severe and terrible' trial, a real going-over if she had given evidence at the Inquest. He would remember very clearly Florence Bravo's humiliating and shaming trial-by-inquest (despite no evidence of guilt) concerning the death by poisoning of her husband, Charles, in 1876. Clarke was seeking sympathy for Adelaide as a woman and he was damning Edwin senior.

Then he took everyone back to dark December and the patient's demise.

'THE LUMBRICOID WORM UPSET EVERYTHING AGAIN'

Clarke glided on to a summary of the medical treatment and Mr Bartlett being 'mentally and morally [in] a condition of great depression' particularly after 'the lumbricoid worm upset everything again' on 26 December. He was building on his case that Edwin was in decline and vulnerable to suicidal thoughts by New Year's Eve.

(No one knew nor had questioned at any stage whether Adelaide was the one who administered Edwin's medication, nor whether she deliberately did not administer certain drugs.)

It was claimed that the purges did not work until repeated on 27 December – when administered by Dr Leach. Lo and behold, the patient 'got relief'.

Edwin had to cope with 'his horror and dread of going to the dentist' and hearing 'that necrosis was setting in.' Clarke's aim seemed to be indicating the downhill trajectory of Edwin's mood, allegedly topped off by Adelaide telling him what had to stop in their relationship. And her story of Edwin 'pretending to sleep or to sulk. Then, soon after midnight, she fell asleep, and once waking, heard her husband breathing in a peculiar manner.'

Clarke stated that it was 'almost the certain history of the transactions of that night', portraying Edwin as having reached the end of the road, the depths of despair.

'IF SHE HAD BEEN A MURDERESS'

Taking a risk, Clarke returns to the subject of Adelaide. He asserts that 'if she had been a murderess' she would never have mentioned Edwin's 'stertorous breathing' to Dr Leach. (Tenuous – if she heard it and went back to sleep, that signifies very little.) Grasping the nettle, Clarke went on to what Adelaide tried to do: pour brandy down Edwin's throat (and/or did she rub it on his chest?).

But it is 'no use; she puts it back on the mantelpiece, where it was found when they [the Doggetts and Dr Leach] came into the room, this wine glass with the brandy in it, a wine glass which only contained brandy; there was no mixture of chloroform with it, but a wine glass which her husband had used for chloroform it well may be.'

So, Clarke tries to remove one suspicion against Adelaide by saying that when she tried pouring brandy down Edwin in the hope of reviving him, it was not given with chloroform.

'THERE WAS NO SCIENTIFIC MIRACLE WORKED BY THE GROCER'S WIFE'

Clarke now taunts the Jury. 'If you believe – and how dare you reject the statement which she in those circumstances made as to what took place on that night – and accept that statement – the whole history is clear. There was no scientific miracle worked by the grocer's wife under circumstances where it could not have been worked by the most experienced doctor.'

Craftily, Clarke uses understatement to describe an action by Adelaide: there was 'unhappily the putting within reach of a man who was broken by illness' the poison. Thus the Defence's submission is that Adelaide was the person who left the chloroform within Edwin's reach. Edwin 'broken by illness' is Clarke's message to the Jury (to make it plausible that Edwin killed himself).

'DISAPPOINTMENT, AND ABSOLUTE AND FINAL SEVERANCE'

Blame placed on the late husband, 'upon whom there had come this disappointment, and absolute and final severance of the effectual marriage tie between himself and his wife.' Clarke repeated himself, saying 'the putting within his reach of the poison which he might have used'. The bottle of chloroform was close at hand.

By addressing the subject of the poison head-on, using a variety of hypotheses, Clarke's daring hope was to sow doubts in the Jurors' minds about murder, openly acknowledging that Adelaide put the bottle within Edwin's reach. Yet, earlier it had been suggested that Edwin put it on the mantelpiece. Whichever, Clarke was emphatic that Edwin swigged down the chloroform of his own volition.

Clarke sought the Jury's sympathy for Adelaide's lack of real friends:

'– but she had one friend – her husband. He did stand by her, strange as his ideas may have been, disordered … and to her at this moment it may seem most strange that he to whom she had given this persistent affection … should be the one of whose foul murder she now stands accused. How strange that such an accusation should have been formulated and tried in court.'

Having suggested how strange it all was, and the absurdity of the accusation against the Defendant, Clarke laid out for the Jury his version of Edwin's final reaction to his wife's putting an 'end' to what he wanted in their marriage. Clarke said of Edwin that 'by his own rash and despairing act, he [was] completely defeated.' The master orator has pushed home his 'suicide' theory.

'TO COMFORT AND PROTECT HER'

Of course, if Clarke has any doubts about his client and about her husband's death, he is not going to voice them. His final appeal to the Jury is nigh and it is as calculated and carefully crafted as his whole performance.

'The spirit of justice is in this court today to comfort and protect her in the hour of her utmost need.'

He expresses confidence that the Judge will deal with 'the evidence which aroused suspicion, and also with the evidence which I hope … has demolished … that suspicion.'

Clarke finishes back where he started, saying to the Jury he hopes their verdict 'tells to the whole world that in your judgement Adelaide Bartlett is Not Guilty.'

DAY SIX
SIR CHARLES RUSSELL – CLOSING STATEMENT
Russell's speech. as wide-ranging and lengthy as Clarke's, emphasised that his 'learned friend' did not suggest an accident had happened to Edwin; Clarke 'confined his case to suggesting the difficulties in the way of the administering of this irritant poison by anyone else, and marshalled his facts and arguments in support of one suggestion, and one suggestion only – suicide, deliberate suicide, on the part of the deceased.'

(Perhaps Russell miscalculated by keeping the idea firmly in the Jurors' minds that his 'learned friend' put Edwin's death down to suicide. Wouldn't it have been better if Russell tried to imprint his own version of what went on in the Bartlett's relationship in December? And between Adelaide and Dyson in December and January?)

Russell highlighted Mrs Bartlett drawing the Reverend into the (tricky) chloroform-purchasing process. 'He was not conscious of having been a party to any possible criminal use of this chloroform, but she knew the injurious effect of the fact that he had procured it for her.'

Adelaide gave Dyson the late Edwin's watch the day he died, maintaining that her husband wanted Dyson to have it. Russell wanted the Jury to query this. 'When did he tell her? Under what circumstances did he tell her?'

(Did Adelaide lie about the watch? Edwin had never specified it should go to Dyson. She gave it to Dyson in January – and when he realised that chloroform had been the cause of Edwin's death, he thrust the late man's watch back at her.)

'HER HUSBAND MAY HAVE BECOME PERSONALLY DISTASTEFUL TO HER'

Warming to a possible motive, Russell described the state Edwin was in by 31 December. 'One cannot but see, looking to his physical condition, the state of his gums, the state of his teeth, the positively foetid breath which is spoken of, that her husband may have become personally distasteful to her; that she had begun to see in Dyson a man of superior education, although apparently of no physical attractions.' (The latter phrase was a put-down of Dyson by Russell, with a touch of sarcasm. However, Dyson's photograph for sale outside the Old Bailey showed him to have lustrous eyes.)

Russell shot himself in the foot by saying that in cases of poisoning 'you can never have – the nature of the thing forbids it – proof' and that 'murders by poison are not committed, like crimes of sudden passion, often in the light of day. They are necessarily mysterious and hidden in their operation.' How was he going to convince the Jury of guilt?

He moved on to his theories, firstly that 'there could be no suggestion of accident in the matter. I remind you that death must have been caused, and could only have been caused, either by the intentional administration, or by the intentional suicide, by the taking of this poisonous irritant. Now, there are two ways in which it may have been administered.'

One way, described in the medical evidence at the police court, was 'that the administration down the throat might have been preceded by a state of insensibility produced by inhalation – a state of insensibility, total or partial.'

He added that there were 'insuperable difficulties' with the theory of suicide suggested by Clarke, in that *if* Edwin took the chloroform when Adelaide was in the room, or when she was out of it briefly (getting ready for the night) she must have seen the effect upon him.

KEY THEORY ALERT!

Russell announced he had taken 'the liberty of suggesting to my learned friend yesterday, at the adjournment, that there was of course another possible view of the administration' of the poison to Edwin. Now Russell put forward a second method. There was 'another way – that, if the draught had been handed to him in a glass, and given to him, as if for an ordinary purpose, with drops of chloroform in it, and water or some other thing, to drink, then it was conceivable that the dying man would have gulped it down, believing in its innocence, and not expecting that the prisoner had administered something which was wrong and injurious.' Breathless after his lengthy sentence, Russell paused.

CLARKE'S OBJECTION

Clarke jumped to his feet at once, beseeching the Judge: 'My Lord, it is with great reluctance, but I feel bound to interpose at this point. I protest against any such suggestion being put forward, for the first time, at this stage of the case, when it was not even hinted by the learned Counsel for the prosecution in his opening, or in the examination of any of the witnesses.'

Clarke added that he *had* been told about this suggestion – but only after he finished with the medical evidence and thus had answered everything raised by the Prosecution. Clarke's protest was that 'this suggestion ought not to be made in substitution of the original suggestion that has been made.'

Russell's reply across the courtroom: he was not substituting a different suggestion, he felt entitled 'to submit any theory which could point in a more probable direction' (than Clarke's suicide theory). Russell did 'not suggest that the theory is one which is free from difficulties either.' He began again, with a rather muddled theory of administration of the chloroform, given 'by the hand of the prisoner, and … taken by the deceased man and gulped down, might possibly have removed some difficulties, but it would not have removed all, because he would be conscious of the presence in his stomach which was causing him pain and anguish, the result of which would probably have been violent exclamations and violent physical effort on his part.'

Russell claimed that this theory had less difficulties than Clarke's one of the man deliberately doing away with his own life – adding that Clarke 'said in his opening that chloroform could not be poured down a person's throat unless he or she, being unwilling, had been rendered practically insensible before.'

The Judge did not allow Russell to expand further on his last-minute theory, death from chloroform and brandy or water, handed to him. (Did Adelaide hand him such a mixture, saying it was a brandy mix for a New Year toast, or did she suggest he drink her concoction as a sedative? Or was it not of Adelaide's making?)

Russell moved on to challenging Clarke's suicide theory of Edwin waiting, until Adelaide left the room (in order to wash and put on a different dress) then drinking chloroform. Russell posed question after rhetorical question.

'What does it necessarily involve? If he takes the bottle, and out of the bottle he takes a fatal dose, is it to be supposed he had sufficient consciousness and self-control to have repressed in that awful moment a cry of anguish and despair? Is he supposed to have re-stoppered the bottle and put it back on the mantelpiece? Or is it supposed – which I understand to be my friend's suggestion – that in the very brief absence of his wife, he stretches from the bed, or gets out of the bed, and takes the bottle, and takes a wine glass, fills the wine glass with a necessary quantity, re-stoppers the bottle, puts the bottle back on the mantel-piece, gets back into bed, takes the wineglassful of chloroform, and puts the wine glass, I know not where? Is that possible? Is that probable? Well, we are only at the very beginning of the difficulty in testing this theory.'

(Challenging questions from the Prosecution – but surely too many for the Jurymen to digest in one go?)

A brief exchange of views between Russell and Clarke as to how long Adelaide was supposedly out of the room just before Edwin died: Russell thinks Clarke's explanation, that Edwin drank down the poison and was back in bed, does not stand up. 'This theory falls to pieces ... on examination, unless you are prepared to believe that when she comes back – the man having taken the fatal dose – she has meanwhile heard no sound, no utterance of pain or distress, that when she comes back she finds him tranquilly sleeping in his bed in such a condition that she, the anxious, the affectionate wife, is able to compose herself at the foot of the bed, and go to sleep.' Of course Clarke is perfectly satisfied with his own, earlier account.

'WHAT BECAME OF THE BOTTLE OF CHLOROFORM?'

Russell left his question in the air.

But soon returned to the bottle. 'Gentlemen, it may be possibly suggested that, if this lady had indeed done this criminal thing, she would have left the bottle of chloroform in close proximity to the deceased' – and if left – cogent suggestions could have been made. 'But ... if you have watched the history of crime' one would see that plans 'have failed because of some short-sighted omission which the criminal has made.'

On he went to the 'grave difficulties' this threw up in relation to the accused, because Mrs Bartlett insisted to Dr Leach that Edwin could not have taken any poison. She continued in that vein until confronted with the fact of chloroform poisoning, revealed in the forensic reports on 26 January. And she was the person who admitted removing the bottle from the room and to a few days later throwing it from a train window.

'A WOMAN OF STRONGER WILL AND FIRMER PURPOSE THAN DYSON'

Russell added that the suicide scenarios did 'not bear the test of critical examination' and turned back to: who could have administered poison to the victim? Time to address what went on between Mrs Bartlett and Dyson.

That 'she had become interested in Dyson is manifest; that she was a woman of stronger will and firmer purpose than Dyson is, I think, manifest.'

Having given this brief assessment of the pair, Russell reminded the Jury that Dyson confessed 'his part' to both Mrs Matthews and the Coroner; also that Dyson made a most serious allegation against Mrs Bartlett. He misquoted Dyson, then corrected himself. In January she allegedly told Dyson:

'If you don't incriminate me, I won't incriminate you', or, I believe the converse is the way it was put: 'I won't incriminate you if you don't incriminate yourself' – 'she was firm to the purpose.'

'THE EVIL COMES INTO HER MIND'

Russell claimed there was no 'shadow of evidence' that Edwin expected a life other than one of 'ordinary duration.' But in December, Mrs Bartlett suggested to Dyson that Edwin could not live long, given his condition. Russell added that, with her feelings for Dyson and the fact of Edwin's new Will, 'the evil comes into her mind to avail herself of this illness' and a medical man, Leach, a stranger to them, who 'would hardly be described as a strong-headed man' is brought in.

'A HUSBAND WHO HAS BECOME DISTASTEFUL TO HER'

'She might take advantage of the opportunity of ridding herself of a husband who has become distasteful to her, and for whom she had ceased to care, that she might clear the way to a union with a man for whom she had of late conceived admiration and apparently affection.'

He said it was not necessary to establish the exact motive, but if the facts drove the Jury to reject other theories of how chloroform was given, and to accept it was 'administered by criminal intent by someone' then they would have to give a verdict based on the view they took of 'the criminal responsibility of the person charged'.

DOUBTS

For some reason, Russell then kept using the word 'doubt' in this concluding part of his speech. 'Doubt' he said – ten times.

'The law requires that you should give – and it rightly requires that you should give – the benefit of any fair and reasonable doubt which, upon the facts, remains in your minds. I ask you to give the benefit of that doubt, if that doubt does remain, but it must be a doubt which would operate upon your minds in the ordinary important affairs of life, and it is not to be a doubt which you may or must conjure up for the sake of having a doubt. It must be a doubt which presents itself to your minds as reasoning men anxious to discharge your duty between the prisoner and the public – the Crown, whom we represent – a doubt which you cannot overcome. Apply your minds, I pray you, gentlemen, in that spirit; consider and weigh the facts of the case in that spirit; and if you come to the conclusion that still a doubt of the nature that I have mentioned remains, in God's name give this woman the benefit of that doubt.'

Why did Russell plant so many doubts, keep on using the word 'doubt' in front of a Judge and Jury? Why add, for bad measure, that if the Jury felt that a 'doubt of the nature' remained (whatever that meant) then 'in God's name give her the benefit of the doubt.' Hardly the words one would expect from a prosecutor, particularly one so accomplished. Was Russell's mind away in Parliament rather than focusing in Court? His overuse of the word 'doubt' and other negations did not help his case. In modern parlance, what was the likely psychological impact upon his audience?

'NOT ALL NEGATION WORDS BEGIN WITH AN 'N'.'

Steven Pinker, linguist and cognitive psychologist, explains the likely impact of specific words upon the human mind in *The Sense of Style: The Thinking Person's Guide to Writing in the 21st Century*.[132]

'To hear or read a statement is to believe it, at least for a moment'.

'Every negation requires mental homework [and] a sentence can have more negations than you think it does. Not all negation words begin with an '*n*'; many have the concept of negation tucked inside them, such as, few [...] instead, doubt.'

After putting so many doubts into the Jurymen's heads, Russell ends by turning minds to their momentous task. If they cannot receive the theory of suicide, and also cannot state 'the exact methods or means' – but feel that 'guilt lies at this woman's door', they should not 'shrink from the responsibility which in that event' will be cast upon them.

RE-ENTER ANNIE WALKER

A highly unusual step in the judicial process took place. Clarke asked for the Judge's permission that Annie Walker be recalled to court by the Defence at this late stage. She had further evidence to give, said Clarke; she contacted *him* – he 'had no communication with her' in advance. The nurse had, of course, been called as a witness by the other side, the Prosecution, on the third day. Clarke's request: that she be asked just 'one question with regard to anything she knew as to the single act.'

The Prosecution made no objection.

'It is very late, but I think one should never shut out anything that may be material,' said the Judge, ordering:

'LET ANNIE WALKER STEP UP!'

Annie, thus recalled, went up into the witness box.

The Judge invited Clarke to put the question.

'Annie Walker, at the time you nursed Mrs Bartlett in her confinement, did you become aware of anything she said to you with regard to its having been the result of a single act?'

When she spoke, the nurse's words of new evidence cast huge and sensational doubt on the veracity of Adelaide's claim (as delivered by Dr Leach) that sexual intercourse between her and Edwin was a 'one-off' in their marriage.

'A PREVENTIVE WAS ALWAYS USED'

Annie Walker: 'A preventive was always used' … always used. Hear the nurse's words echo, even in the crowded courtroom, and then hang in this historic space.

Her words caused the Judge to express utter disgust that women had bought tickets and were seated in the public gallery for each day of the Trial, listening to such unsuitable matters. A reporter made it his business to note that they had knitted diligently for four or five days, but then these women …

'LAID ASIDE THEIR NEEDLES AND HALF- …'

'… laid aside their needles and half-completed work and endeavoured to look unconscious that evidence of a character totally unfit for publication, but considered of the greatest importance, was being tendered and discussed.'[133]

Why on earth Clarke asked for Annie to be recalled is a mystery – isn't it? Had he misunderstood what she wished to add? Did he think she was going to say Edwin and Adelaide had sex only on one occasion? What Annie knew, and returned to Court to say, was that there was just one connection without a preventive, on a Sunday afternoon. On all other occasions when the Bartletts had intercourse, 'a preventive was always used.'

How much would this revelation damage the Defence's case on Adelaide's behalf – and rubbish the story she had pitched to Dr Leach?

THE JUDGE'S SUMMING-UP

Dyson was not in court but 'other witnesses were seated here and there, or clustering below the jury box, Mr Bartlett [senior] and Dr Nicholls amongst them … The summing-up, as could have been seen by the gestures of the Judge, was characterised by pronounced news, but among at least three-fourths of the reporters … and of the public, the utmost straining to hear would not catch one complete sentence in a dozen. The prisoner, sitting with closed eyes and sunken head, did not betray a vestige of interest in the charge to the Jury, and indeed could not have heard many of its terms.'[134]

Thus many in court could not hear the Judge's quiet words, but all that he uttered was noted down for the official record. He asked the Jury 'in the name of justice' to refuse to have anything to do with the last-minute theory put forward by Russell. He dismissed another theory by saying there would be so many difficulties for anyone trying to administer the drug to someone partially insensible, and to get them to swallow it, 'that no skilled man would venture upon it unless he were a madman.'

Some present may have pondered on whether a woman ventured upon it …

Surprisingly, the Judge quoted a line from a sixteenth-century poem by Alexander Pope: 'Fools rush in where angels fear to tread'.[135]

The quote was apt. The Judge knew – and assumed others did too – that the poem's next lines were 'the ignorant and the presumptuous will sometimes attempt that which no human being who understood the conditions of the problem would think of trying, and will sometimes blunder into success.'

The Judge was applying these lines to the prisoner, meaning: did she succeed in that most extraordinary fashion? And he continued, '… because the conditions and chances are all against it'.

All of this referred to getting the balance right (if of murderous intent) between administering sufficient chloroform to produce anaesthesia during sleep and using not so much of the poison that the power of swallowing was lost. If a person lost the swallow reflex, chloroform would not go down into the stomach.

THE BOTTLE AND THE GLASS

The Judge confessed to personal experience of a dreadful craving for something that would bring sleep. He told the Jury it struck him as 'possible that [Mr Bartlett] might get hold of the bottle and pour some in a glass and drink it' and – if done in the dark – more may have been poured than intended. He added that he thought his was 'a more reasonable explanation than that of suicide', the theory which the learned Counsel had been instructed to present to them. The Judge was thus suggesting that Edwin had taken an accidental overdose.

Unfortunately, many of the Judge's thoughts put into quiet words had not reached the audience, but perhaps someone belatedly asked him to speak more loudly. 'After the Judge had been speaking for more than an hour and a half he became more audible.'[136]

'WHAT IS THE HISTORY OF THE CHLOROFORM BOTTLE?'

Now he approached 'by far the most important part of this inquiry … what is the history of the chloroform bottle?'

Throwing in a welter of words about what might or might not have happened just prior to Edwin's death, concerning the missing bottle of chloroform and a glass left in the room, the Judge emphasised that a 'very strong factor in her favour' was that the prisoner (or someone else) made 'no attempt to clean out that glass.'

'I am still keeping to the theory of non-criminal administration – that the bottle must have been, as she says it was, on the chimney-piece in the course of the evening before she settled off to sleep, and he took the chloroform. I see no difficulty if it were so taken – accidentally ... in supposing that he could have so far lifted himself up as to have taken it without disturbing her, whether he was bent on suicide, or bent, more probably as it seems to me, on allaying his restless craving for sleep.'

The Judge said it was proved that 'soon after four o'clock in the morning that bottle was not there.'

He expressed confidence that 'the glass which must have been made use of in connection with it was still in its proper place, and was found by Doggett; he smelt it; he sniffed at it; and he gave that piece of evidence which, I think, is an important piece of evidence in her favour – he smelt the smell of paregoric or ether. It had brandy in it, no doubt, but the smell was, beyond all doubt, the smell of chloroform – that smell lingered about it.'

So, key words from the Judge: paregoric or ether; brandy no doubt; chloroform. In a wine glass; smelt (but not kept as evidence, the glass was washed up on New Year's morning by the servant).

How Edwin could have unstoppered a bottle of chloroform, poured some into a glass, drunk it down (with or without brandy) and died – all without disturbing Adelaide – was not addressed by the Judge.

'CRIME IS SELDOM ARMED AT ALL POINTS'

He added that it was 'true that crime is seldom armed at all points; its designs generally break down at some place where you least expect it; but if that woman's hand poured that chloroform out of that glass into that man's throat, she must have been strangely constituted, according to the instincts of criminals in general, if she was not possessed with the desire of obliterating the traces of what had been in the glass.'

(Well, perhaps Adelaide *was* 'strangely constituted'? Or, *if* she gave the glass, did she forget to take it away?)

The Judge anticipated where listeners' minds might go with his line of thought.

'And it is not as if there could be any suggestion of a formed design in her mind to allow death by chloroform to be attributed to accidental administration. It is clear that from no point of view was that her plan, and therefore you cannot suggest this was a clever thought that it would be better to let the smell linger there in order that the notion might gather ground.'

By 'notion' the Judge meant the idea that Edwin took the poison accidentally.

So, whether Edwin did or did not take the chloroform himself, why was the glass left in the room? If Adelaide was the person who poured brandy and chloroform into it and gave it to Edwin – saying something like '… here're your drops, drink them down in one go and they'll give you a good sleep', or '… here's your brandy, let's toast the New Year!' – then we have two possible methods. And the question of the glass: perhaps she forgot the glass if, for example, Edwin shouted out, she took the glass from him, he lurched and slumped down, she had the devil's own job to move him onto the small bed, to turn him flat on his back. If she did any or all of that, did she then prop him up for a while?

If that was how it was, or something like that, Adelaide might have been more shaken than she had imagined she would be. She did remember to remove the bottle and she made up the fire. Why pile up new coal? Had she set light to something incriminating? Did she feel shivery? Need to do the steadying, routine task of banking up the fire, to compose herself? Or were the Doggetts plain wrong about the state of that fire?

Perhaps, with all the drama, Adelaide just forgot to go back for the damn glass. It was washed up later that fateful New Year's Day by Fulcher, the servant.

'A SORT OF CURIOUS FATUITY SEEMS TO HAVE HUNG OVER THE CASE'

Back to the bottle of chloroform. Why (around breakfast time) had the bottle disappeared, into the second, never-searched drawer – or been put elsewhere by Adelaide?

The Judge thought it was 'difficult beyond measure to account for the disappearance of that bottle' and that they would never know where it went.

He ridiculed PC Ralph's search of the Bartlett's rooms. 'A sort of curious fatuity seems to have hung over the case at its earlier stages. The Coroner's Officer – a grown-up policeman – who was sent there … to aid in the discovery of truth' did not remember to look in the drawers.

The Judge declared: 'if that man [Mr Bartlett] took that poison non-criminally, the bottle must have been on the mantel-shelf.' (Yet the search was inadequate from the start.)

'THE PERSON WHO HAD A LARGE FATAL BOTTLE OF THE STUFF'

Talking about Adelaide, he commented how strange it was that 'the person who had a large bottle of the fatal stuff … should have said nothing about it.'

'MODESTY AND RESERVE AND DELICACY'

He counter-balanced by saying there was 'modesty and reserve and delicacy' in her story to Dr Leach on 26 January, namely of her need to stave off Edwin's ardour by the use of chloroform on a handkerchief.

Time to refer back to the evidence from the experts. 'As far as I remember' said the Judge, 'the smallest recorded dose which is supposed to have killed a person is either two ounces or one ounce and a half.' If that previous case had not happened, 'death from so small a dose would have been supposed to be almost impossible.' He pointed out that 'very large doses are apt to defeat their own ends if taken with suicidal intent, because they make the patient sick.'

'STEADILY TAKING ADVANTAGE OF THE HUSBAND'S WEAKNESS'

Deep into his summing-up the Judge was scathing of Dyson's portrayal of Edwin supposedly encouraging him to carry on with his wife, with Dyson 'steadily taking advantage of the husband's weakness.' And the Judge laid bare the kissing of Adelaide in the presence and the absence of her husband, and Dyson 'justifying all this to himself by the miserable pretext that he was listening to the maudlin nonsense of the husband, and accepting his invitation to succeed him when he should be no more.'

'ALMOST REVOLTING IMPROBABILITY'

The Judge said Dyson should have 'stamped it out' and he scorned how 'they got to that state of intimacy when the possible death of the husband and the possibility of Dyson succeeding him were matters of familiar discussion.' All this was, said the Judge, discreditable to Dyson himself and to the Bartletts; Dyson's stories had 'some features of almost revolting improbability.' And now the Judge, not impressed by Dyson's evidence, addressed the Jury directly.

'Whatever may become of the case by your verdict, no human being can say that the actors in such a drama as this, when the very thing had occurred which had been the subject of discussion between them, and had occurred under very suspicious circumstances ... [neither] of them has any cause of complaint if grievous suspicions are entertained that he or she, or both of them, has had a hand in it.'

By 'it' the Judge meant Edwin's death, by 'he or she, or both': Dyson and Adelaide. Dyson was coupled up with the prisoner by the Judge – even though the worried young man had been found 'not guilty'. Clearly the Judge wanted the message to get through to Dyson that he did not have 'any cause of complaint'.

SEX AND 'DOMESTIC FURNITURE'
The Judge moved on to muck. 'The case is full of unpleasant subjects ...'. (Well, it is bound to be, it is a murder trial.)

French letters were 'unpleasant' and there was 'a very unpleasant book that formed one of the articles of [Mr Bartlett's] domestic furniture ...'. The Judge made that book (yes that one) sound like a table – or perhaps more suggestively – a bed). Much was made by him, from so little, about that book, *Esoteric Anthropology (the mysteries of man)*. Handed many moons ago by the audacious Adelaide to George Matthews; given back to her in quiet outrage by Alice Matthews.

'IT IS READING SUCH AS THIS THAT HELPS TO UNSEX THEM'
Here it comes again, mention of that book by Thomas Nichols. The Judge decries Annie Walker, 'who seems a respectable woman and she says there is not a word immoral or improper' in this book. He thunders on about the book having a passage on procuring abortions.

'It scatters its poison and does its mischief. The women of the present day are used to strange things ... and it is such reading that helps to unsex them, and to bring them to a place like this day after day to listen willingly to details which, even to men of mature life ... are distasteful and disgusting.'

The Judge has criticised the author and the nurse, both of whom gave evidence. But primarily he directs his ire at any women who reads the book – and all women with the audacity to attend such trials. He pities the prisoner, 'the unhappy woman, made in early life the companion of a man who could throw such literature in her way.' The Judge thus blamed Edwin and displayed no thought that Adelaide, an intelligent, strong-minded woman and a voracious reader, was well capable of selecting her own reading matter. And capable of consulting Mary Gove Nichols, as she did in order to arrange for a birthing nurse, Annie Walker.

Rant over, the Judge rights himself by reminding everyone, including himself, that 'we have sterner matters here to deal with than pity' (for the prisoner).

'ONE NEVER KNEW WHERE FACTS ENDED AND INFERENCES BEGAN'

With regard to young, eager Dr Leach's crucial and lengthy evidence about his numerous visits to the patient, the Judge turns sardonic.

'One must make great allowance for a man who is evidently possessed of a self-consciousness that not even the solemnity of this inquiry could still for a moment, and which undoubtedly detracts from the value of his evidence, because one never knew where facts ended and inferences began.'

'A NOT VERY STRONG-HEADED MAN'

Serious talk nonetheless; hopefully Dr Leach was suitably chastened (if present). However, remember back to the Inquest in February, when Coroner Mr Braxton Hicks found Dr Leach to be a tricky witness. Slippery but seemingly not in the dishonest sense, more like soap slipping through the hands. Now, the Judge intended to put flesh on the bones of his concerns about Leach during this Trial:

'One never knew when one was getting the unvarnished efforts of memory or the impressions of a not very strong-headed man painfully haunted by the idea that he is the central personage in a drama of surpassing interest.'

The Judge concluded, for now, his views on Dr Leach by saying that one of the great difficulties of the case – for reasons 'very different from those which apply to Dyson' whom the Judge felt had not told the whole truth at times – was that 'you cannot trust … the impressions or statements of Dr Leach.'

Having made his frustrations abundantly clear about the deceased's doctor – such a crucial witness – the Judge repeated that Adelaide made no mention of having had chloroform, until she told Dr Leach on 26 January. That was the day she elicited Leach's sympathy with allegations about how her life had been with Edwin.

'A POINT OF EXTREME IMPORTANCE IN HER FAVOUR'

The Judge pointed out that Adelaide urged a post-mortem be held as soon as possible after Edwin's death, according to Dr Leach. No one questioned the accuracy of the latter's recall on that point. And – believing Dr Leach – the Judge said that the prisoner's urgent insistence on a prompt post-mortem was 'a point of extreme importance in her favour.' This was a crucial tipping point.

Unfortunately, there hadn't been a fly on the wall to see whose hand poured a large quantity of chloroform down Edwin's throat …

The Judge emphasised the conduct of Adelaide as 'a devoted wife' who was attentive to her husband despite the state he had been in, 'with his wretched hypochondriacal melancholy' and 'all the irritability and moral disturbance which attend such a condition.' The Judge disclosed that he personally, for twelve months of his life, did not get 'one tolerable night's rest'; he knew also what discomfort such misery brings to people around a patient. (In modern parlance, one could say the Judge was over-identifying with both the deceased and the accused by this point.)

However, when mentioning the French letters (condoms) it was obvious the Judge did not buy a certain story from the Defence. That was the story of what he now described as a 'morbid romance of a non-sexual connection' between husband and wife – that 'baseless illusion is swept away by the one sentence which you heard in the witness box today.' By that he meant the new evidence from Annie Walker, that 'a preventive was always used.'

What the Judge did not state, or perhaps comprehend, was the fact that, even though the couple had consensual sex in the past, if Adelaide's feelings had changed and hardened from say, June onwards, then Adelaide may have decided to poison her husband with chloroform. Russell had outlined that distinct possibility, but the Judge was not on the same page.

MORE DOUBT

Nearing the end of his summing-up, the Judge reminded the Jury that if they thought the prisoner guilty it would be their 'bounden duty to act', however painful the consequences. But if they thought her innocent or if they were 'in a state of honest and conscientious doubt' then they should acquit her.

There was that small but niggling word 'doubt' yet again. Surprisingly, Russell had used it ten times from the 'wrong' side, the Prosecution. Here was the Judge, from his position of authority in the Trial, rightly reminding the Jurymen to consider their doubts.

It was still Day Six of the Trial, Saturday, 17 April 1886. The Judge having finished speaking at seven minutes to three, the Jurymen retired to consider their verdict.

The prisoner, by some mistake not being at once removed, was condemned for a while to witness, as far as one whose eyes were kept studiously shut could witness, the behaviour of the ladies and gentlemen for whom she furnished such an enjoyable entertainment.

'LORGNETTES AND EYE-GLASSES WERE LEVELLED AT MRS BARTLETT'

The ladies were in for it again, this time from reporters. 'All around was bustle, excitement, noise, the animation of a crowd who had no cares in the world, and no visible sense of the gravity of the occasion. Lorgnettes and eye-glasses were levelled at Mrs Bartlett by ladies, and two or three of the sisterhood stared point blank at the prisoner through the framed glass of the dock, loudly describing their observations to their friends and acquaintances.'[137]

'UNSEXED WOMEN' AT CRIMINAL TRIALS – A PROTEST'

'A Barrister' wrote straight to the press after the verdict. 'The law of England no longer permits any criminal to be tortured; but to judge from what occurred … the worst of tortures are sometimes inflicted on the unconvicted prisoner. The behaviour of the women, who have … formed a large proportion of the crowd in court, has been so disgraceful as to call forth from Mr Justice Wills some strong expressions on their conduct; but on Saturday these persons outdid themselves. For some reason or other the prisoner was not removed from the dock until three minutes after the jury had retired; and during that time was keenly scrutinised through eye-glasses and opera-glasses ... in a manner that must have been as painful to herself as it was discreditable to civilisation.' Some women went 'up to the glass partition which separates the dock from the court, in order to gratify their unwholesome tastes by staring through it at the wretched prisoner'.

The Barrister's view was that a judge should have had 'a few of these unsexed women "cleared" from the court'.[138] Presumably for the sake of example to all the other women, as a deterrent.

'COULD SYMPATHISE THEIR PLIGHT, IF NOT THEIR SOLUTIONS'

Although the women were perceived as scrutinising a woman in a situation very different from their own, perhaps they viewed Adelaide as a woman with thoughts and feelings similar to their own. Fervent, hidden wishes and desires which had brought Adelaide – and them – into this place. In a review of the book by Mary Hartman, *Victorian Murderesses: A True History of Thirteen Respectable French and English Women Accused of Unspeakable Crimes,* Kathleen E McCrone suggested that the women who attended court or read avidly about the trials of Adelaide and other middle-class women 'could sympathise with their plight, if not their solutions'.[139]

A tortuous three minutes for Adelaide sitting there in court, a humiliating process; wondering what would come next.

'The female warders, meanwhile, stood in the rear consulting, and the Inspector in the dock at length went up to the forlorn prisoner and spoke to her. She faintly smiled, at once rose and retired from the gaze of the joyous throng.

At this period in the proceedings, the opinion and hope of the majority of at least the gentlemen present was that the prisoner would be acquitted and this had been their opinion throughout the week. Time would soon settle the question.

A few minutes after four a cry of "Hats off!" in the doorway by which the jury would enter, produced an instantaneous hush. The judge came in and took his seat; the twelve jurors solemnly filed into their places, the prisoner was brought up again, and again sank into her chair in the old attitude, perhaps more ashen of hue than previously, but always firm and composed'.[140]

ANTICLIMAX

'It was only a respite: there was no verdict yet. The jury wished to ask questions and, these answered, they left the box once more, and the prisoner, this time, was at once removed.'

THE TRIAL VERDICT

'The supreme moment of the Trial had at last arrived'.

The twelve men had returned to court from their deliberations, the Judge had taken his seat and 'the prisoner had been conducted to the front of the dock, and stood there. Her face was overspread with a death-like pallor. Her eyes were not, throughout the crisis of her fate, raised to jury, judge or people. The small dark figure stood firm, and from first to last there was no tremor of body, no quiver of lip – no movement of any description. The female warders, one on each side, softly moved quite close to the prisoner, each quietly taking an arm to support her if needs be when the dread words were pronounced.'[141]

The Clerk of the Court asked the question.

'Do you find the prisoner, Adelaide Bartlett, guilty or not guilty?'

The Foreman of the Jury had their answer.

'We have well considered the evidence, and although we think grave suspicion is attached to the prisoner, we do not—'

At that signal of the verdict, the tiny word 'not', someone rushed from court and shouted out the news to the huge crowd outside.

'– think there is sufficient evidence to show how or by whom the chloroform was administered.'

'Then you say that the prisoner is not guilty, gentlemen?'

'NOT GUILTY'

The Judge then 'made an emphatic protest, in most indignant tones – not about the verdict, of course – about the cheering in Newgate Street, soon overlain by a cheering hubbub in the courtroom, with handkerchiefs, hats and papers being waved – everyone ignoring the Usher's shouts of 'SILENCE!'

Whether anyone other than reporters noted Mrs Bartlett's reaction and condition is not known; she 'received the verdict calmly. She had stood – the only woman in court with an uncovered head – at the front of the dock, a hectic flush on her usually sallow and colourless cheeks'.[142]

Mr Sheriff Evans and the Under-Sheriffs roared, again unsuccessfully, for 'SILENCE, SILENCE!'

The Judge declared the noisy reaction from the spectators an outrage and he could hardly be heard, thanking the Jury for their attention. Then a mistake. Whether by accident (with all the distracting, disgraceful clamour) or by design, he omitted to say whether he concurred with the Jurymen's decision.

'SOBBING'

Meanwhile, Edward Clarke, arms stretched out across his table, head down, had tears of relief pouring down his strained face. Years later he wrote in his memoirs: 'I found myself sobbing. I dropped my head on the desk before me and some twenty minutes passed before I recovered myself.'[143]

OVER AND OUT

On 24 April 1886, the *People's Weekly Journal* featured Adelaide's run to freedom. The report can be laid out to read like a breezy poem, as follows:

'Round after round of ringing cheers,
accompanied by waving of hats, were given,
drowning the continued demonstration outside.
The prisoner retained her marvellous self-command
even now.
Without opening her eyes, she paused
a moment,
bowing her head somewhat,
and seemed about to faint:
then, as if suddenly realising
that she was a free woman,
turned decisively round,
and led the way
with uncertain step
(the female warders assiduously supporting her)
out of the dock ...
the Judge was rebuking the people
for their behaviour ...
The young lady before mentioned,
who was to take Mrs Bartlett home,
hastened to the Governor amidst the tumult,
and, being admitted to the dock,
ran with beaming countenance
down the stairs
to rejoin her friend, who had just descended them,
a prisoner at liberty.'

In the manner of a celebrity avoiding the modern-day paparazzi, Adelaide left by a FRONT exit, with alongside her the young lady of 'beaming countenance' (presumably Miss Wood, sister of Adelaide's solicitor).

Meanwhile crowds jostled at a BACK door, where a decoy hansom cab was supposedly awaiting the former prisoner.

If they had any desire, money and energy left, spectators could still buy, from hawkers on the crowd-filled street outside the Old Bailey, those stunning photographs of a woman. Mrs Adelaide Bartlett, the newly-released young widow, escaping from everyone's clutches at last. Over, out and onwards.

PART EIGHT
'UNREBUKED TO FREEDOM'

Chapter 32

CORRESPONDENCE AND OPINIONS

LETTER FROM THE JURY FOREMAN

Surprisingly, the Jury Foreman in the Bartlett case, Frederick Eden Elton, wrote a letter on 19 April to a London newspaper and, not surprisingly, it was seized upon by many others.[144]

Elton disclosed that the Jury's expression of views was 'the result of a compromise. Eleven of our number were in favour of a verdict of not guilty, with a rider that we were of the opinion that, considering the state of health Mr Bartlett was in, or imagined he was in, he administered the chloroform to himself with a view of obtaining sleep or committing suicide; but the twelfth Juryman would only consent to a verdict in the form in which it was given; and the majority, rather than subject Mrs Bartlett to all the agony and expense of a second trial, gave way upon the point.'

So, one Juror held his ground against the eleven.

Somehow the Jurors discounted the following disclosures they heard in court, that Adelaide allegedly:

- said to Dyson that Edwin would not live long
- requested Dyson buy chloroform
- protested to Dyson that the bottle was just as he had bought it (i.e. not opened, not disposed of)
- told Dr Leach that someone had bought chloroform at her request; that after her husband's death she put the (opened) chloroform bottle in her drawer and later threw it away.

'WILFULLY OR UNINTENTIONALLY'

A Norwich newspaper editorial bluntly and unsympathetically declared that 'there was no circumstance adduced in the course of the trial which pointed directly and unmistakably to murder'. And that indeed 'there were many points ... on the theory that the wretched creature who finished his useless life in Claverton Street had perished, wilfully or unintentionally, by his own hand'.[145]

As for the Jury, the Verdict was 'hampered by the perverseness of one of their number' who held 'a cross-grained view of the case' and declined 'to yield it under pressure of the majority. It is a pity ... that some method of deciding a disputed verdict by a majority vote has never been incorporated in our English law. The plan might be open to objections and liable to abuse, but it would save us from any decisions at once inconsequent and unjust.'[146]

'MRS BARTLETT AND HER SEX'

Under that explicit headline, the *Shields Gazette*'s editorial on 19 April claimed that the conclusion of the case would 'take nobody by surprise ... In Scotland, this would be a verdict of not proven'. Strikingly its view was that since 'the Bravo case there has been no English criminal trial which has similarly excited the public'.

'QUITE AN ABUNDANCE OF NAUSEATING MATERIAL'

One would need to know the works of Zola to understand a particular newspaper editorial point about the Pimlico Poisoning case: that a novelist of 'the Zola type might find in it quite an abundance of nauseating material'.[147] Similarly, to appreciate how the characters of those involved in the Pimlico Mystery would 'command' Zola's interest.

Zola was the most prominent of French novelists in the late nineteenth century; his sequence of twenty novels, *Les Rougon-Macquart*, documented French life through the fictional portrayal of two titular branches of a family, one violent and one passive, related to each other through one key character.

Although the editorial in the *Shields Gazette* was an apt reference to the vicissitudes of individual's and families' lives, it is unlikely that the person who penned it had any inkling of the people in Adelaide's family and their true natures – nor knew of the French connection – but sometimes fact is far zanier than fiction.

HAVING IT IN FOR THE WOMEN

The Bartlett case was labelled in the same newspaper as 'this unwholesome domestic tragedy'. Dyson's behaviour was considered caddish; Mr and Mrs Bartlett's married life not resembling that of decent folk … and many women attended the Trial having 'laden themselves with lunch baskets' as if for a jolly picnic. 'Withered old women and young maidens have alike shown themselves oblivious of decency. They sat for hour on hour contemplating the agony of a poor creature, who sat pale, bowed, and crushed utterly.' (However, Dr Leach felt, and Dyson knew, that Adelaide was made of tougher stuff.)

The editorial declared that these women 'cast an unmerited stigma on their sex. All womankind, for the time being, suffers in reputation through their prurient curiosity'.

And it continued with a warning to such women. 'The interest of a certain class of females in criminal trials which are disgusting in their details is scarcely explainable ... an ardent lover who caught sight of the being of his worship knitting socks in the Old Bailey ... would surely retire from his suit whilst there was yet time! He would argue that she was both depraved in taste and deficient in modesty'.

That editorial writer was so indignant that it is hard to tell whether he deemed those women wrong for listening to such disgusting detail or for knitting in court. Probably both – women couldn't win in a male-dominated world ...

The principal woman in this case had been saved by primarily one man (with the help of his team).

As mentioned earlier, Adelaide's Trial appears in Mary S Hartman's book *Victorian Murderesses: A True History of Thirteen Respectable French and English Women Accused of Unspeakable Crimes*. Many of these women were in marriages through arrangements made about them and for most, divorce was not a viable option in any way. They felt trapped by power and circumstances.

However, the conventional view of women in England and France at the time differed greatly from the analysis Hartman provides. And the way in which many men dealt with women in public had a particular slant.

As Hartman puts it:

'Adelaide's defense ... called no witnesses and produced no evidence. They did not have to. Adelaide and her counsel found it unnecessary to construct an explanation by stepping into a fully developed and popularly embraced rendition of middle-class womanhood and heterosexual marriage ... part of such a defense reinforced and further defined the very terms it borrowed. Consequently, while Barrister Clarke used heterosexual marriage ideals to defend Adelaide, his own 'appropriate' modelling of a male representative simultaneously condemned Mr Bartlett and affirmed his own authority'.

Hartman captures the essence of what Clarke, representing male authority, was all about.

'Clarke's basic contention was that a woman like Adelaide was incapable of murder. Nothing she could have said and no evidence Mr Clarke could have presented would have carried the same, deeply engrained message or would have rung so true to the ears of the jury.

'But more important, her silence allowed Dr Leach and Dr Clarke to tell her story, to lend her credibility by mouthing her words, to take her representation on their own backs, thereby elevating her believability by dint of their own trustworthy positions and reputations.

'However convincing Mrs Bartlett's testimony might be, her silence would be more convincing because it dovetailed with the image of a perfect middle-class wife whose silence allowed her 'husband' to speak for her.'[148]

FLAIR

On 19 April the *Pall Mall Gazette* praised Edward Clarke's expertise and declared that 'no greater forensic triumph has been scored in our time'.

Clarke had 'a special flair for cross-examining doctors – a flair he reinforced by most industrious research' wrote Edgar Lustgarten seventy-two years later in *The Murder and the Trial*.[149]

'THE HANGMAN'S CORD'

There is little reason to think that Clarke took on Adelaide's case for money. After all, in 1877 he had defended Patrick Staunton (tried, with others, for the murder of his sister-in-law) and there is no evidence of money being available for Staunton's defence. The principal reward for Clarke always was the satisfaction of successfully using all his skills and endeavour in constructing a comprehensive defence for those in danger of being hanged. Adelaide had played Dyson like a fish on a line, and Clarke's tactics were to be 'friendly and sympathetic' towards the still-Reverend when he became the key witness against Adelaide.

Clarke's graphic description of his strategy in relation to Dyson: 'the more closely I could associate his actions with those of Mrs Bartlett, the more I could strengthen the reluctance of the jury to send her to the hangman's cord while he passed unrebuked to freedom.'[150]

'AN ABUSE OF HEMP'

On the subject of Dyson, a declaration in many newspapers was that to have hanged Adelaide and not hanged him 'would have been an abuse of hemp'.

'A SNEAK AND A LIAR'

One newspaper said of Dyson that he was:

'... a parasite of the Bartletts. They fed him, and they seem to have provided him with money. He must have known that whilst it is not right to kiss another man's wife behind the back of her husband, it is free love with a vengeance to kiss her in his presence. He admits that he bought the chloroform ... and he must have known that he was doing wrong, or he would not have purchased it secretly' and thrown away the bottles. He is 'a sneak and a liar'.

'ONLY A JURY OF WOMEN WOULD HAVE CONVICTED HER'

And a great deal about patriarchal views was packed into just one sentence.

'Mrs Bartlett is, I am told, a pretty woman – small, with frizzy hair and large blue [sic] eyes; they were during the trial generally cast down, but occasionally she raised them with such effect upon the male sex that, even if the evidence had been stronger against her than it was, only a jury of women would have convicted her'.[151]

That ending made another dig at women, suggesting that envy and jealousy would have resulted in Adelaide being found guilty if it had been up to a hypothetical all-woman jury. And it was written smug in the knowledge that no women were allowed to sit on juries at that time in England.

A SUICIDE – AND MARRIAGE IN MIND

Many newspapers carried the 'London Letter' with its insights and snippets on aspects of the Pimlico case, including a piece about Mr Justice Wells and his 'impressive' summing-up. One of 'the newest made of the Judges, he has never before presided at anything like a sensational trial. He is a man of fresh colour, blue eyes, and pleasing expression; a slight hesitation of speech somewhat detracts from his delivery; but his language is weighty and well chosen.

'As the learned Judge spoke of the severe sleeplessness from which he had suffered some years ago, it was impossible not to remember that his Lordship's own brother ... committed suicide under the depression induced by long insomnia'.

This 'London Letter' declared that Dyson was being 'deluged with correspondence, not wholly it is said, from the male sex. Mrs Bartlett, besides the tender of other kinds of consolation, is said to have received many offers of marriage during her incarceration'.[152]

LETTER FROM ADELAIDE TO CLARKE
After her acquittal Adelaide was driven away for a stay with Mr Negus Wood, her solicitor, and his sister at 66 Gresham Street in the City of London. From there she wrote a letter of thanks to Edward Clarke on 24 April; it was not published until 1927 – and that was an abridged version. It has one small misspelling by Adelaide. Apart from her brief outburst against Edwin senior at the Inquest, and two different photographs of her, this letter is all that is left of her in the public domain.

'Dear Sir,
'Forgive me for not earlier expressing my heartfelt gratitude to you, I feel that I owe my life to your earnest efforts, and though I cannot put it into words, the feelings that fill my heart, you will understand all that my pen fails to express to you. Your kind looks towards me, cheered me very much, for I felt that you believed me innocent. I have heard many eloquent Jesuits preach but I never listened to anything finer than your speech.

'My story was a very painful one, but sadly true, my consent to my marriage was not asked, and I only saw my husband once before my wedding day ... I am much gratified that Dr Stevenson has written to say that he concurs in the verdict, he wrote so kindly of Miss Wood, who has been a true friend. I received great kindness at Clerkenwell, from the

Governor to the lowest, they did their best to comfort me. Assuring you that I shall ever remember you with feelings of deepest gratitude,
I am,
Sincerely yours,

Adelaide Bartlett'

Words and phrases jump out: Jesuits; consent not asked; only saw my husband once before my wedding day; Dr Stevenson concurs; kindness at Clerkenwell.

Perhaps she had been a Roman Catholic (RC) at some stage – but there is no known evidence as to whether it was a RC, Protestant or secular school which she attended in Belgium. Her story is that she was married off after just one meeting. Dr Stevenson had 'gone public' in writing that he agreed with the verdict of the Jury. She was appreciative of those who helped her in the forbidding prison.

This abridged version of her letter was published in the *Trial of Adelaide Bartlett*, edited by Sir John Hall.[153]

For some reason (possibly Clarke deciding to keep it private for some years) the final, more personal sentence in Adelaide's letter – these closing words were omitted by Sir John Hall:

'I have not been a good woman and my temptations have been terriable ones, but although I have not kept my vows as I should have done, you will judge me mercifully.'

This final sentence, not revealed until 1939 appeared when the full letter was published in *The Life and Famous Cases of Sir Edward Clarke*.[154]

On to the essence of Adelaide's closing sentence. She could not have made it any clearer, she knew herself well and her words were an admission of something, but of what? Not keeping her vows: obviously a very different kettle of fish from murder.

Of course, this letter after her acquittal was solely for Edward Clarke, not written for public perusal down the centuries, yet the words are still mulled over.

'AND MY TEMPTATIONS HAVE BEEN TERRIABLE ONES'

A minor matter: 'terriable', another spelling error. Unfortunately for sleuths, Adelaide did not divulge the temptations to which she succumbed. It is not surprising that she would not divulge them, after her many months of silence and finally Clarke's toil and tears.

The next line, an admission of not keeping her vows. She did not enlighten Clarke as to which ones, religious and/or marriage vows?

'BUT THOUGH I HAVE NOT KEPT MY VOWS AS I SHOULD HAVE DONE, YOU WILL JUDGE ME MERCIFULLY'

Was any of that a confession of some sort, deliberately vague, opaque? Followed by 'you will judge me ...'. An order, a plea, a belief?

'FOR I FELT THAT YOU BELIEVED ME INNOCENT'

Adelaide seems to reveal so much to Clarke in so few words. She does not write that she is innocent, only that she felt he believed she was – and that was exactly what she wanted him to believe, obviously. She will admit she has not been good; she glances back to terrible temptations, her vows left behind.

Adelaide is strong in some ways (as emphasised in court by Russell). She has confidence in Mr Clarke, believes he is merciful. She ends her letter by showing it – and telling him what to do: 'you will judge me mercifully'.

DYSON TO DO LAW?

Newspapers found plenty more to say about the case, just days after the verdict. On 19 April the *Evening News* – apparently with no sense of irony – suggested Dyson would 'in all probability' study law, but only after a good rest abroad.

'THE TREMENDOUS ENTHUSIASM WHICH THE LADY'S ACQUITTAL EVOKED'

On 25 April in the *Referee*, the column 'Mustard And Cress' emphasised that the Jury decided 'there was no proof that the fair Adelaide, or rather the dark Adelaide, had given her husband the fatal dose', adding that the most mysterious part about the Pimlico Mystery was 'the tremendous enthusiasm which the lady's acquittal evoked'.

'HER METHODIST MASHER'

Dyson was depicted as 'her Methodist masher' (a 'masher' at that time meant a man who made sexual advances) whom she sent to buy chloroform for her to make her husband 'insensible'. The chloroform 'purchased by Dyson got in some mysterious way a little further than Mr Bartlett's nose … To say the least of it, a lady who looks upon herself as sacred to another man during her husband's lifetime is hardly a heroine to be applauded to the skies'.

And the columnist (presumably male) added that 'Mrs Bartlett has beautiful eyes, and is an interesting young woman. I think this, and the disgusting, cowardly conduct of the man Dyson, went a long way towards making Mr Clarke's task a comparatively light one'.

This columnist found it difficult to believe that Mr Bartlett could have administered chloroform to himself, got onto the bed again and died,

'... all without attracting his wife's attention sufficiently to make her ring the bell and call for assistance. If Mr Bartlett wasn't chloroformed by somebody else, he chloroformed himself, and how he did it is now 'the Pimlico Mystery'.

The writer turned to the acquitted. 'Mrs Bartlett is proved innocent. No word must ever be said against her again'. (Yet here we are, all these years later, still thinking, writing and reading about the mystery.)

'She disappears from the case, and when we argue it out in the future we must confine ourselves to finding out how and why Mr Bartlett elected to swallow the chloroform obtained with so much cunning and duplicity by the dreadful Dyson. It was at least unfortunate that the means of suicide for the unhappy man should have been provided by this new Tartuffe'.

Tartuffe, a character in the famous comedy of the same name (meaning 'Impostor') by Molière, first performed in 1664. The word 'Tartuffe' is still used for a hypocrite who feigns virtue, particularly of a religious nature. The columnist's use of 'Tartuffe' was extremely apt in the context of the triangle of Edwin, Adelaide and Dyson. In *Tartuffe* the husband, Orgon, was full of admiration for Tartuffe and trusting of Tartuffe's attentions to Orgon's wife, Elmire.

'Mustard And Cress' returned to commenting on Adelaide and women, in that '... the moral seems to me that injured innocence stands a much better chance of being vindicated when it is young, pretty, and of the female sex'.

SWITCHING THE ROLES OF MR AND MRS B
The columnist strode into the realm of suppositions, turning the case on its head for a completely different perspective: imagining how it would look if the accused spouse had been a MAN.

'Suppose ... that Mrs Bartlett had arranged that at her decease her husband should marry a young and pretty governess who was in the habit of spending the day with him when Mrs B was out – who called him by his Christian name, wrote him erotic poetry, and confessed that she was madly in love with him. Suppose it was proved that the governess went out, and by telling a lot of lies procured chloroform at three different shops, and brought it home to Mr B.

'Suppose one night Mrs B, having ordered a haddock for her breakfast the next morning, was found dead, being at the time alone in her room with Mr B. Suppose in Mrs B's inside was found some of the chloroform which the girl Mr Bartlett was going to marry on his wife's decease had purchased.

'If you can suppose all this you have turned the Pimlico Mystery upside down, and all you have to ask yourselves is "Would Mr Bartlett have been enthusiastically cheered when the jury said that he wasn't guilty?"

'I make these remarks not to dispute the verdict for a moment ... My only object in re-arguing the case is to show that injured innocence has a better chance when it is a pretty young woman than when it is a plain, middle-aged man, and that sentiment has a great deal to do with public opinion'.

A perceptive piece. Then back, acidly, to Dyson.

'Rev Masher, it is announced, is to quit religion and study for the Bar ... One thing is to be hoped sincerely, and that is, if he ever goes courting again it won't be a lady whose husband is still alive ... and that he will be careful, if he does get into the confidence of a married couple, not to supply the wife with a wholesale quantity of chloroform'.

'Mustard And Cress', not yet finished with the case and taking a detour, waxed lyrical.

'The other night I was attracted by a crowd at the corner of Oxford Street, surrounding a young girl who was singing in a voice which must have been distinctly audible at one and the same time at the Marble Arch and Holborn Bars. I never heard such a voice in my life – you could hear the drums of the bystanders' ears breaking whenever she stopped between the verses. She was singing from a broadsheet of songs … for copies of which she asked one penny'.

First of all, she sang 'Harbour Lights'. He continued: 'Imagine my surprise, when that song was concluded, at hearing the young woman strike up:

'The Lights o' London'
'While lying thinking on my pillow,
My thoughts I could not resist:
That half the world, while they live in splendour,
They don't know how the rest exist.
They don't know half the poor man's troubles,
They don't care how he's trodden down,
They treat his care like any bubbles
Beneath the Lights o' London town.'

CHORUS:

'You'll say these words are truly spoken –
There are troubles that are never known
And many a heart's in secret broken
Beneath the Lights o' London town.'[155]

'Mustard And Cress' continued:

'I waited when the song was over, expecting this Patti of the Pavement to strike up 'In the Ranks' or 'The Romany Rye' or 'Mother-in-Law', but she didn't. She said: "Look 'ere, ladies and genelman, I've got a proper song 'ere wot I'll sing yer. It's called 'The Pimerlico Mystery; or, The Wicked Parson'." And then this Diva of the Ditch, this Tietjens of the Turnpike-road, this Grisi of the Gutter, this Malibran of the Macadam, struck up a merry ditty concerning a recent case and the 'naughty parson who taught her how to wrong and how to write' – which was slightly cerulean and extensively tepid – and just as the young ladies in the audience (it was 11 pm) were beginning to giggle and titter like the ladies in court upon which Mr Justice Wills so heavily seated himself, a stalwart sergeant came along, and the serio-comic star of the streets, the Albani of the Asphalte, the Prima Donna of the Queen's Highway, was "moved on", and I heard no more'.

'Mustard And Cress', astonished by the volume of the performance by the youngster, compared her with some fine singers of the era. Whether this was admiration or ridicule need not be decided.[156]

And we leave that spirited young woman singing away on a corner in Oxford Street, the street where Edwin senior lived at the time of his son's death.

'THREE OR FOUR VERY COMMONPLACE PERSONS'

Two days after the verdict a leading newspaper, The Times, was critical of some recent juries that had announced a rider to verdicts. However, the paper's view was that in the case of Adelaide Bartlett it considered the Foreman's statement understandable and excusable, saying it was or ought to be, a verdict of 'not guilty'; how Mr Bartlett 'met his death the Jury do not know'.

The paper was snobbish about the key players, describing the Pimlico Mystery as 'a mystery still … Three or four very commonplace persons are actors in it, and they weave a plot which in all probability will never be unravelled'.[157]

The Times did not state which 'three or four' people, but assume that two were Adelaide and Dyson. The third might be the late Edwin, but perhaps not; the paper may have meant the actors were alive rather than dead. It is likely that Edwin senior was in mind. He, as far as is known, fits the bill of ordinariness. But from what is now known (and you will soon see about the former reverend) Adelaide and Dyson were definitely unusual people. It is likely too that there was much more to Edwin than just his allegedly conventional views. However the Judge, for one, could make neither head nor tail of Edwin. Dr Leach, for instance, had not helped the Judge know what made Edwin tick.

The Times was incorrect in its analysis; the key players were not 'commonplace' at all.

And Dr Leach was something else again.

Chapter 33

DOCTOR ALFRED LEACH

For everyone in court during Adelaide's Trial, searching for evidence within Dr Leach's words was like desperately panning for gold. Water running through, stones left behind, precious few nuggets. The absolutely reasonable expectation was that Leach, as a professional man, would give his evidence in a concise and clear manner. But hopes were soon dashed.

'I WAS DEALING WITH NO CRIMINAL'

Less than a week after Adelaide's acquittal, a newspaper[158] printed excerpts from Dr Leach's 'long letter to a contemporary' about Adelaide. Firstly 'concerning the disappearance of the fatal bottle of chloroform and his not searching the room thoroughly'. Dr Leach had 'suspected no foul play. I was dealing with no criminal. Had I suspected, I should have searched nowhere; I should simply have advised the landlord to send for the police to make a thorough search at once'.

Yet he knew that by her removal of the bottle, 'an innocent woman must have laid herself open to the gravest suspicion'. He supposed that Mrs Bartlett noticed the bottle on the mantelpiece and put it 'out of sight – probably into her pocket. A tale hangs to that chloroform she does not desire to make public in the interests of herself, her husband and others'.

'VERY IMPRUDENT PRUDENCE'

For weeks in January 1886, Dr Leach had asserted that it was probably chlorodyne not chloroform which killed Edwin. His amateur and incorrect assessment led to Adelaide keeping *schtum* about the purchased and used chloroform. The doctor described her as acting 'from very imprudent prudence … to keep both from me and others her secret, until the analyst shall have spoken'. The phrase 'imprudent prudence' was an obscure way of voicing his belief in Adelaide's innocence.

'TOO STRONG A FOOD FOR THE DIGESTION OF A BRITISH JUDGE AND HIS JURY'

On 24 April, a letter from the irrepressible doctor about the Bartletts was printed in the *Westminster Times*. Obfuscation and generalisation, an exasperating read. Dr Leach, expressing an intention to write 'one word concerning the dead man', wrote many – among which he gave just one concrete example of what his patient said or did.

'I may state that there are undisclosed facts in this case too strange for belief by any but eye-witnesses, and though all within my knowledge are distinctly evidence in favour of Mrs Bartlett, her legal advisers evidently considered them too strong a food for the digestion of a British judge and his jury. In one respect experience has justified their opinion. This much I feel it a duty to state in vindication of my patient's widow. In conclusion, one word concerning the dead man. Much has been written in the papers and much said from the Bench tending to present the late Edwin Bartlett in a very odious light.

'I knew him only during the last twenty-one days of his life; I must state that he was not so black as he has been painted. He was a man of the most extraordinary ways and ideas, and since his death we have all learnt that his ideas were stranger than even I knew them to be. He was shy and reticent, especially before strangers, but once he believed in anybody his belief became an implicit faith, and to use a metaphor, his whole heart seemed to go out to them, and his gratitude for trifles was unbounded. There was, too, something peculiarly "taking" in him, and, although a self-made man, he was retiring, diffident, and in no sense unmannerly. I confess that, with all his oddity, I took more than an ordinary interest in the welfare of my late patient.'

What was all that about? Dr Leach's words gave with one hand and took away with the other. After his vague, verbose evidence-giving, the doctor hinted at his patient's 'oddity' without offering up specific words to describe how Mr Bartlett's 'ways and ideas' seemed so 'extraordinary'.

It sounds as though Dr Leach continued believing the story of Adelaide being 'given' to Dyson and in thinking Edwin's ideas on marriage (and mesmerism too?) actually were 'extraordinary'. Was Edwin just very different from anyone else whom young Dr Leach had encountered? The letter referred to Edwin's trusting nature – 'once he believed in anybody his belief became an implicit faith' – but without mentioning that Edwin's trusting nature could explain his faith in Dyson having honourable intentions towards Adelaide.

Perhaps Adelaide picked up a newspaper and read Dr Leach's abstract portrait of her late husband that day, before penning her thank you letter. Her letter, not to the doctor, to her life-saver, Mr Clarke.

The *South Wales Echo* on 29 April had a correspondent's interview of Dr Leach, who described himself as 'a great admirer of Mrs Bartlett's courage' and said how she boasted to him that she 'had more than once pinned a mad dog ... before which a crowd of men was flying, and either succoured the poor beast or held him till he was secure.' When Dr Leach asked if she was weary, after sitting up with her husband night after night, she replied: 'I have nursed a sick St Bernard puppy for six weeks. Surely I should not flinch when instead of a dog I have my husband.' The latter phrase gives food for thought.

Dr Leach spoke of admiring her 'pluck' and felt that her 'calm unostentatious nerve under the most desperate provocatives to fear, and her self-abnegation are amazing.' He certainly had a way with words, but it had not served him or others well in court; it created frustration and confusion.

'Two hours after her acquittal I called upon her to proffer my congratulations.'

Apparently Adelaide did not talk about herself; she was sorry for 'poor Mr Dyson' and 'how pained she was whenever Mr Clarke or the judge said unkind things about him'.

So either Adelaide cared about Dyson – or was shedding crocodile tears. Dr Leach, succinct for once – but probably wrong in saying 'she pities rather than blames him.'

He moved on to the subject of Edwin's character, starting by damning him with faint praise: Edwin was 'not half so bad as he was described at the trial', then generalising.

'He was odd and eccentric beyond all measure; but he had many amiable qualities, and was keen, intelligent, and even interesting when not in the presence of strangers. There was, indeed, something that made people like him.'

Dr Leach's words throw some positive light on Edwin; however, by not mentioning specifics he left most of the man behind a closed door. Of Dyson: he took to Mr Bartlett, and 'a real friendship existed between them.' (If so, it was a friendship in parallel with Dyson's inappropriate relationship with the man's wife.)

'HIS ABSURD CRAZE'

Dr Leach continued, adamant that Dyson was drawn by degrees 'into the absurd situation disclosed in the evidence and found himself entangled before he had time to consider how it all came about. I don't mean that Mrs Bartlett took any active part. It was her husband who determined to work out his absurd craze.'

The entangled Reverend, the passive Adelaide and the blamed Edwin. That was how Dr Leach could have put it, in just a few words.

WAX

Look at the public exhibits that Easter of 1886: Adelaide Bartlett and George Dyson. On show at Reynold's Waxworks in Lime Street, Liverpool. Models on display, gawked at by the curious, who wanted their money's worth after forking out for the entrance fee.

One wonders whether the wax models bore any resemblance to the humans – and how long Adelaide and George stayed out front before being removed, melted down, then the wax returned to the limelight, channelling the next notorious set of characters.[159]

Taking stock, one can say Adelaide probably felt Edwin was, at best, stolid and rather boring as the years passed by. Ultimately too that she found him repulsive, particularly by the winter of 1885. For whatever reason, he had made his unconventional choice of partner; they shared a small range of interests, including the breeding of very large dogs and the reading of the Nichols' esoteric works, and evidence in court from some was that the couple seemed happy – before December, at least. But in essence he was a grocer, with the essential routines and steady habits provisioning required of him. Adelaide felt frustrated and at a loose end. Leach felt that Edwin was extraordinary – but perhaps the fact that he felt convinced that things Edwin said were 'preposterous' shows how he misread his patient's vulnerable and pathetic situation that December.

The doctor viewed Adelaide as merely a dedicated and over-solicitous carer, nursing a hypochondriac – not as a danger to her husband.

Dr Leach's stance seems astonishing in that it absolves Adelaide of responsibility and attributes to Edwin an 'absurd craze' – Leach at his infuriatingly vague and sweeping worst. Bearing in mind that he spent so much time with Edwin during his patient's worst days (and reflected from 1 January upon the possible cause of death) Dr Leach's evidence would have had great weight IF he gave facts about Edwin rather than teasers.

Although there was criticism of Dr Leach at the Inquest and in the two courts, there was some 'sympathy' from Clarke: an acknowledgement of the complexities presented by the Bartletts to the doctor. And recognition from Russell, acknowledgement that the doctor had been 'most anxious to give full information to the Jury and to the Coroner' concerning the key witness.

Russell added that Dr Leach, 'under that crust and appearance of self-consciousness', answered questions 'without favour on one side or the other.'

'EVER DARING IN HIS DUTY'

Sadly, but unsurprisingly, the high level of curiosity and dedication Dr Leach exhibited as a doctor in 1886 brought about his demise in September 1892 when he was only thirty-five years old. Reports were of him as one of the most prominent witnesses in 'the Pimlico Mystery' and how it was to him 'that both husband and wife made those startling confidences, the repetition of which gave the trial its chief sensation. Dr Leach was killed a few days ago by inhaling sewer gas whilst investigating the causes of a patient's diphtheria. He was ever daring in his duty ...'.[160]

The obituary in *The British Medical Journal* fleshed out the man, revealing that he had written a book, the *Letter H*, concerning pronunciation and the aspirate. 'He was a good linguist, speaking Arabic, Italian, and French.' [161]

Chapter 34

ADIEU, TO YOU AND YOU AND YOU

In her book *Edwin, Adelaide & George: The Bizarre Bartlett Poisoning*,[162] Jeannette Hensby posits that Edwin was gay, attracted to Dyson. Edwin seemed to have just male friends, but such is the way for many men. Edwin and Dyson took a day trip to Calais when the Bartletts were staying in Dover. The two men wrote fulsomely to one another in September 1885, for instance – but florid prose was not unusual for those times. Precious little is known about their friendship or about Edwin's relationships with other men (apart from the very regular contact between father and son) although there are facts and opinions which were provided by his friends to the newspapers, to try to mitigate misrepresentation of the late Edwin.

'SHE SHOULD TELL US IN THE INTERESTS OF SCIENCE ...'
Adelaide the enigma; bored but never dull, complex and quixotic, mysterious and mystifying; innocent or guilty?

The Chief Justice of England, Lord Coleridge, wrote to Clarke about Adelaide, attributing to the esteemed surgeon and pathologist Sir James

Paget a wry comment along the lines of 'now that she's been acquitted and can't be tried again, she should tell us in the interests of science how she did it!'

Linda Stratmann, in *Chloroform: The Quest for Oblivion* offers a solution. In the chapter 'The Crime of Adelaide Bartlett', Stratmann describes the case as the 'most celebrated chloroform crime ever'. Her use of the word 'crime': she regarded it as a crime, not as a case of suicide? Read her book, with its suggested solution, and ponder ...

HEADGEAR

Back to the third so-called 'commonplace' person. The unworldly Dyson was by no means 'commonplace'; his metamorphosis – another astonishing story – will be revealed later. Meanwhile a prosaic titbit: the Reverend was in north Wales at Easter and someone bothered to tell a columnist about his attire, Dyson having 'almost completely dropped his clerical garb. I suppose he affects the same costume as that adopted at the Old Bailey in the latter days of the trial. First of all he appeared in severe Wesley-like headgear, but in a day or two he found it expedient to drop the broad brim altogether and adopt the useful collapsible polo'.[163] A 'polo' hat: a softer version of a helmet-shaped piece of headgear worn when on horseback playing polo.

Dyson had entered the Trial as prisoner on trial, the 'Preacher On Trial', wearing the hat of his religion. As key witness, he came back down to earth under a collapsible hat; perhaps it symbolised his state of mind. Or was it a ploy, presenting himself as a humble person? Someone likely to lose his Methodist living – if not his religion.

'PURE FICTION'

It seems doubtful, with such huge public interest and her distinctive looks, that Adelaide would have stayed in Britain after Edwin's money was available to her through his Will.

On 1 May 1886 the *Northampton Mercury* declared that although Mrs Bartlett 'felt the severe strain upon her, the story of her subsequent illness and hasty departure from England is, so far as I can learn, pure fiction. Mrs Bartlett is lying *perdu* [sic – should be *perdue*] in or near London, and will not depart hence until she has seen the last of her law suits'.

EDWIN'S WILL: PROVED

The failure of Edwin senior's *caveat* against Edwin's Will led on 12 May 1886 to the Will being proved at the Principal Registry by (it's that man again) Edward Negus Wood, solicitor. Edwin's Personal Estate was £3,858.16s. 6d (in old money three thousand, eight hundred and fifty-eight pounds, sixteen shillings and sixpence).

Finances secured, did Adelaide feel the world was her oyster? Or would she go forth with much trepidation?

On 29 May a weekly comic magazine, *Ally Sloper's Half Holiday*, trumpeted that Adelaide was living in Brighton under an assumed name – which would not give her anonymity, as 'the photographers have been too busy to give her much chance of escaping recognition'.

The comic-strip character Ally Sloper (who sloped around alleys, picking up gossip) asked the readers, in French:

'Où est, Dyson?'

So, where was Dyson? He had headed to the north of England, back to parts he knew as a younger, carefree man.[164]

HAVING IT IN FOR THE JUDGE: A LETTER FROM DYSON

Dyson sat down in Breedon House at Goole (an inland port town in Yorkshire) on 10 June 1886, wrote a long rebuttal and sent it to the *St Stephen's Review*, a weekly journal.[165]

Dyson's letter was taken up by many newspapers, filling an entire column. Primarily a response to the general outcry against him – 'the cause' of which, said he indignantly, was the summing-up at the Trial. (He had it in for Mr Justice Wills, the Judge.)

LETTER TO THE EDITOR

'Dear Sir – It is probable that by this time I have heard the utmost the world has to say against me. It is never its custom to condemn a man unheard, and, as I have never yet spoken, I feel emboldened, in the name of common justice, and that inherent chivalry upon which, as a people, we pride ourselves – the supposed lack of which has brought such unanimous censure upon me – to ask permission to speak a word in self-defence through your column.

'Your journal is, as far as my knowledge goes – the fact has only just come to my knowledge – the solitary exception to the 'universal howl' that went round the Press against me; and its few words in my defence furnish the condition upon which I had determined that the question of my speaking out, or silence, should depend.

'When, on the Monday after the trial, I read the leading articles of a few London dailies, I saw that the inevitable had happened, and that the outcry bid fair to be general. This did not surprise me; it was the natural effect from an efficient cause – and the cause was the summing-up of Mr Justice Wills.

'Previous to that, from the very day of my arrest, throughout the protracted magisterial inquiry, and up to the last day of the trial, I received abundant evidence of a growing and widely-extended sympathy, not with my follies, but with my misfortunes, and because of the atrocious charge that lay against me. This was strengthened by the fact that the weary spinning out of the inquiry at the police court merely served, so far as it touched my evidence, to establish its truthfulness, even to detail.

'But in one short hour the tide of feeling turned madly against me, not – and I say it with emphasis – not upon the facts (for the facts were the same) – but upon the *interpretation* of the facts that Mr Justice Wills was pleased to make.

'Mr Editor, it is ever an ungracious task to have to defend oneself, especially when one has a conviction that it is an attempt to overcome prejudice with reason. Though I am glad to feel that in anything I may say with regard to his Lordship's strictures, I am considering the well-weighed words of one who by his position was, of course, placed infinitely beyond the bias of prejudice or dislike, for "Brutus is an honourable man."

'And if I sometimes feel that even in my case he "erred on the side of severity", I take comfort from the reflection that "he is wise and honourable, and could, no doubt, with reasons answer me."

'On even a cursory view of the summing-up, it is evident that my offences, in his Lordship's eyes, were these:

I. That the case against me was dismissed.

II. The possibility, in his judgment [sic], amounting to certainty, that I committed perjury in the effort to shield myself.

III. That I exhibited a want of chivalry, because I did not close my lips and refuse to give evidence.

IV. That his Lordship, because the Crown refused to prosecute on such trivial evidence, should visit his disappointment upon me, seems to me a little unreasonable – for how could I help it. If it was a blunder, as he evidently thought, it was not my blunder. Indeed it was the issue of all others that I dreaded most; and the Newgate authorities, from the Governor downwards, could testify to the bitter mortification with which I received my discharge.

'By Mr Justice Wills's gracious admission, I am "no fool" and so could not fail to see that by such a course I was placed in an invidious position, and the way prepared for that bitter animus which his lordship unconsciously fanned to a white heat.

'That the Crown should have kept me so long under the odium of the capital charge, exposing me to the mercy of witnesses who betrayed no small amount of animus, and then at the eleventh hour have thrust me into a position, in which I was deprived of all power of defence, either by myself (with due deference to his Lordship) or by my counsel: this I say, was needless cruelty, and if Mr Justice Wills had possessed a trace of the chivalry, with the lack of which he taunted me, he would at least, considering my position, have spared himself the trouble of that little imaginary trial, in which he suggested how hardly it would have gone with me if, &c, &c.

'If it was a disappointment to him, because the biting epithets which he had prepared during that "careful consideration" of the case before he had heard it, could not be thrown at me in the dock, it was unfortunate for the dignity of his position that he should manifest that disappointment, by casting them at me when, as he significantly expressed, "by my acquittal I had been transferred from the dock to the witness box."

'With regard to the second intimation to the effect that where my evidence was not corroborated by other witnesses, it must be received with very great caution. Mr Justice Wills has answered himself. For it so happened that wherein my evidence could be tested by that of other witnesses it was invariably confirmed; and it does not need even the thirty years' experience in judging of probabilities which Mr Justice Wills announced had been his, to show that such being the case, my evidence, where it could not be compared, was by every probability equally reliable. I say that this was an altogether gratuitous assumption that does violence to the facts of the case; and it could only have been guaranteed by such a contradiction on the evidence itself as never appeared.

'The third charge, insinuation, or whatever it should rightly be called, viz., that of want of chivalry, seems to me, considering the position of the speaker and the gravity of the case, simply preposterous. To say that "in giving evidence I gave no trace of chivalry", is to fling out one of those specious catch-phrases that (as the event showed) are admirably calculated to raise a popular fury, but which, to say the least, sound oddly coming from the Judicial Bench. For, translated into plain English, that word in such a context means simply this: that in a case of such a kind, where there is a woman concerned, it is the duty of the witness either to close his lips altogether, or to distort the facts in her favour, or to conceal any evidence that might damage her case. Explain or twist his Lordship's statement as I may, I somehow cannot get away from this conclusion. So that in one breath I am charged with perjury, and in the next censured for speaking the truth.

'Now, I ask any impartial person to consider my evidence, and say whether from the beginning to end there is the slightest effort to raise any prejudice against the other party in the case.

'But more closely, I deny that my evidence is at all open to the suspicion of being "partial" or "adulterated by motive". If I was accessory, every word that damaged Mrs Bartlett reacted equally upon myself. Being "no fool", I clearly saw that, and the fact had been duly impressed upon me by my legal adviser.

'Moreover, it may be interesting to some of my censors to know, that when I stood up to give evidence before the Coroner, I carried in my pocket a letter from one of the jury, warning me of the probable issue, and telling me that a bitter animus pervaded the minds of the jury, which he was endeavouring to allay. Yet, with that cheerful fact before me, I did not hesitate to state such facts as that I had thrown away the bottles, or that the chloroform was given to Mrs Bartlett without Mr B's knowledge, two *prima facie* damaging facts that could never have been known but for my voluntary admission.

'If, as he affirmed, it was my determination that "the Rev G Dyson should suffer as little as possible" by this inquiry, I would ask Mr Justice Wills how he reconciles the above fact with his generous estimate of my character.

'In conclusion, I do not hesitate to say that the course I took in the matter, in not refusing to subject myself to cross-examination in the witness box was favourable, rather than prejudicial, to Mrs Bartlett.

'Let any who doubt this ask themselves what would have been the result if the two chief actors, or those who are considered to be the two chief actors, in this case, had both refused to open their lips, or submit to be questioned, as to their share in it?

'I commend this question to Mr Justice Wills's "thirty-years' experience" and the clear and unbiassed [sic] judgment [sic] with which it has enriched him.

GEORGE DYSON, BA'

Dyson's venting of feelings was sniffed at by the *Manchester Evening News* (18 June).

'We should have thought that the Rev George Dyson would have desired to withdraw … for a season from the public ken, but it seems we were mistaken. Since the celebrated trial, he has been writing under the stinging words of the judge whose summing-up entered deeply into the soul of the Crown witness. What seems to have affected him more than anything is that doubt was thrown on his word, and that he should be charged with lack of chivalry … Mr Dyson's letter will not alter public opinion in respect of his conduct, and he would have displayed more wisdom if he had kept in retirement.'

Dyson put the blame on the Judge, primarily on his summing-up. No mention of Dyson's own responsibility in the matter, by purchasing an unusually large amount of chloroform from three chemists, lying when he did so. In the letter he calls those actions his 'follies'; feels sorry for himself, for his 'misfortunes'. He describes the evidence as 'trivial'. He comes across as arrogant. The only reference to the deceased is in his phrase: 'without Mr B's knowledge'. Dyson is not even respectful enough to give the name of the man he had called his friend: Edwin Bartlett. As an alternative view, consider that Dyson dissociates himself from the death in order not to be subsumed.

Dyson's letter, with its emphatic, self-confident style, can soon be compared with his literary efforts in later life.

The Wesleyan Conference would meet that July; attendees discuss Dyson and decide his fate. How he must have continued squirming at his plight! Raging privately about his situation – a bad one, even though he was a free man.

That month, the lawyer Edward Beal (at Edward Clarke's request) edited and produced the report of the Trial. Its Preface was written by Clarke, who acknowledged the respective contributions, including those from Mr Justice Wills (revision of the report of his summing-up); Charles Russell (opening speech and reply); Mr Sidney Plowman of St Thomas' Hospital (supervised the report's medical references).

Clarke's hope was that the volume would be found useful by students studying the administration of law. It covered 12–17 April 1886; Adelaide and Dyson in the dock and the subsequent Trial of Adelaide Bartlett.[166]

WHITHER ADELAIDE?

Where did Adelaide go, when she had the money? Perhaps she changed her name, or parts of it; perhaps she left England for ever. On SS Liguria, a steamship leaving London in 1887 for a voyage to Australia (via Plymouth, Devon) was 'Madame de Thouars', age 38, a 'foreigner' (ie not English/'Scotch'/Irish). The ship docked at Adelaide, then at Melbourne, where Madame was due to disembark before the ship continued to Sydney. Did Madame de Thouars, whoever she was, actually stay on board until Sydney? In the summer of 1888, advertisements were placed by a Madame de Thouars in the *Sydney Morning Herald* newspaper,. For example on 3 August: 'MADAME DE THOUARS, Dressmaker and Milliner, just arrived from Paris. Charges moderate, 143 Phillip-st.' Subsequent adverts were for her French bonnets and hats at one guinea each. And she was still at that address in 1889, listed in the Sands Directory [see Sands Directories, Sydney and New South Wales, Australia, 1858-1933]. So, who was this Madame de Thouars and where did she go? *Does anyone know?*

OSCAR WILDE

A change of focus …. In 1895, Sir Edward Clarke was the lawyer for Oscar Wilde in his court appearances. Adelaide's Judge, Mr Justice Wills, presided over the final trial of Wilde: 'one of the most sensational trials ever held at the Old Bailey'.[167]

He sentenced Wilde to two years' hard labour.

DEATH OF WILLIAM CHAMBERLAIN

Adelaide's Uncle William's unusually long and highly successful career in the city was acknowledged in many newspapers when he died – thirteen years after Edwin Bartlett - on 7 January 1899 at Shortlands, Kent. He was seventy-seven. William worked for almost sixty years at the London Stock Exchange and must have 'enjoyed good health' as the saying goes. Respected by his colleagues, they penned fulsome testimonials.

One can see that Edwin Bartlett's work ethic, application and dedication would have found favour with William – and vice versa. Whether Uncle William put pressure on Adelaide, or on Edwin, to marry is not known; now spare a thought for him. He had to endure the distress of Edwin's sudden death, the many months of strain and newspaper coverage. William Chamberlain kept away from any publicity and all the press furore, but surely read with horror about the Inquest, the police court appearances and Adelaide's Trial.

PART NINE
TIME FOR GEORGE DE THOUARS

Chapter 35

A STICK-UP AND A LOCK-UP

FAREWELL FREDDY

When Freddy recited the following lines as a young schoolboy in 1869, did he long to travel the world?

'Secondly, tell me, without any doubt,
How soon I may ride the whole world about.

'You must rise with the sun, and ride with the same,
Until the next morning he riseth again;
And then your grace need not make any doubt,
But in twenty-four hours you'll ride it about.'

Freddy de Thouars, Adelaide's younger brother, took on both lengthy roles in 'King John and the Abbot [sic] of Canterbury' (Anonymous, Olde English). Clever, confident Freddy.

After 1871, he was not heard of again in England. Soon he went halfway around 'the whole world'. And when there, he *would* ride a horse.

HELLO GEORGE

Circumstantial evidence points strongly to Frederick George, Freddy, having transformed into George Gustave, known as George de Thouars, arriving in Melbourne, Victoria, south-eastern Australia. In 1872, George was on the same ship from England as landowner John King, who offered him work at Nambrok. It was a property with a house, worker accommodation, farm buildings and some 13,000 acres, a few miles from Rosedale, Victoria. King was one of those involved in the early years of what was termed 'pastoral leasehold settlement'.

That phrase wrongly ignores the taking-over of huge areas of Australia by white people – and the dispossession and slaughter of huge numbers of the population, the First Nations Australians. The Ancestors and Elders, past, present and emerging and all the First Nations people, Custodians of the country (including what is today called 'Gippsland') are hereby acknowledged and accorded due respect.

After Nambrok, George worked at a coal yard and then as a tanner in south Gippsland and Broadford, north of Melbourne. Did he ever hear from Henry Edward or from his sister? Did he know about Adelaide's marriage?

Then he made 'work' for himself, advertising locally, inviting people to send stamps to the Post Office, promising that by return he would send details of a way to make their fortunes. When the spotlight was cast on his scheme a few years later, a suspicion in the neighbourhood was that George had sold the stamps, aiming to make his fortune – rather than telling others how they could get rich. However, the scheme/scam did not work out to his advantage. He may have been warned off …

It is January 1880 and the twenty-two-year-old stands five feet seven inches tall, has very white teeth, black curly hair and bow legs. Surely the young, self-styled 'George De Thouars' feels pleased with how he looks? Handsome, smart and bright.

'ANOTHER BUSHRANGING OUTRAGE'

The main article in the Melbourne *Age* on 17 January 1880 featured a 'French half-caste'. The second article called him 'Black George', who on 15 January called at Holey Plain (as it was then called, now Plains; seven miles from Rosedale) where he had been employed by the Crooke family. The area may have been called Holey Plain because of the holes made either by 'yabbies' (crayfish-type crustaceans) living in the waters there, or by carts causing wheel ruts.

George had been dismissed for alleged 'deceit' at Toorak (where the Crookes had a house) - or was it for leaving the place unattended when he should have been guarding it? Or for 'keeping company with magsmen' [confidence tricksters] or 'being with swindlers at the races'? The newspapers weren't sure which, if any, of the alleged misdemeanours applied.

Now George was out looking for Edward Jolley Crooke,[168] who managed the family properties and staff for his widowed mother. Reporters thought George (some three years older than Edward) envied the son's privileged position. Staff told George that Mr Crooke would arrive there some days later; George did not believe them. Thinking that Mr Crooke was responsible for his dismissal, he shouted out on several occasions during the day that he would shoot him. Allegedly, after George had been to the men's quarters, he took one or two women into a room in the main house (ie away from the men) and said he would shoot them too. This sounds deadly serious. Jolly frightening.

The police had a photograph of him. Not part of a police record – he did not have such a thing.

THE CHRISTY CONNECTIONS

It is likely that George's photo had been handed out as part of the publicity for the Christy Minstrels, a 'black face' troupe, back when he was a member of that travelling troupe in the area. They performed in Sale, a town in the Gippsland region of Victoria. Remember Freddy swaggering onto the stage, singing with aplomb in the Christmas entertainments at the English School in Hampton Wick village? The thought of George onstage with the Christy Minstrels in Australia takes us, amazingly, full circle back to Freddy in 1870, singing Stephen Foster's minstrel song 'Massa'.

And hark back to the original Christy's, formed in 1843 by Edwin Pearce Christy in New York.

When touring with the troupe in Australia around 1879, George was variously named as the Blossom, the Vinditti or Vidette (sentinel), the French boy, and (a fine compliment) the 'Maori Sims Reeves'. John Sims Reeves was the most famous English operatic and ballad tenor vocalist of the mid-Victorian era. George was a young man with a good tenor voice; Freddy as a schoolboy had been in excellent voice, singing and reciting for audiences. The Australian newspapers quoted George's stage-names and continued to describe him as French and a 'half-caste'. Photographs of Sims Reeves show him as a handsome man with dark eyes, dark moustache and wavy hair. George certainly resembled the famous English tenor.

Shockingly, here was 'George de Thouars' waving 'a six-chambered revolver' with which he persuaded seven people into a room. After locking the door he kept them there for many hours. At 2 a.m he made them swear not to tell on him until 9 a.m. He took a rifle, demanded a horse, food and water.

'SURRENDER OF DE THOUARS'

'He gave himself up on Tuesday, probably because he found the search becoming too warm for his safety'.

So said the *Gippsland Times* on 23 January, trying to take heat out of the outrage by adding that the matter came to 'a rather tame, not to say ludicrous climax, the offender having voluntarily surrendered himself' to Mrs Salter at the 'halfway house' on the road to Port Albert. George reminded Mrs Salter how kind she had been to him in the past when he worked in that area; she called out to her husband, and George handed his weapons to Mr Salter. George asked the couple for food, and read the newspaper accounts of his own exploits; he told them he disagreed with some details. Next morning, off he went with Mr Salter to Sale Police Station and gave himself up.

Young George's fate would now be in the hands of the law.

THE NED KELLY EFFECT

The prisoner was a 'mild looking, pleasant-spoken young man ... more the look of a respectable harvest man than a bushranger. He told his story in a frank and open manner'.[169]

The term 'bushranger' was originally used for those escaped convicts who hid in the Australian bush. The notorious Ned Kelly and his gang, sought for murders and bank robberies, were much on the minds of officials – and of the public, many of whom were petrified, others furious about the crimes and the methods used. Consequently those who were bushrangers (or seemed to be) risked heavy punishments.

Just as his father had been in the late 1840s, George was described as a Creole, one newspaper adding that he had 'an exceedingly swarthy countenance, quite justifying the assumption of a negro alloy'.[170] George insisted he was 'not a Creole, but a Frenchman of noble extraction.'

Under the name George Gustave de Thouars he was put before Mr English, JP, on 22 January 1880 at Sale Police Court. Remanded in custody for eight days and remanded again, he appeared at Sale Assize Court before Mr Justice Stephen and twelve Jurymen on 17 February. Charged with robbery under arms, George was unrepresented, because he had misunderstood the Judge's explanation about being entitled to have a lawyer. George pleaded not guilty, claiming he went to the Crookes' place to ask for harvesting work and to try to sell the revolver he carried for self-protection when selling jewellery.

Witnesses were called to give evidence against him and – as his father 'Henry Desbury' had done in 1848 and 1849 – George cross-examined them in an eloquent, confident manner. His stage presence and mastery of his case was clear; however, the evidence against him stacked up. Station overseer Arthur Stanner told the court that when they were in the men's quarters he asked George to leave. This uninvited visitor, losing his temper, held out a pistol. Not in charge of his emotions and being inexperienced, 'his pistol hand shook as with the ague', said Stanner. The story of that 'stick-up' day continued as evidence: young Tom Job was allegedly ordered by George to find 'the best horse on the station', mount it and to show him that it could gallop.

Mrs Crooke's sister, Mrs Chepmell, rushed out on to the verandah of the main house, grabbed a stick and tried a stand-off with de Thouars, but soon went back in and locked the door. George threatened to break it down with an axe – and was soon shown the way into the drawing room by another door! It might seem rather farcical, but was doubtless frightening (perhaps for George too, by that stage). George demanded that Mr Crooke's 'Henry' rifle be brought to him and, holding the gun to a man's head, he asked for and was given a quick lesson on how to use the 'Henry'.

Having shepherded the men into a hut, George blocked the doorway by lying across it, resting, until 1 a.m. He then rode off, but returned an hour later. Taking a Bible or prayer book from the hut, he got the seven men to swear on the book that they wouldn't leave or tell on him until 9 a.m. He made the folk at the homestead swear in the same way, then left the station on horseback.

One of the station men, David Rintoul, hurried into Rosedale at 6 a.m to raise the alarm. Senior Constable Keon wired 'the Chief Commissioner, Superintendent Kabat and all the chief police stations in Gippsland'. They began the tracking-down of de Thouars, who meantime had gone towards Longford and left the horse, with plenty of food and water, at Mrs Chepmell's.

FIFTEEN YEARS' IMPRISONMENT WITH HARD LABOUR

George de Thouars was found guilty and sentenced by Mr Justice Stephen to fifteen years' imprisonment with hard labour, as a deterrent to others – the Ned Kelly Gang effect. And whether there was prejudice against George on account of his colour or supposed ethnicity is not known. Noises of astonishment arose from many in court …

George and onlookers were not the only people shocked by the severity of the sentence and many in the community were stirred into at least thinking about action. All knew for certain that he would experience terribly harsh conditions during incarceration.

Did Freddy/George's siblings know about his imprisonment? Henry Edward, living in the same country …. were he and his brother in contact since arriving, in the previous decade, from England? If not, did the older brother read about this George character and think: that must be our Freddy? And, would they have contact with one another again, after George's lengthy imprisonment?

DETAILS OF PRISONER
No.18033 'DE THEUARS' [sic] George Gustave

'5' 5"; 10 st 7; date of birth: 1860. Native Place: Tours, France. Build: stout. Brown mark lower left arm. Lost part of little finger of left hand.

Religion: Wesleyan. Read or write: Both. "Per Superb to Melbourne in 1873, single, no relatives in this colony".

Sentence: 15 YEARS H.L. [Hard Labour] subject to a special case review.

Date of Conviction: 17.2.1880 [17 February 1880]

Sentence confirmed, namely 15 years H.L. Supreme Court, 5 May 1880.

Offence: Robbery under arms. Where and before whom tried: Sale Assize Court, Justice Stephen.

18.2.80 – ATTEMPTED TO HANG HIMSELF AT SALE GAOL.

On 3 March transferred to Melbourne Gaol; admission to Pentridge Prison on 5 March 1880.

Shouting in cell. 3 days S.C. [Solitary Confinement]

28.7.80 – Wilfully disabling himself. 7 days S.C.

10.9.80 – [?] papers [?]

16.10.80 – Class 2

24.7.82 – Insolence. [?] 2 days.

Insolence, 3 days S.C.

Attempting to abscond. 3 mos [months] H.L., first 14 days in S.C. With bread & water rations only.

20.2.86 "TO FREEDOM" See P.A. Book [Prison Account Book]. Cash 10/- [10/- : Ten shillings in silver coins, probably produced at the Melbourne Mint, which was part of the British Royal Mint.]'

[VPRS 515/P0000, Central Register For Male Prisoners 17912–18398 (1880) Prisoner: GEORGE GUSTAVE DE THEUARS, Vol 31 Page 124, Prisoner Number 18033]

As shown in his police/prisoner record, George tried to hang himself on 18 February 1880 in his cell, using torn-up strips of blanket to make a 'rope' and noose. He was unconscious when found by Sergeant Irwin, who called the assigned local doctor, Reid, to attend to the prisoner. George was visited by Superintendent Kabat, who had led part of the initial search for him after the stick-up. Kabat recounted afterwards that the prisoner 'declared he could have borne a sentence of death' but could not bear the thought of fifteen years in prison.[171]

Later that month a letter in the *Gippsland Times* from 'Humanity' of Rosedale asked: could nothing be done 'to secure some considerable mitigation of this terrible sentence?'. The newspaper did not let up in its support for young George, declaring that 'for eighteen hours seven people should have sheepishly obeyed his orders, eaten their meals and taken their sleep, without once finding an opportunity of disarming [him], evinces an almost incredible pusillanimity'. Lack of courage may be, but who can say?

One wonders, if it was thought relatively easy, why they did not overpower him – but perhaps in reality he terrified them. Was George's acting so good and/or his temper so bad that they were frightened stiff? And, after all, who would argue with a gun? The consequences of his behaviour, plus the deterrent effect intended by Judge Stephen, were that George received harsh punishment.

'DROPPED IN FOR THE PENALTY DUE TO OTHERS'

The *Gippsland Times'* editorial on 8 March 1880 described the 'unconscionably severe sentence upon a mere youth' who had 'dropped in for the penalty due to others, and society has taken the first offender who would colourably be indicted for bushranging as an atoning sacrifice for the misdeeds of others'. It called for a 'philanthropic gentleman' to prepare a 'Memorial' (a statement of facts, as the basis of a petition).

During June, the Reverend GW Kelly, 'Humanity', was said by the newspaper to be gaining signatures for said Memorial in support of George. It would be sent to the Governor in Council. The stated grounds of this petition were that George was a foreigner and had been unrepresented in court – whereas if he'd had a lawyer to call witnesses, they would have attested to his previous good character.

TEMPER

In the Memorial it was claimed that George, who had a revolver for protection when selling jewellery, went out to Holey Plains to try to sell it, was ordered off the station and lost his temper. The stick-up and hours of incident were followed by his cooling-down, leaving the stolen horse with food and water, stumbling around in the bush then surrendering via a woman.

By October 1881 the signatures of lawyers, ministers of religion, men of all classes – and even several of the Jurors from George's Trial – had been added to various petitions. In May these were presented to State Governor Phipps. His disappointing response was that when the prisoner had 'served some years of his sentence, a mitigation might be sought with more prospect of success'.

George must remain in prison. What next?

'HIS FOOLISH FREAK'

Five years on, George still in prison, suffering, brooding, working, reading, writing, counting down the days of fifteen years, was without hope. On 15 April 1885 the *Gippsland Times* had things to say on his behalf. 'The severity of the sentence' came when the Kellys 'were then in the full tide of their criminal career of murder and robbery' and that no more 'unlucky time could have been chosen by de Thouars for his foolish freak'.

'THE DE THOUARS INCIDENT'

On 3 August the newspaper printed a letter from 'Humanity'. This endorsed the articles about the 'unfortunate young man'' (on whose behalf people had put their names to petitions on at least four occasions) and reasoned that efforts for his release must, this time, 'originate in Sale or thereabouts'. 'Humanity' had read that Mrs Crooke of Holey Plains intended to pay for a Memorial window in the new church at Sale, 'in testimony of the worth of her deceased husband. If she is the Mrs Crooke of the De Thouars incident, would it not be a graceful, as well as a Christian act on her part, to set the example on his behalf?'

'Humanity' thus recommended that Mrs Crooke now support the efforts being made by hundreds of people to secure George de Thouars' release from Pentridge.

The wealthy landowner, John King (a grandson of Governor Philip Gidley King) featured in Freddy/George's life at various stages in the 1870s and 1880s.[172]

John King's letter, published by the *Argus* on 7 August 1885, showed his concern for and loyalty to his ex-employee. It stated that he was 'one of the few witnesses summoned' by George in 1880 – but not called upon, because George had misunderstood the Judge's question. The history that King gave in his letter was of the young man being on the 'same vessel' as King and his family arriving in Melbourne from England in 1872. George, became their servant, 'leaving by his own accord' after eighteen months.

King commented that during the 'Holey Plain' hold-up, George used much bad language – 'being a Gascon'. He was adamant that George's action was 'unpremeditated' and that his pistol was small, like 'a mere toy'. However, King's opinion was that the Petition (his name was one of over five hundred on it) should not have been presented so soon after 'the Kelly episode'. Now, five years on, John King considered it the right time to ask the Governor if he would reconsider George's harsh sentence.

Chapter 36

STRAIGHT OUT OF PENTRIDGE

George, released from suffering, walked free on Saturday 20 February 1886; his sister Adelaide sat newly locked up in England.

George de Thouars, not only a singer but also a skilled writer. In January 1887 he walked into a newspaper office – not armed with a gun, but rather with a penned account. The *Gippsland Times* in Sale soon announced that 'by way of assisting him, as he was short of funds, the proprietor of this journal purchased the right of first publication' of his narrative. It became 'A Peep into Pentridge'. George's journal had been 'found to be more interesting than first thought'.[173]

MORE THAN JUST 'A PEEP INTO PENTRIDGE'

The 'Peep' came out in two parts in the newspaper; those people unable to get a copy soon petitioned the *Gippsland Times* to issue it as a pamphlet. Instead, it was reprinted in full in the newspaper and George received an unnamed, probably small, sum of money for his work. His descriptions and insights concerning Pentridge Prison were impressive and had an impact on many readers. The *Melbourne Herald,* crusading on behalf of a prisoner for whom George was seeking help, reprinted the manuscript.

Source of the title of George's extended journal, 'A Peep into Pentridge', was not mentioned. It was adapted from the title of a work by renowned English orator, Henry Hunt, published in 1821: *A peep into a prison, or, The inside of Ilchester Bastille: dedicated, without permission, to William Hanning, esq., high sheriff, and the magistrates of the County of Somerset.*[174]

Henry 'Orator' Hunt was born at Upavon in the county of Wiltshire, England. A wealthy farmer, a radical who advocated parliamentary reform and repeal of the Corn Laws, his brilliance and passion as a public speaker helped carry the message of working-class people to national prominence. In 1820, Hunt was convicted of 'unlawful and seditious assembly' and locked up in His Majesty's Jail at Ilchester. There he wrote three volumes of memoirs, initiated a campaign for reform of the prison and issued a pamphlet against the insanitary conditions, abuse by staff and the 'unchecked immorality' among prisoners.[175]

Two formal inquiries were held into the running of Ilchester prison, one result being the removal of the Governor, William Bridle, from his post.

Why had Hunt landed up in 'Ilchester Bastille' as he called it? An estimated 80,000 people had gathered in the St Peter's Field area of Manchester on 16 August 1819 to hear him speak about parliamentary reform.

Magistrates ordered that Hunt must be arrested – and mounted cavalry officers were sent into the huge crowd to break up the meeting. Terrible events surrounded the attacks upon some of the huge crowd; it is thought that seventeen people died (although the exact number is not known) and many hundreds were seriously injured. The tragedy was called the 'Peterloo Massacre', solemnly mocking the cavalry who rode into the unarmed crowd, in the manner of the Battle of Waterloo (fought four years earlier). Hence: the Peterloo Massacre at St Peter's Field.[176]

Following his arrest, conviction and sentence, Henry Hunt's time at Ilchester prison led to his furious writing during incarceration. The conditions, which included insanitary, overcrowded cells and a lack of ventilation, were described in detail in his '*peep*', the Ilchester Bastille exposé.

From that background to Hunt's '*peep*', back now to George in the State of Victoria, Australia. George, or an editor or journalist in Gippsland, knew about Hunt's Ilchester Bastille pamphlet (published almost forty years before George's birth) and suggested the alliterative title 'peep' for George's narrative, protesting against the conditions in Pentridge.

George also wrote in his manuscript about the authors whose works were in Pentridge Prison's extensive library, one being Dumas.[177]

The Frenchman 'Alexandre Dumas père' was of part-African ancestry – and this was of great significance to him. It is highly likely that Dumas' work resonated on various levels with George de Thouars when he sat in the library in Pentridge Prison; people of colour have major roles in Dumas' work and imprisonment features vividly. He became famous around the world for his novels, particularly *The Three Musketeers* and *The Count of Monte Cristo*, the latter an adventure story with hope and vengeance among the themes. A man, wrongfully imprisoned, manages to escape. He acquires a fortune and begins to exact revenge.

'Chapter One: Marseilles – The Arrival'. A young man leans over the ship's bulwarks. 'He was a fine, tall slim young fellow of eighteen or twenty, with black eyes, and hair as dark as a raven's wing, and his whole appearance bespoke that calmness and resolution peculiar to men accustomed from their cradle to contend with danger'. Picture it striking a chord with young George (he had told police he was born in Tours, France) who went to sea from London, on a voyage halfway around the world. And Dumas' story, when first serialised in English in 1846 surely resonated too with George's father, Adolphe (allegedly a naval man, born in 'Marsailles' he said, for his Gloucester prison record).

Many of the plot devices in *The Count of Monte Cristo* were recycled from 'Georges', a novella by Dumas. Covering 1810 to 1824 and set on the

Isle de France (Mauritius) a large island in the Indian Ocean, 'Georges' was published in England as 'George; or The Planter of the Isle of France'. In part it is about race and racism, and is likely to have had a powerful impact on George de Thouars in terms of the novella's title, the author's heritage, George's possible roots, his background and experiences.

George had stated to the police that his father, 'Henry de Thouars', a teacher of languages, was born in Port Louis on the island of Mauritius (the French and English languages were already widely spoken there).

So, an intriguing mixture of fact and fiction – or did George give the facts? Was he truly George, not Freddy? Whoever he was, he may have not known which was what in the family stories.

And what stories truth and fiction make.

PENTRIDGE, BY GEORGE

The account by George de Thouars of life in Pentridge was harrowing and chilling, throwing light on institutionalised cruelty in a carefully-planned regime. Men were only supposed to be known by their cell number; men in 'A' Division had to wear a hood when exiting their cells. Exercise to be taken alone. Punishment cells were underground and prisoners used Morse code for communicating with one another via cell walls.

This 'Pentridge' writer was also using the extensive library to study languages, George taking any opportunities to be in that quiet room for brief times away from the harshness. He comes across in his account as a man of intelligence who must have had a good education. Calling for reform, many of his concerns about prison systems (for instance the folly of putting young people in with hardened criminals) are issues *still* highlighted around the world today.

TWO OUT, ONE BACK

According to George's written account, after 20 February 1886 he was no longer prisoner number 18033. He had been discharged by special authority, released with only the things he had worn when taken into prison in 1880. His clothes, now rotten, were tied together with string.

He felt fortunate to have been given 10/- (ten shillings): a distressed sixteen-year-old, released at the same time, had nothing and knew nobody in Melbourne. George must have given him 5/- but the youngster soon had to return to prison, penniless. George's help was not enough and – as is the reality for many ex-prisoners today – the sad result was a big door opening up and the lad being taken back into prison.

WHAT LIFE?

By April 1888, George de Thouars had gone … not far. He married Helen Kimber in Victoria and worked as a gardener in Prahran, Melbourne. Helen was a widow some years older than George and had three surviving children. She died in 1895 at The Alfred Hospital, her death registered with the name Kimber, surname of her first husband. This may indicate that her marriage to George did not turn out to be a happy one for her.

Constance Kent, after voyaging from England to Australia and changing her name to Ruth Emilie Kaye, had trained as a nurse at The Alfred Hospital at Prahran from 1890. (It was named after Prince Alfred, who was shot and injured in 1868 when in Sydney on a royal visit; Henry James O' Farrell was hanged for the assassination attempt.)

Did George de Thouars find some sort of peace during the rest of his life? Who knows what happened – and where did Freddy/George's life end?

PART TEN
GOODBYE GEORGE DYSON

Chapter 37

'MISCONDUCTED HIMSELF'

Dyson: clever, much cleverer than he was thought to be in 1886. He used his considerable brain to negotiate a way through the Trial that April; he can be viewed as a naïve young man when he met Adelaide. And, at best, stupid to do her bidding. At worst, what was he?

Dyson gathered and composed himself after the dreadful shocks: Edwin's sudden death and the link to chloroform poisoning; his own regrets about purchasing the chloroform that killed his friend; the post-mortem; the Inquest; his remand and the police court hearing. He told friends he was innocent. Then he and Adelaide were in court for their Trial.

He must have gauged that as a witness he might make the best of a very bad job by completely distancing himself from Adelaide. And by not speaking ill of Edwin – otherwise he could be deemed to have shown malice towards his so-called friend with a wish to subdue Edwin, or worse.

Dyson spoke out for himself, for his life.

Having become both calculating and careless through infatuation, he had been determined to have his wits about him, trying to save his career and – Lord *help* him – his neck. How deeply Dyson must have regretted that Sunday when he first welcomed the Bartletts into his flock!

Where did he go and what did he do after Adelaide's Trial and after the publication in June of his letter criticising the Judge? Dyson was a terribly relieved and temporarily chastened young man, in search of anonymity and a new start in the world.

Yet the case was not only personal, it was 'a major embarrassment to Wesleyanism'.[178]

And the case, sensational on many levels, continued to mystify reporters and a fascinated, appalled public.

1885 had been a momentous year for Dyson: meeting Adelaide, academic studies completed, promotion to a larger church, the delicious allure of Adelaide, the relationship with her and Edwin. Hugely thrilling and stimulating for a young, inexperienced chap – until he was brought back down to earth by Edwin's perturbing illness in December. Then the death on New Year's morning.

From January 1886, the still-Reverend Dyson, after his sickening realisation that Edwin's death may have been by murder, had the urgent necessity to cut himself off from Adelaide and to try to avoid being incriminated. And he rapidly recalibrated in an attempt to save himself.

However, in addition to the courts he was at the mercy of the Wesleyan Methodist Church. When its leaders met in Conference that summer of 1886, their verdict endorsed the judgement which had issued forth from the London District Meeting earlier that year.

Dyson: 'guilty of wilful falsehood and … misconducted himself in a manner so discreditable as to render his continuance among us under any circumstances utterly impossible'.

Out he went – and off. [179]

PART ELEVEN
BEING 'JOHN BERNARD WALKER'

Chapter 38

A SCIENTIFIC AMERICAN

The former Reverend Dyson crossed the Atlantic and headed west. He travelled across the United States and lived in the Pacific state of Oregon. It must have been a big shock to his system, after a lifetime of study, to have to become a manual worker. Such is the lot of many immigrants; his life became one of physical toil until (so the story goes) some of his drawings were seen and his nascent technical abilities given an opportunity to develop.

ON THE REBOUND
The Trial less than a year behind him, in March 1887 'JB Walker' married Eliza Belle Wilson ('Bella') a local woman, in Benton County, Oregon. In Corvallis, Benton, she gave birth in April 1889 and the baby was, no real surprise here, named George.

Put the man's actions to the test and scrutinise stories of others. When shaking off the past and constructing a different persona, many people hold on to some element of their birth names. They often take away an identity with one hand and give something to themselves with the other. In this case, 'John' was the new first name George Dyson bestowed on himself, using his father's name, John. He used 'Bernard', the name of his friend, Bernard Curtis, as his new middle name. He jettisoned the name 'Dyson'. Hey presto he had morphed into 'John Bernard Walker'; John Bernard Walker (JBW) from now on …

He held on to his old forename 'George' by donating it to their son. He inserted 'Bernard' as the baby's middle name – obviously an important name from Dyson/Walker's to-be-kept-secret past. And so Bella, 'George Bernard Walker' (their brand-new son) and JB Walker formed a new family. The surname 'Walker' may have been taken on, unconsciously or deliberately, from the nurse Annie Walker, a witness in Adelaide's Trial. Adelaide had allegedly said that Nurse Walker went to America – but no.

Dyson, now John Bernard Walker, *had* gone to America. And as J Bernard Walker, by golly, he 'got on'.[180]

THE *SCIENTIFIC AMERICAN*

By 1895, JBW was a 'Journalist' and had an editorial, editor-in-chief role with the prestigious *Scientific American* magazine for many years.[181]

Did Walker gain any electrical or engineering experience in Oregon, or just an interest in all things mechanical which developed when he moved east in the USA?

NATURALISED

Casting off his homeland, England, and the shame of both a ruined life and being cut adrift by the Methodist Church, Walker 'abjured all allegiance and fidelity … to the Queen of Great Britain and Ireland'. On Christmas Eve 1898 at the State Court, White Plains, New York, he became a naturalised citizen of the USA.

Legally, the very English, ex-reverend George Dyson was now the all-American Mr John Bernard Walker.

By the 1900 Census, living at Mount Vernon in Westchester County, New York were JBW, Bella and son George, now eleven years old.

And the man who had been Dyson, what a brain he proved to have …

He wrote that very average poem to Adelaide in 1885, but having applied himself for years as a schoolboy and into his late twenties at college, he was a fully-fledged pen-man. And a person with, to use a cliché, boundless energy; prolific and confident.

Unfortunately there seem to be no photographs of John Bernard Walker within the public domain.

In September 1907, SS *Lusitania*, the British ocean liner owned by the Cunard Line, made its maiden voyage from Liverpool to New York. That December, Walker, listed as forty-nine, married, returning to the Standish Arms Hotel, Brooklyn, made the crossing back from England to New York on the same ship. (The redesignated RMS *Lusitania*, on its usual North Atlantic crossing, was sunk by a torpedo from a German submarine on 7 May 1915 and 1,198 people drowned. Its sinking led indirectly to the United States entering World War One.)

For the 1910 Federal Census, Walker gave his status as 'divorced'. Living in Columbia Heights, Brooklyn and employed as a journalist, he boarded along with twenty-three other people. Bella also lived in New York, in Manhattan; she gave her status as 'widow'.

MOVING ON

From 1911 onwards, articles in the *Scientific American* were under their authors' names, thus Walker's numerous contributions to the magazine are evident. And on New Year's Eve, 1911 the *New York Times* asked various local 'names' for their selection of the five greatest achievements of the year in the USA. Surely John Bernard Walker, formerly George Dyson, was sparing a thought for the late Edwin Bartlett on that 31 December – and on every 31 December? How strange and disconcerting it must have felt each New Year to remember his late friend, whom he had prayed for on New Year's Eve, 1885 – not knowing that by the next day Edwin would be dead.

'OUR BARREN YEAR'
This New Year's Eve, Walker has more to say than the other invitees.

'The thing that looms large out of the year 1911 is that nothing at all looms large. We have had our X-Ray year, our "wireless" year, our flying year, but this year we have our barren year.'

Perhaps a depressing time for him personally, as well as a poor past year technologically, in his opinion. However, he revs up, acknowledging the achievement of those who constructed the Panama Canal and then, among other things scientific, highlights a passion – alas, soon putting a dampener on it:

'A VERY MEDIOCRE YEAR'
'Steamships, both for peace and war purposes, have attained undreamed of size; the orders are out for the first 1,000 foot boat, and that means larger changes than most of us would think.

'With the increasing size of steamships comes the making of mammoth internal combustion engines … Several ships now [being built] will be driven by engines of 3,000 horsepower – a notable advance. And these are about all the things that loom above a very mediocre year.

J. Bernard Walker'

It was as though he was thirsting for more excitement, ever more technological innovation and endeavour, yearning for something for himself perhaps. And for what many call progress.

'AN UNSINKABLE *TITANIC*'

In 1912 he visited Colon, the port city founded during the building of the Panama Canal. Catastrophically, in April that year came the shocking sinking of a huge steamship, the British liner RMS *Titanic*. On her maiden voyage from Southampton to New York, she struck an iceberg in the North Atlantic Ocean and sank. More than 1,500 people died.

Astonishingly, within just three months Walker completed and had published *An Unsinkable Titanic – Every Ship Its Own Lifeboat*.

His introductory question is clear: 'Why did this ship, the latest, the largest, and supposedly the safest of ocean liners, go to the bottom so soon after collision with an iceberg?'

A thought: had Adelaide been his iceberg? Meaning, did Dyson/Walker feel that he sank because of running into her? Adelaide, with much more to her than just the visibly attractive woman one noticed.

The man who'd had to save himself wrote: '... every ship its own lifeboat.' Worth saying that again, to savour its meaning.

'EVERY SHIP ITS OWN LIFEBOAT'

Every ship should be self-righting; able to save herself. Form and function.

Here, a brief comparison between Walker's life then and his life before. It was a holing that Dyson had survived back in April 1886, a near-destruction.

'GOING TO JAIL WITH A CHANCE OF BEING DROWNED'

Walker's *Titanic* story includes a rueful quote which evokes memories of Dyson.

'Boswell, that faithful, if over-appreciative chronicler, tells us that Dr Johnson once described an ocean voyage as "going to jail with a chance of being drowned".'

Gallows humour, yet a reality in terms of being in confinement with risks all around. And surely any mention of 'jail' dredged up memories – albeit self-induced – of Dyson's time in prison on remand. Reality being that, back in 1886, he felt perilously close to being locked up for the rest of his life – or hanged by the neck until dead.

ANOTHER SHIP ... ANOTHER WIFE?
'J Bernard Walker, editor-in-chief of the *Scientific American* of New York, and Mrs Walker are at the Hotel Central for a few days en route for Hamburg, where they will be the guests of the Hamburg-American Line. The Walkers' trip ... has been timed for the maiden voyage of the *Imperator*.' (The *New York Times*, 25 May 1913)

'Mrs Walker': presumably his second wife. They were off to northern Germany to view the awesome SS *Imperator*, largest passenger ship in the world (at that time). It was the year before World War One began.

John Bernard Walker became an even more authoritative figure on war, weapons and strategy, engaging in debates and planning at the highest level alongside politicians and the military. He chaired the Navy Committee of the National Security League (then an extremely influential non-partisan organisation) founded in December 1914 primarily to promote US military preparedness.[182]

AMERICA FALLEN!

In 1915, J Bernard Walker's *America Fallen! The Sequel to the European War* was published. In the first chapter, he envisages a world in which the war will end with a Treaty of Geneva in 1916, signed by the peace plenipotentiaries of thirteen nations. Still available today, Walker's story is of the 'invasion literature' genre; a cautionary tale told in Dyson's sermonising style about military ill-preparedness in the USA. Walker envisages destruction of the Panama Canal, writing with first-hand knowledge of its construction having visited it just the year before. Dramatic chapter titles include 'The Capitulation of New York' and 'The Capture of Washington'. *America Fallen!* – in many ways an extraordinary publication.

PITTING HIS BRAIN

The USA did not enter the First World War until 1917. Walker had continued using the power of his pen, writing with emphatic confidence, warning about the war and developing his eclectic interests. These were primarily around engineering, whether in relation to architecture, transport, or whatever might be the next invention. Mere mortals could not envisage what the next invention would be and how it might change the world for humans. Dyson was always on the lookout for inventors' projects, pitting his brain against a problem, searching for solutions. That was how the man had spent his working days and late nights ever since being Dyson the student. And now always keeping busy, occupied – perhaps keeping demons away.

In June 1925, Walker arrived back in New York from St John's, the capital city of the Canadian province of Newfoundland and Labrador. Listed as a sixty-seven-year-old 'widower', home: 233 Broadway, New York.

THE DEATH OF JOHN BERNARD WALKER

As John Bernard Walker he re-entered England in 1928 to re-visit Dyson's old haunts and returned to the States in July. He was seventy when he died that October. His remains were placed in a niche at Fresh Pond Crematory and Columbarium, in Middle Village, Queens County, New York.[183]

THE 'POISONING CASE'

How did that story of George Dyson becoming John Bernard Walker reach daylight?

Dr John A Vickers has written extensively about the history of Methodism and has had important roles in the Wesley Historical Society and the World Methodist Historical Society. The information in articles by Dr Vickers provides a springboard from the world of Dyson in 1886 into the world of Walker from 1887.

Vickers' account starts with finding a typescript of the diary kept by Helen McKenny, whose father was Minister of Wesley's Chapel in City Road, London.[184]

On 19 February 1886, McKenny's entry referred to 'the distressing poisoning case of Rev Dyson'. She was writing during that terribly tense time for Dyson: around the Inquest and before the Trial.

Knowing nothing more, Vickers looked up the 'Minutes of Conference' of the Methodist Church. Dyson was listed in 1885 – but by 1886, no sign of him in the Minutes. A friend of Vickers knew that the 'poisoning case' referred to the Bartletts and pointed him towards more source material. Thus Vickers learned why and how Dyson disappeared from the list of men 'on trial as Probationers' in the Church.

A correspondent sent Vickers a transcription of a letter sent to Edgar Lustgarten, the respected British broadcaster and notable crime writer. The letter was from a Miss Evelyn Curtis, of Bournemouth, who in 1928 had met Dyson (by then Walker – she must have known that?) when he visited her father, Bernard. To recap, Bernard and Dyson were firm friends for years before the Bartlett case hit international headlines.

One wonders whether during their last-ever meeting these old pals conversed as Bernard and George, or as Bernard and John.

Vickers pieced together the stories of Dyson's emigration, his change of names to John Bernard Walker and his highly successful career. And of Walker's visit to Britain in the early summer of 1928, visiting old haunts and spending that precious time with Bernard. Evelyn recalled Walker as 'a little old man, frail, very courteous and kind, and, I think, sentimental.'

He wrote to her as he travelled around England, visiting architectural splendours, perhaps feeling that this would be his last visit. That October, Walker died in New York.

Vickers read the obituary sent by Miss Curtis to Lustgarten. Walker died on 17 October 1928. Apparently, when Bernard Curtis wrote a letter of sympathy to Walker's son, George, the reply was that his father had made Bella very unhappy and they divorced (no mention of in which year).

Vickers did not have the opportunity to speak with Miss Curtis; she passed away before a meeting could be arranged. The story which she conveyed (and which Dr Vickers compiled from her documents and from subsequent research) provides a large puzzle piece for an extraordinary life – lived in at least two parts by George Dyson and John Bernard Walker.

'BEAUTIFUL AND ACCOMPLISHED MATE OF …'
Very sadly and almost unbelievably, another shock, another piece of puzzle. A newspaper front page announces:

'EDITOR'S WIFE KILLS HERSELF

Beautiful and Accomplished Mate of

Scientific American Man

Inhales Gas.

'New York, 21 August – Mrs John Bernard Walker, wife of one of the editors of the *Scientific American*, and for years recognised as one of the most beautiful and accomplished musicians in Brooklyn, was killed by illuminating gas in her home at Flushing, L.I.

'When Walker returned home from New York he found all of the doors of the house fastened from the inside and was compelled to cut a piece from a rear door before he could gain an entrance.

'He detected an odor of gas as soon as he entered, and traced it to the kitchen where he found Mrs Walker, fully dressed, lying dead on the floor'.[185]

Another newspaper turns the clock back for us to that shocking afternoon on 19 August 1916.

'Returning to his new home here, J Bernard Walker ... found his beautiful young wife dead upon the kitchen floor with all of the gas jets turned on. Mrs Walker had been suffering from melancholia'.[186]

Presumably this poor woman had been the second wife of John Bernard Walker? Her death was from the inhalation of 'illuminating gas', a mixture of combustible gases formed during such heat-producing processes as coke-making from coal. Until the 1920s, illuminating gas was used for lighting houses and streets, also for cooking.

A Missouri newspaper, the *Sedalia Democrat*, 21 August 1916:

'WIFE KILLS SELF

Spouse of the Editor of the

'Scientific American'

Committed Suicide

BEAUTIFUL MUSICIAN IN BROOKLYN, N.Y.

Mrs John B Walker Hastily Inhales

Fumes While Her Husband Is

Away – Had Been Sufferer

From Melancholia.'

He found her lying in front of the gas stove, oven door open and gas pouring from half a dozen jets.

'A physician stated that Mrs Walker had been dead more than two hours'.

Coroner Vogel confirmed the case was one of suicide by inhaling illuminating gas.

'Walker and his wife were married in Brooklyn about seven years ago and had no children. Some years ago Mrs Walker became a sufferer from melancholia and was placed in a sanatorium. About six months ago she returned to her home in Brooklyn apparently greatly improved in health but soon became nervous and, with her husband, removed [i.e. they moved] to the house in which she died, one of the finest houses in Flushing.

'Mrs Walker, who was 36 years old, was an accomplished violinist and pianist.'

So, her end came in 'one of the finest houses in Flushing' on Long Island, in the New York borough of Queens. Was it a little, or rather largely, like an empty palace? Perhaps she felt isolated, unable to relax or sleep.

How long had she suffered from 'melancholia' and how long was her stay in a sanatorium? Someone may know.

Another report added that 'in an effort to restore her to her normal mentality by a change of scene, Walker had closed their home in Brooklyn and taken an estate in Flushing for the remainder of the season'.[187]

A question: in a room, or rooms, filling with illuminating gas, six jets on – for about two hours – would there not be an explosion when her husband entered the house?

None of the newspaper reports named this woman in her own right. She was just listed as the wife, Mrs John Bernard Walker.

THE SECOND WIFE?

Searches reveal her. Ernestine V Miller born on 8 July 1880; what was her middle name? Her mother and father: Althea and William. At the time of the 1900 US Federal Census the family lived in New Jersey; her sisters were Marguerite and Althea, her brother Walter. Althea will appear a little later in the story, writing an incendiary letter about her late sister's marriage.

In April 1910, Ernestine was single and living at home in Brooklyn, Ward 20, Kings, New York, with her parents and siblings. She was employed as a lawyers' stenographer.

Presumably she married John Bernard Walker at some point between that April and her death in August 1916.

She lies buried in Flushing Cemetery, Queens County; the inscription: 'Ernestine Walker the beloved wife of John Bernard Walker born 8 July

1880 died August 18, 1916'.

For the second time in his life, Dyson/Walker's attendance was required at an Inquest concerning the sudden death of a person to whom he was close: Edwin Bartlett in 1886, Ernestine V Walker in 1916.

Fact – not an accusation.

Time to talk money. Ernestine: rich, poor or somewhere in between? Did she have money of her own, or had the couple been well off through his work?

Searches turn up a Probate date in October 1916 concerning the administration of her estate and a petition by John B Walker to the Surrogate's Court of Queens.[188]–

'DIED SEIZED AND POSSESSED'

The transfer of property, of which Ernestine 'died seized and possessed or in which she had any right, title or interest' was transferred to the petitioner, who signed as 'John B Walker', of the Standish Arms, Columbia Heights, Brooklyn. Ernestine's father, William W Miller, of 280 Dean Street, Brooklyn, was named as another next of kin.

There were relatively small amounts in various savings banks, plus her jewellery and clothing. 'The deceased died seized of a one-half interest in the following real estate'. It detailed parcels of land at Broadway-Flushing in the Borough of Queens. The value was said to be $8,000 (eight thousand dollars) and the whole interest was for sale. The deceased had no life insurance and the petitioner applied for an order exempting the estate from tax.

After Ernestine's death and the Inquest, then his administrative role as executor, John Bernard Walker picked himself up, somehow. Back when his original self, George Dyson, way back in 1886, he had done so, somehow. Now John Bernard Walker, widower, he threw himself back into production. It was 1916 and his homeland, England, was at war.

Dyson/Walker, the sort of chap who would need to keep on working relentlessly, not only through curiosity, but also to stave off whatever feelings might otherwise engulf body and soul. Work and work – otherwise memories and emotions might sink him.

'OUR MOST DETERMINED EFFORT'

Did Dyson grow to love science when in Britain? The energetic Walker, from his thirties, developed his passion for innovation and championed a host of ground-breaking projects. He had a particular 'thing' about ships: writing about them, making recommendations for improvements, travelling in the newest, speediest and largest of them.

As indicated earlier he had been involved in strategic planning at the highest level in the United States, alongside politicians and military leaders. As Chairman of the Navy Committee of the National Security League, he was described as 'one of the best authorities in this country on scientific matters'. He stated that Germany could construct 1,200 submarines in a year – and we must 'make our most determined effort against the submarines, or we may ultimately find ourselves in this country face to face with the German fleet and her veteran armies 10,000,000 strong.' Walker, referring of course to Americans and the USA, was being quoted in an English newspaper.[189]

With his self-invention, his new name and making a name for himself as a prodigious writer and editor in New York, he displayed great foresight and confidence after being in such a parlous situation in 1886 in England. He left his past behind and crafted a completely different life in another country and into a new century, keeping on writing until the last years of his life. His work is still available today.

Full of energy, facts, opinion and passion, John Bernard Walker's writing makes compelling, thought-provoking reading.

When he was young, George Dyson perhaps felt 'driven' to try out certain things. His relationships with Adelaide and Edwin resulted in him taking a disastrous course. Maybe Dyson/Walker felt by the end of his life that he had atoned for his sins and been a mainly decent, diligent human being.

'BELLA'

By 1915 Walker's first wife Bella, 'Eliza Walker', was living on her own with two servants in Brooklyn. In 1920, in the Bronx, New York, with her son George, his wife and their grandson (another George, just three months old). Bella's status was given as 'married'. Were she and John Bernard still married? By 1930, she was still living with the family but they had all moved out to Morris, New Jersey. Her status was given as 'widowed'. John Bernard Walker's death was in 1928; presumably they had divorced at some stage? In 1910, he declared his status as 'divorced'. And, as stated earlier, he and a 'Mrs Walker' – presumably Ernestine – travelled to Germany in 1913 to view the SS *Imperator*.

Walker's previously beloved Bella died in 1934.

'MORE INTERESTING THAN THE BARTLETT CASE'?

And there comes to light another incredible slant on John Bernard Walker – called out in the piece as 'Dyson'.

'I THINK THE STORY OF WHAT HAPPENED TO GEORGE DYSON WAS MORE INTERESTING THAN THE BARTLETT CASE. HE WAS TO THE END A BRILLIANT AND ALSO A SINISTER PERSON.'

In 2001 a question (on the genealogy.com website) about George Dyson and his life after Adelaide's Trial drew a reply from a Jeffrey Bloomfield. He stated that Richard Whittington-Egan wrote a biography, *William Roughead's Chronicles of Murder*, which included Roughead's essay about Adelaide Bartlett – and also this response in a letter to him from the United States:

'107 West Underwood Street,

Chevy Chase, Maryland.

December 20, 1939.

Dear Mr Roughead,

'I have just finished reading your book *Murder And More Murder*[190] with a great deal of pleasure. On page 238 you speak of writing about the Adelaide Bartlett case … I am very much interested in this particular case – especially in George Dyson. You probably do not know that he came to America directly the Bartlett case was over. He changed his name and had a most interesting career and became a very well-known man. I think the story of what happened to George Dyson was more interesting than the Bartlett case.

'He was to the end a brilliant and also a sinister person.

'Mrs Belloc Lowndes knows the whole story and is deeply interested.[191]

'I would probably never have known that George Dyson was the well-known man in New York except the fact that he married my sister, a young and beautiful creature, and she died six years after her marriage quite mysteriously.

'George Dyson was twice her age when she married him – against all wishes of her family.

'We did not know anything about him at that time – and only three years ago [1936] did I know the true facts. My mother, shortly before she died, told me and I have all the proofs – a letter from my sister's lawyer, a photograph of George Dyson in his clergyman's robes and many other facts that are almost unbelievable.

'If you would be interested in writing this as a sequel to the Bartlett case it would make startling news – because as I have said he was a very well-known man in New York.

'Knowing what I do now I am sure my sister did not die a natural death. If I had only known at the time of her death in 1916, I would have had a thorough investigation. My mother was too heartbroken about it all and did nothing – it is indeed a strange world!

'She sent me the *Trial For Murder Of Adelaide Bartlett* and I can picture George Dyson telling his story and giving away the woman who loved him. Of course he was guilty too. Knowing his ambitions for power and money he would not hesitate.

Sincerely yours,

Mrs Charles A. Mason.'

What a letter!

Bloomfield tried to verify whether Mrs Mason ever lived in Chevy Chase, Maryland, but he had no success. He checked the 'social register of New York City for 1911 and 1916' but could not find relevant information (a JB Walker and Ernestine V Miller marriage and her death). Bloomfield concluded that 'the letter may be a hoax, but it was a very complex one if it was meant to be one.'

He was to the end a brilliant and also a sinister person', wrote Mrs Mason about Dyson/Walker. Was he? Was he either, both, neither? Any truth whatsoever behind her suspicions; any evidence? Mrs Mason (born Althea Miller, sister of Ernestine) had found out in 1936 from her mother that John Bernard Walker had been George Dyson until 1886. Althea Mason knew that Ernestine married him 'against all wishes of her family.' If they married in 1911, he would have been about fifty-three and Ernestine thirty-one years old or so – not 'twice her age', but yes, an older man.

There was Althea, writing to Roughead in 1939 after the commencement of World War Two. Writing that angry, sad letter twenty-three years after her sister died. Did Althea's opinion of her brother-in-law change after Ernestine's sudden death – or had she always disliked Dyson/Walker and found him sinister?

Dr John A Vickers has written extensively about the history of Methodism and edited the online version of the *Dictionary of Methodism in Britain and Ireland;* he has important roles in the Wesley Historical Society and the World Methodist Historical Society[192] .

With regard to Evelyn Curtis and her father, Bernard, there was the revelatory letter written by Evelyn to Edgar Lustgarten with an obituary from the *Scientific American* about John Bernard Walker. As noted earlier, Evelyn met Dyson/Walker on his visit to England early in 1928.[193], [194]

WRAPPING UP

At Christmas 2017, I felt the urge to 'do the Bartletts' again, pore over books and search online for any new insights or clues as to her father. At any one time there are various mysteries I am trying to crack and put back together in a new form. Seeking answers about alleged murders may not seem to be a healing process after suffering a bereavement, but for many who have lost someone it is a compulsive process. The deceased person cannot be brought back to life, yet answers about long-dead others may help the newly grieving.

I had been with my beloved sister Gill when she died on Christmas Day, 2016. As adults she and I used to pursue leads about our family history – she called it 'getting out the knitting' – spending a few minutes separately or together in our busy lives, peering at census returns, thinking laterally about spellings and ages, our family tree taking shape in our heads and on charts.

Making sense of facts and feelings; letting some things lie.

Broken parts of inanimate objects can be mended with care, as in the Japanese art of Kintsugi, the mending of pots in ways which do not hide the repairs. Hearts and minds can be mended; they won't be the same again but the dead person can be remembered and honoured in new ways.

With the Bartlett case came the added poignancy of my searches being at the time of year so ghastly for Edwin Bartlett. His December decline, his final New Year's Eve, his death in the early hours of New Year's Day, 1886. I imagined the shrinking of Edwin's world down to that tiny bed in front of the fire, shut away from family and friends, not well enough to go to work. Work, long his priority, had occupied most of his attention from when he was a teenager. I thought about his plight: painful teeth and gums, depression, sleeplessness, agoraphobia, and labile reliance on Adelaide.

My usual pattern was enthusiasm for researching a case for a few weeks, then it ebbed away. In January 2018, it did not; I looked forward each day to doing more 'knitting'. Edwin, Adelaide and Dyson were not going back to the nineteenth century, they kept popping up in my waking thoughts as they had in my father's, years ago, along with images of Lord Alfred Paget, a 'prominent Englishman'. Ivor had calculated that Adelaide's mother could have become pregnant when Queen Victoria's court, including Lord Paget, visited France in early 1858.

Search results (Findmypast website, and newspapers) for 'Adolphe Collot de la Tremoille de Thouars d'Escury' and variations thereof, made me do a double-take. Up came 'Henry Desbury', courts in Gloucestershire, a violent assault and bigamy. 'Henry Desbury', 'a foreigner of a very dark complexion', 'a man of colour', 'a Creole', 'a black man', an 'ebony Adonis'. A man who had lost an arm and wore a wooden one.

Of Eleanor and Adolphus' four children, not surprisingly it is Rodolphe's life and death ... so young ... that most touch my heart.

Whether the four men, Cox, Otto, Chambrun and Collett were personally known to Rodolphe or were men he admired from afar was not discovered by me for a long time. They were in his thoughts just before his fatal shot. Serendipity untangled the story: reading George Saunder's *Lincoln in the Bardo* (see Bibliography) I found mention of an article, 'Personal Recollections of Mr Lincoln', by the 'Marquis de Chambrun'. I guessed that the newspaper report of Rodolphe's 'de Chambrien' was a misspelling of Chambrun – and yes, here was the same man.

I often had to edge forward in time to make sense of events then go back to 'slot in' facts, as with the New York Naturalization Index entry of 17 March 1868 from the Common Pleas Court, New York County. 'Rodolphe De Thonars': former nationality French; no birth date, no occupation, no arrival date; address 160 Fulton St, NYC – the street on which Mlle A De Doré lived. His witness: David Mannon, 83 Nassau St. (And now I recollect that Rodolphe and Adele married less than two months after that date.)

Julia received the late Rodolphe C de Thouars' pension payments from 1911.

His Will answered some queries and raised others. I doubted that Walter ever lived in France but found his baptismal record for 26 March 1847 in France. Until I read Rudolph's Will I had no information to suggest Walter was a criminal. *If* he was a prisoner in France, what crime and what sentence? Did he ever go to New Caledonia – or go direct from France to Australia after 1870?

I hope someone knows much more about the life of Helen/Ellen d'Escury (Eleanor and Adolphus' third child); I could find so little.

As for Clara and Adolphe's first child, known as Henry Edward, he lived a relatively ordinary life – certainly when compared with several family members. Except that as, allegedly, a 'citizen of France' he became an alien in a foreign land hence his adult life in Australia may not have been straightforward. He claimed that he was born in Orleans, France. Like many in his family, did he change some facts about his origins in order to survive? Or perhaps his parents told him that Orleans was his birth place; official word is that there is no record of that.

'GRAND SLAM'

Of Adelaide, Mary S Hartman wrote that 'she effected a kind of grand slam by enlisting the unwitting aid of a doctor, a clergyman and a lawyer to serve her ends'.[195]

Adelaide's first match was her marriage to Edwin, Mr Thomas Edwin Bartlett: boring ninny, cuckolded weirdo, oppressive husband? Or compassionate businessman, generous, fun-loving son, friend and husband? Edwin never got to shut up shop one final night, retire and go home to his slippers by the fire, a lifetime's work done, to stay put in a suburb or steam off on a well-earned tour of foreign parts. Did he do away with himself – or did Adelaide do something? What would he have made of a longer life?

'God only knows the machinations of the human mind, and no human being can tell the machinations of it.' So said 'Henry Desbury', up before the court in 1848. Anyone in court at the Trial of his daughter in 1886 could have uttered the same words about Adelaide. By the mid 1880s Edwin may have thought he knew her inside out, but after being married for ten years, had Adelaide had enough?

SIMILARITIES AND CONTRASTS

Adolphe's son Rodolphe, a man with unspecified injuries from his years as a soldier, a bigamist like his father. Adelaide, undervalued, oppressed nurse-wife, according to her; scheming, lying, cheating wife, according to some others. Frederick/George Gustave (Adelaide's younger brother) the violent bushranger, according to police and the Judge; a foolish incompetent according to many press reports.

Dyson, naïve, gullible? Self-serving, according to Clarke, to the Judge and newspaper reporters. Dyson as John Bernard Walker, forceful; an innovative scientific writer. Dr Leach, naïve yet arrogant, impulsive, abstract; knowledgeable – and maddeningly confusing.

MAKING CONNECTIONS

For some people in these stories, crime was a part of life. 'Henry Desbury' and three of his sons, Walter, Henry William and Frederick/George, committed crimes and all four men were imprisoned. Which of Adolphe's children knew one another – or at least knew of one another? When money, inclination and invention aligned, did they keep in contact, by letter, telegram, telephone, in good times and bad, read newspaper articles about their trials? Walter (Eleanor's son) was in Australia by 1884; his half-brothers, Henry Edward and Frederick/George (Clara's sons), lived there from the 1870s. Did they know of one another's existence, did they meet up? And did Adelaide ever join her brothers there?

THE HOLLOW AT THE HEART

Adelaide's disappearance: the hollow at the heart of this whole story.

Obviously I hoped to discover where she went and what she did after escaping from the limelight, but I could not find out. Someone may beaver away and uncover the story – if it has not already been found. Although it might sound surprising, this huge hollow does not bother me; it just sits quietly among the satisfactions of finding other members of her family.

I imagine Adelaide displaying a 'rather warm, fiery disposition' – like father, like daughter – which leads me back to 'nature, nurture' questions. Does that type of disposition travel in the blood and genes through generations, or is it 'just' learned behaviour in families? Probably both, yes?

Although 'Henry Desbury' was treated fairly by the Judge prior to the bigamy trial (in that he was permitted by Special Order to send letters to potential witnesses) it is highly likely that Adelaide and her father's side of the family encountered racial prejudice, overt or indirect. In addition, they may have expected insults, felt slighted, been wary, developed numerous ways of defending themselves in a primarily white world; add those factors to the evidence that Adolphe, Adelaide and Freddy/George were intelligent, hot-tempered and impulsive.

NEAR THE MARK

I found this description of Adelaide in the *New York Times:*

'Mrs Bartlett is a good-looking, girlish-faced, dark complexioned woman, with big dark eyes, thick black hair, and a contour of facial outlines which suggests negro blood. She bore a French name before she was married, and is very probably of Martinique or other French colonial mixed extraction. She has a contemplative, earnest expression of face, which one cannot help liking.'[196]

This reporter in the United States had cut to the chase. Living in a country where there were people of every hue was a very different experience from reporting on Adelaide in Britain. That reporter might not have been correct on Adelaide's origins, but his description was far more detailed on the subject of her heritage than any report found in the British press.

Of Clara and Adolphe's four children, Freddy's performances on the school stage made me feel as pleased as a parent would about his talent. One of the times I miss my father most is when finding references to someone like John Sims Reeves, the English singer with whom George de Thouars was compared. Ivor would have read about Sims Reeves; he, George and my father had fine, light tenor voices. And I am touched by the two photographs of George. In the first, full of youthful hope; in the second, trapped so much like Adelaide.

POEM
'PHOTOGRAPHS

The eyes have it,
eyes alluring, eyes pleading.
Was it manslaughter, murder,
or suicide,
a man taking his own life?
So many lies before and after
a man died.

'Adelaide looks up,
way beyond the camera,
as though something
has been lost.
In another pose, same clothes,
she looks hopeful,
wistful.

'Not knowing
that Edwin's death, her life,
her intriguing face,
her Trial, all will endure,
in books, blogs,
and plots.

'George looks out, defeated by
the stick-up aftermath.
Captured by the lens.
A gaze of consternation,
as if looking for a door left ajar,
longing to slip away.
A look of
"Who, me?"
A look of
"I cannot face …"'
(Rose Storkey)

WHAT ABOUT THE WOMEN?

Imagine being Eleanor Caroline Hampton, Maria Margaret Bearcock, Clara Chamberlain. What on earth was life like for them, being with Adolphus/Henry Desbury/Adolphe?

There is so little in the public domain about Clara Chamberlain. Was she unaware of her husband Adolphe's chequered past? What did Adelaide inherit from her, in terms of disposition? And I know nothing about what Eleanor and Clara thought of him. Maria Margaret said in court in 1848 that she 'freely' forgave him. For almost killing her? For lying and marrying her when he was not free to do so? She may have been pressured by him to say she forgave him. She had a son with him five years later; perhaps she loved him and was happy.

When and where was Adolphus born, England, the Netherlands, Belgium, France? Somewhere in the Dutch Empire, Indonesia for example? Did he have another wife – or wives – and other children? Which of his known children were born in France? We know that Adelaide was registered as having been born there.

When and where did Eleanor, her daughter Helen and her son Walter die? I am almost certain that Freddy became George de Thouars. When and where did he die?

Adelaide experienced serious illnesses and death in her immediate family, as do many children; and loss, both her parents and aunt Ellen dying when she was young. Arrangements within the Chamberlain family for her care were either not made or did not work out, hence Adelaide's ending up out at Hampton Wick with the Wellbeloves.

In the village community, she and Freddy may have been on the receiving end of prejudice about colour and race. Working as a confectioner's assistant to William Wellbelove, her 'adoptive' father, while her younger brother was excelling at the boys-only school. Adelaide was perhaps bored, resentful that she was not in education, frustrated by a lack of opportunity to use her talents and certainly isolated by difference and temperament. Later, underestimated by her husband and yet put on a pedestal by him, she may have felt lonely, haunted by deaths, illnesses and losses which had occurred at crucial stages in her development. She held the secrets of her father and was perhaps practised in lying.

Was Adelaide a feminist, a passionate advocate of women's freedom from oppression in marriage? Did she have a personality disorder or psychopathic tendencies? From remarks she made to people, she felt undervalued, frustrated. A clever person with too much mind-numbing, ego-crushing, frustratingly boring spare time. Time spent waiting for the man of routines and regular orders, the stocktaker, the methodical mixer for tea-drinking customers. Adelaide waited at home for the man who wanted a steady life and a steady wife. She told other people that she'd had to agree to an arranged marriage, a 'compact'.

Adelaide probably dwelt on hurts, fantasised about revenge, hatched schemes. Would you or I do the same, in her situation? There is the well-known saying, 'the devil makes work for idle hands' – but free time can also be used towards positive, enjoyable ends – dog walking, for instance. Adelaide, allegedly having no say about the arranged marriage, had no need to earn a living. She had ample free time to ponder on what might have been ... and what might be. Would Edwin have 'let' her earn money? Did she want to do so and plotted her way out? Perhaps she fell in love with George Dyson and was sincere in her conduct towards *him* – until the rot set in after Edwin's death. I believe Dyson when he told the Court in April 1886 that Adelaide had shouted at him 'OH DAMN THE CHLOROFORM!' that January. And it leapt out at me as a title for this book. She stamped her foot upon getting up from the chair and stamped about so loudly that Alice Matthews went to see what was going on.

In May 1886, Edwin's Will was finally proved. Adelaide could take the money, spread her wings and go free, go as anyone, go anywhere in the world.

DYSON AKA JOHN BERNARD WALKER

In January 1886, the Reverend commenced what might be described as 'Project Save George Dyson'. After the Trial he sloped off, began his re-invention – and what a life he lived. I have not changed my early analysis of him: 'wet behind the ears'. I see him as a quick learner, shrewd if not wise. Sad about losing Edwin, Adelaide, Ernestine? Sad at rarely being in Britain after 1886?

Did he and Bella divorce? Did he and Ernestine marry?

SO, WHAT ABOUT THE CHLOROFORM?

Christianna Brand according to Megan Westley 'proved' that chloroform can be suspended in brandy and swallowed without harm. Is that so?

If so, there is still the mystery of whether the death was through murder or suicide.[197]

CONSTELLATIONS

Research on family constellations, intergenerational transmission of trauma, systemic entanglements, and the ensuing effect on individuals down the generations is of importance to a wide range of academics, therapists and historians. Whether trauma experienced by ancestors can be *inherited*, and our own trauma passed on to descendants, is hotly debated. The study of epigenetics continues.[198]

POEM
'START, STOP
Where to stop? where to begin?
Family constellations
are like wrinkled walnuts
in their skin,
lying in connected chambers,
ear-curved, hidden,
hard to extract whole,
sometimes in pieces,
all walnut nonetheless.'
(Rose Storkey)

'When Does a True Story End?' is the heading of the Epilogue in Angela
Bourke's book, *The Burning of Bridget Cleary*. The author says that she
knows more 'about the subsequent lives of some of these people than
I have written, but it is not the business of this book to pry into or make
public the family affairs of people yet living'.[199]

Adelaide's family go on through the generations; I do not look for them.

When I reached December 2020 and 'started to finish' this book, I
thought deeply about Edwin's pain and misery. I wanted to stop editing
on 1 January, in memory of him. On 3 January, still going, I looked at
'The Pimlico Mystery' on Wikipedia and saw that someone had entered

numerous details about Adelaide's family. Almost, but not quite, time for me to stop.

ON BEING EDWIN BARTLETT

Back to Edwin: the story from Edwin's friend, Mr Tombs (Tombs), about Bartlett and Baxter working in the city of Birmingham together is a true one, I hope. Tombs said Edwin was full of fun (as Edwin senior told the court in April 1886) and that Edwin implicitly trusted his friends. Edwin was possibly duped into thinking that Adelaide would have a dowry of £1,000, but it was allegedly only £200. Tombs showed the grocer businessman to be more complex, interesting and light hearted than Edwin is often portrayed in studies of the Pimlico Poisoning. Hopefully more will emerge to illustrate the true character of the fellow.

The death of Thomas Edwin Bartlett led to a mystifying murder trial and the acquittal of Adelaide. I wish Edwin's life had been long and happy; it was not. I hope he rests in peace.

Illustrations

1. Adelaide Bartlett looks up… sad, a little lost. 1886.
Credit smallprint: Adelaide Bartlett © Getty Images/Hulton Archive

2. Adelaide Bartlett 'wistful, of course not knowing that her past will live on.' 1886.

3. Thomas Edwin Bartlett (always known as Edwin). This drawing (from a photograph) featured in many newspapers in 1886.

4. *George Dyson*

5. *Dr Alfred Leach (Edwin's doctor).*
This drawing featured in many newspapers in 1886.

6. 'George de Thouars' 1870s cartes. NB image reversed here, to show how author considers George looked - if photo negative was 'flipped' before printing. (Original photo, courtesy of Victoria Police Museum, can be seen online.)

7. 'George Gustave de Thouars' photo from his prison record (courtesy of PROV)

8. No.18033, 'DE THEUARS George Gustave' (Handwritten record, including photo, courtesy of Public Record Office Victoria (PROV), Australia)

9. The Pimlico Poisoning Case: illustration of key alleged incidents.

FAMILY TREE

ADOLPHUS m ELEANOR CAROLINE HAMPTON
children: RODOLPHE, WALTER, HELEN, MODESTUS

ADOLPHUS (as 'HENRY DESBURY') 'm' MARIA MARGARET
BEARCOCK
child: HENRY WILLIAM DESBURY

SUSANNAH AYNSLEY m WILLIAM ROBINSON CHAMBERLAIN
children included WILLIAM, CLARA, ELLEN
ADOLPHUS, as ADOLPHE m CLARA CHAMBERLAIN
children: HENRY EDWARD, ADELAIDE*, FREDERICK GEORGE, CLARA
junior

SARAH m EDWIN BARTLETT senior
children included THOMAS EDWIN (known as EDWIN**)
*ADELAIDE m EDWIN**
Their child, unnamed (born November or December 1881) did not
survive

WIDER FAMILY DETAILS -
AND RELATIONSHIPS

The HAMPTONS
Hannah MUSPRATT married Robert HAMPTON.
Hannah died 1853. Robert died 1856.

CHILDREN included Reuben born 1808 and Eleanor Caroline, baptised 1820 (with three brothers).

ADOLPHUS 'COLLOT DE THOUARS D'ESCURY'
Adolphus born about 1807, married Eleanor Caroline 1844. Eleanor's place and date of death not found. Adolphus died 1860.

CHILDREN of Eleanor and Adolphus:
1. Rodolphus Hampton d'Escury born 1845, married Adèle de Doré born 1842?, Baptist Marriage, May 1868. Date of Adèle's death not found.
Rodolphe married Julia M Harrison born 1848, married July 1869; Julia de Thouars died 1922, Washington DC. Child of Julia and Rodolphe: Helene Caroline, 'Nellie', born 1869 or 1870. Rodolphe died August 1870.

2. Walter Henry Prout de Thouars d'Escury born 1847, married Sarah Ann Riley 1884. Walter's country and date of death not found.

3. Helen born 1848, married Louis Verguet 1874. Helen's country and date of death not found.

4. Modestus Felix born 1851, died 1851.

Maria Margaret BEARCOCK (MMB) born some time between 1824 and 1829. 'Married' January 1848 'Henry DESBURY' (aka Adolphus – see information above, and below re Adolphe).

CHILD of MMB and 'Henry Desbury' (Adolphus): Henry William DESBURY (HWD) born July 1853; HWD's place and date of death not found. MMB (as MMD, 'widow') married 1868 David John Falconer Newall (DJFN) born 1825. She became MMN.
CHILD of MMN with DJFN: Catherine Falconer Newall born 1872, died 1941. MMN died 31 January 1886. DJFN died 1901.

THE CHAMBERLAINS
Susannah AYNSLEY born about 1805, married 1822 William Robinson Chamberlain (WRC) born 1799. Susannah died 1862; WRC died 1860.

CHILDREN of Susannah and WRC included: William (WC) born 1823, married Emily, WC died 1899. Clara born 1834, married January 1853 Adolphe 'Collot de Thouars d'Escury'. Adolphe died in 1860. Clara died 1866. Clara's sister Ellen died 1868.

CHILDREN of Clara and Adolphe:

1. Henry Edouard (known as Henry Edward) de Thouars d'Escury born 1854, married 1: Henrietta Wagener. 1882. CHILD: Clara Amelia born 1885 died 9 March 1886.

Henry Edward married 2: Ada (née Wilkinson?) Barclay. Ada died 1924.

Henry Edward died 1927.

2. Adelaide de la Tremoille de Thouars d'Escury born 1855 Orleans, France. Married 1875 (Thomas) Edwin Bartlett born 1845. Adelaide's place and date of death not found.

Edwin's parents: Sarah and Edwin Bartlett. Other children of Sarah and Edwin senior: Charles Joseph born 1848; Frederick Oscar born 1849. CHILD of Adelaide (and Edwin?) born dead Nov or Dec 1881.

Edwin died 1 January 1886.

3. Frederick George de la Tremoille de Thouars d'Escury born 1858. 'Freddy' as George de Thouars married 1888 Helen Kimber [surname from her first marriage]. Helen died 1895, buried as Helen Kimber. Frederick George's place date and of death not found.

4. Clara de la Tremouille (Clara junior) born 1859, died 1873.

DYSON

Mother: Louisa née Brown? Father: John Dyson. George Dyson born 1858. Married 1st (as 'John Bernard Walker' – JBW) March 1887 Eliza Belle Wilson known as 'Bella'; CHILD: George Bernard Walker born 1889. Bella and JBW divorced (?) – date not found. JBW married? 2nd: Ernestine

Miller died 1916.
JBW died 1928, New York.

LOCATIONS

UK: London (Bunhill Row, St Pancras, Primrose Hill, Dalston, Hackney, Stoke Newington, Herne Hill, the Stock Exchange, Merton Abbey, Wimbledon, Putney, Pimlico, Clerkenwell, Old Bailey). Hampton Wick, Croydon, High Wycombe, Rode, Chatteris.

France: Orleans, Paris, Marseilles, Nice. The Netherlands. Belgium: Antwerp. India: Bengal, Darjeeling (now in West Bengal). Canada: Winnipeg and Maniota. USA: New York City and State; Washington DC; Oregon. Mauritius. New Caledonia. Australia: Victoria: Melbourne area, including Pentridge; South Australia, including Adelaide; Queensland. New Zealand: Wellington, Timaru, Lyttleton.

ENDNOTES

1 Mary Wollstonecraft, *A Vindication of the Rights of Woman: with Strictures on Political and Moral Subjects* (London: J Johnson, 1792).

2 Sir Alfred Joseph Hitchcock (1899–1980) was an English film director, producer, screenwriter whose work spanned six decades and his name lives on through the images and words.

3 The village appears as 'Rode' in the Domesday Book. The spelling was labile from an early date: it is 'Roda' in assize rolls of 1201, 'la Rode' in a charter roll of 1230; by the eighteenth century 'Road' was regarded as the usual form. It reverted to the older spelling 'Rode' under Somerset County Council in 1919. The name derives from the Anglo-Saxon 'rod', meaning a clearing. The parish was part of the Hundred of Frome'. RODE (Wikipedia, 2021)

4 *The Suspicions of Mr Whicher: A Shocking Murder and the Undoing of a Great Victorian Detective* (Walker & Company, 2008) by Kate Summerscale won the Samuel Johnston Prize for Non-Fiction in 2008.

5 *Literature, history & culture in the age of Victoria.* The Victorian Web (2009).

6 *Sussex Advertiser,* 26 December 1843.

7 *Hereford Journal,* 16 August 1848.

8 *London Evening Standard,* 16 August 1848.

9 *Hereford Journal,* 16 August 1848.

10 *Hereford Journal,* 16 August 1848

11 Robert Blake, *Disraeli,* (London: Eyre & Spottiswood, 1966)

12 *London Evening Standard,* 15 August 1848.

13 *Bristol Mercury and Western Counties Advertiser,* 31 March 1849.

14 *Cheltenham Chronicle and Gloucester Advertiser,* 4 April 1849.

15 *Cheltenham Chronicle,* 5 April 1849.

16 *ibid.*

17 *ibid.*

18 *Cheltenham Journal and Gloucestershire Fashionable Weekly Gazette*, 2 April 1849.

19 Under canon law (the body of rules for the faith and practice of a religious, particularly a Christian church) the strict original meaning of 'bigamy' was marrying a person after the death of the first spouse. Of course, in countries where only one marriage is permitted at a time, bigamy now has the meaning of marrying again when one's first spouse is alive and there has been no ending of the first marriage.

20 William Shakespeare (1564–1616), English poet, actor and playwright; regarded by many as the greatest English dramatist of all time. Desdemona featured in *The Tragedy of Othello, the Moor of Venice* (London: Thomas Walkley, 1622) – *Othello*: a play, a tragedy written between 1601 and 1604.

21 *Gloucester Journal*, 31 March 1849.

22 *Wilts and Gloucestershire Standard*, 3 April 1849.

23 *Ibid*

24 Hermione Hobhouse, *Prince Albert, his life and work*, (London: Hamish Hamilton, 1983) p. 91.

25 The Crimean War (February 1853–October 1856) was a joint European response to Russian expansion southwards and also into Western Europe.

26 The East India Company, an English (later British) joint-stock company, was formed in 1612 and its trading in commodities became vast. From 1757, it ruled the beginnings of the Indian part of the British Empire. Just as they had been for its counterparts, the French and the Dutch, trade and politics were part and parcel. The Boston Tea Party of 1773 (in Massachusetts, USA) was a protest by the Sons of Liberty following the Tea Act that year, which allowed the British East India company to sell tea, from China, within American colonies without paying certain taxes. The Government of India Act 1858 led to the British Raj having control of the subcontinent. The Company was dissolved in 1874 after recurring financial problems.

27 Anne de Courcy, *The Fishing Fleet: Husband-Hunting in the Raj.*

28 DJF Newall was a Fellow of the Royal Geographical Society and illustrated his own books. Some, still regarded by scholars as being culturally important, are reproduced from the originals. The published works include:

Preliminary Sketches in Cashmere; or, Scenes in 'Cuckoo-cloudland' [with illustrations]. Originally published in 1882. (Reprinted London: British Library, Historical Print Editions, 2011).

Tales Of The Pandaus, By A Wandering Cimmerian [a pseudonym of DJF Newall] illustrated; (London: Harrison And Sons, 1884). The Cimmerians were mythical people living in perpetual mist and darkness near the land of the dead; members of an ancient Nomadic tribe who overran Asia Minor in the seventh century BCE (from Greek mythology). His imaginary tales, loosely based on Hindu fables, were written by Newall in various places, including the forested area around Khajjar, the hill station in Chamba district, India.

29 *Derby Daily Telegraph*, 5 February 1889.

30 *Gloucester Journal*, 16 February 1889.

31 *Isle of Wight Times*, 14 February 1889.

32 *Daily Telegraph & Courier*, 6 August 1900.

33 *Evening Express*, 7 May 1901.

34 Abraham Lincoln (1809-1865); 16th US President.

35 Henry Clay Whitney, *Life on the circuit with Lincoln*, (Estes and Lauriat, 1892).

36 The 131st New York Volunteer Infantry Web Page: see Facebook.

37 General Thomas Jonathan 'Stonewall' Jackson (1824–63) was one of the best-known Confederate commanders in the American Civil War. His nickname came from his being like a stone wall in the face of the enemy.

38 The conditions in January 1863, as described in a post on the 131st New York Volunteer Infantry Facebook page, with McBeth's letter from a Collection of the New York Historical Society.

39 The summary of Rodolphe's US Army record was provided to the 131st New York Volunteer website by Gregory Tavormina.

40 Andrew Johnson (1808–75) was seventeenth president of the United States for four years from 1865. A Southerner – but a Unionist – he opposed citizenship for former slaves, some four million people. He came into conflict with Cabinet officials and removed the Secretary of War, Stanton. As a result, Johnson was impeached by the House of Representatives for 'high crimes and misdemeanors' – the first US president to be impeached. Then the Senate voted: thirty-five 'guilty' to nineteen 'not guilty' – one vote short of the two-thirds majority required to convict him.

41 His names were incorrectly transcribed as 'Rodolph C Heun' on the Ancestry website and misspelt as 'R C de Thonars' in the *New York Herald*, 21 July 1869. The wedding was conducted by the Rev JW Wenner. See also: 'New York, New York City Marriage Records, 1829-1940' database, *FamilySearch*. New York City Municipal Archives.

42 Lucien-Anatole Prévost-Paradol (1829–70) was born in Paris, France. A moderate liberal, he became one of the main opponents of the Empire. He took on the post of envoy to the United States but was still much criticised by Republicans in France. Shortly afterwards, the Franco-Prussian War occurred. He shot himself on 19 July in Washington and died the next day. An assumption was that he was devastated by the declaration of war – but some writers considered he was in favour of France trying to check the ambitions of Prussia and that a combination of factors led to him killing himself.

43 Jacob Dolson Cox (1828–1900). His life changed from that of an academic in Ohio to an

officer in the American Civil War, to a political career back in Ohio; he was Governor from 1866 to 1868. He moved on to Washington and was at the heart of the national government as Secretary of the Interior from 1869 to 1870.

44 William Tod Otto (1816–1905) was an American judge, for thirty years a friend of President Abraham Lincoln. Otto went on to become a diplomat and then Reporter of Decisions of the Supreme Court from 1875 to 1883.

45 Charles Adolphe de Pineton, Marquis de Chambrun (1831–91) was born in Marvejois, south of France. The article (found among his papers after his death in 1891) was published as *Charles Adolphe Pineton de Chambrun: Personal Recollections of Mr Lincoln,* (USA: *The Century Magazine*, January, 1893). The foreword states that although Chambrun was a liberal 'he was, from family traditions, attached to the legitimist branch of the royalist party that centred around the Comte de Chambord'.

His book: *Impressions of Lincoln and the Civil War: A Foreigner's Account,* by 'Marquis Adolphe de Chambrun' (USA: Random House, 1952). Chambrun's trajectory towards the powerful had been through his father-in-law, Monsieur de Corcelles' friendship with Charles Sumner (1811–74). This lawyer, academic and radical Senator from Massachusetts was leader of the anti-slavery movement in the state, railing against the influence upon federal government of the southern slave owners. Sumner was leader of the Radical Republicans in the Senate, a cauldron of politics during the American Civil War.

46 Eustace Jules Collett (1838–95) born in Nice, was a French civil engineer/topographer – skills he put into action when serving in the American Civil War as a private; he was a keen freelance artist and his two sketches of General Lee are of historical importance. During the war he contracted malaria and suffered rheumatism thereafter. He was buried in Arlington Cemetery, Washington, with' Grand Army Honors'.

47 This refers to James C O'Connor, who lived in Washington City, Ward 3 and was a Clerk in the War Department (1870 US Census).

48 *Revue des Deux Mondes*, a French monthly literary, cultural and political affairs magazine published in Paris since 1829.

49 Gregory Tavormina provided information about 'Rudolph de Thoures' to the 131st New York Volunteer Infantry Facebook page. 'A truly sad and tragic newspaper article about a suicide of what turned out to be a former member of Company K. [It] said he was known as Count De Thomas in his native France. One of his aliases was Rudolph Callat Henri.' He was recorded in the regimental rosters as Rudolph De Thoures.

50 Fortunately, Berthemy had not left the States and soon after Prévost-Paradol's death was asked to return temporarily to the role of French Ambassador. Berthemy was in post until the arrival of Jules Treillard later in 1870.

51 An 'Envoy Extraordinary and Minister Plenipotentiary' is a person, for example a diplomat, invested on behalf of his or her government, with full powers of independent action in a

foreign country; 'plenipotentiary' from the Latin plenus, 'full', and potens, 'powerful'. An envoy was usually ranked second to ambassador. Prévost-Paradol was Ambassador for a short period – just months – in 1870.

52 The name Adèle is the French form of the German Adel meaning 'nobility; Adal, 'noble'.

53 Transcription of a New York City Marriage Record – see FamilySearch film number 001543714 (The Church of Jesus Christ of Latter-day Saints operates this genealogy organisation); see also Findmypast (UK-based online genealogy service). 'Marriage returns 1866-1882 at First Baptist church of Brooklyn and the Baptist church of Elizabeth, NY' and also Article: 'Marriages By A Brooklyn Baptist Minister, 1868-1870, Vol 116, Issue 3, Page 133, published 1985. Both of her other marriages took place in Brooklyn.

54 The New York Genealogical and Biographical Record image in the document *Marriages By A Brooklyn Baptist Minister, 1868–1870* (Brooklyn Marriages, Volume 116, Issue 3, p. 133, published 1985).

55 *Daily Telegraph*, Sydney, 22 August 1888.

56 *New Zealand Police Gazette,* published weekly from 1861 to 1990 and distributed to police stations. See Archives New Zealand website.

57 Chalcot Terrace (now Chalcot Crescent). The Brown family, in the film *Paddington* (Director: Paul King, 2014) based on the books of Michael Bond about the fictional Paddington Bear, lived at 32 Chalcot Crescent, renamed in the film as 'Windsor Gardens'.

58 The National Archives of Australia (at Canberra and online): citizenship records for all States from 1904.

59 Adelaide of Saxe-Meiningen (born in 1792) and William married in 1818; she died in 1849.

60 Henry Edward only publicised his whereabouts some years after the amendments to the Naturalization Act, 1917 (which required foreigners to acquire citizenship) and to the Nationality Act 1920 (which required him to formally identify himself).

61 A copy of Adelaide's birth certificate was kindly sent to me by the local authority in Orleans, France; my father loved the copy he had in the 1960s.

62 Sir Edward Clarke, QC, MP, *The Story of My Life* (London: John Murray, 1918).

63 Stephen Collins Foster (1826–64) was sometimes referred to as 'the father of American music' and known for his parlour and minstrel music, first performing as a minstrel when just nine years old. 'He often attended negro camp meetings and there studied the music of the colored people'. *The Frederick Harris Music Co Limited, Oakville, Ontario, Canada. The Commonwealth Book of Favourite Songs* (Alfred Lengnick & Co Ltd, South Croydon, Surrey, England). His enduring, evocative songs – some with what today is deemed to be racist language – included 'Oh, Susanna(h)!' and 'My Old Kentucky Home'. The lyrics of verse three of 'Massa's in de cold, cold ground' began 'Massa makes de darkeys lub him, cayse he was so

kind. Now dey sadly weep above him, mourning cayse he leave dem behind'.

64 Thomas Ingoldsby [pen-name], *The Ingoldsby Legends, or Mirth and Marvels* (London: Richard Bentley and Son, 1840). The legends were written by Richard Harris Barham (1788–1845), a clergyman.

65 *St Neots Chronicle and Advertiser*, 27 February 1886.

66 *Lloyd's Weekly Newspaper*, published in London from 1842, had a proud history of crime news, shock and horror – but also literature and much more. Its circulation figures took an upward trajectory from 1855 until after the gruesome 'Jack The Ripper' murders in 1888.

67 Edgar Allan Poe (1809–49) is known for his macabre mystery stories and as the first, or one of the first, writers of detective fiction. What would he have made of Adelaide and the story surrounding her?

68 Charles Delauney Bravo (born Turner in 1845). He died of antimony poisoning at Balham, London in 1876. The case generated huge public interest, increased newspaper sales and resulted in numerous books being published about the alleged murder. Two inquests were held and the details extracted from his widow were considered so scandalous that women were barred from attendance. It has since been suggested that Florence, who feared that another pregnancy and miscarriage would kill her, had been alluding to unwanted penetration (including anal) to which she was allegedly subjected by Charles – and she had confided in her doctor.

The first Inquest returned an open verdict i.e. a verdict of a coroner's jury affirming the occurrence of a suspicious death, but not specifying the cause of death. The second Inquest resulted in a verdict of wilful murder. No one was ever arrested or charged, but the impact upon Florence Bravo of the humiliating questioning was profound. After her move to a house with a sea view near Lumps Lane in Southsea, Hampshire she continued her descent into alcohol misuse and died in 1878, at the age of thirty-three, just two years after the death of Bravo. The house was demolished in the twentieth century and a new one built in its place.

There are numerous books about the Bravo case, including: John Williams, *Suddenly at the Priory* (Heinemann, 1957); James Ruddick, *Death at the Priory: Sex and Murder in Victorian England* (Atlantic Books, 2001) and Antony M Brown, *Poisoned At The Priory: The notorious death of Charles Bravo* (Mirror Books, 2020).

69 Mary Gove Nichols, née Mary Sargeant Neal (1810–84). Publications included: Mary Sargeant Nichols, *Mary Lyndon; Or Revelations Of A Life. An Autobiography* (New York: Stringer and Townsend, 1855).

Mary SG Nichols, *A Woman's Work in Water Cure and Sanitary Education* (London: Nichols & Co, 1874).

70 Thomas Low Nichols (1815–1901). Publications included: TL Nichols, *Esoteric Anthropology (the mysteries of man): A comprehensive and confidential treatise on the*

structure, functions, passional attractions and perversions, true and false physical and social conditions, and the most intimate relations of men and women. Anatomical, physiological, therapeutical and obstetrical; hygienic and hydropathic (New York: NY Stereotype Assoc., 1853).

TL Nichols, *A Biography of the Brothers Davenport: With Some Account of the Physical Phenomena Which Have Occurred in Their Present [sic], in America and Europe* (London: Saunders, Otley, and Co, 1864).

71 TL Nichols and Mary Sargeant Gove Nichols, *Marriage: its History, Character, and Results; its Sanctities, and its Profanities; the Science and its Facts. Demonstrating its Influence, as a Civilized Institution, on the Happiness of the Individual and the Progress of the Race* (Cincinnati: V Nicholson & Co, 1854).

72 Peter Squire and Albert Herbert Squire, *Squires' Companion to the British Pharmacopoeia* (London: J & A Churchill, thirteenth edition, 1882).

73 Yseult Bridges née Guppy (1881–1970), author. My parents spent many happy and interesting times visiting her and her husband, Michael, in Rye, Sussex (now East Sussex). My father valued her intelligence, her crime-writing skills and treasured their lively discussions about those alleged murders in which they had a mutual research interest (including the case involving Constance Kent, the Bravo case and the Bartletts).

74 Yseult Bridges, *Child of the Tropics: Victorian Memoirs* (London, Collins and Harvill Press, 1980). Hers was a 'privileged' upbringing, but of course involved separations of the type that cause stresses for many. In the 1930s, Yseult wrote two novels based on Trinidadian life. She began writing her memoirs in the 1940s when living in Africa with her husband, a British diplomat, and she experienced many cultures in her lifetime. See Bibliography for details of Yseult's book about Adelaide; also see the research and published works of Jak Peake concerning Yseult Bridges.

75 *Framlingham Weekly News*, 27 March 1886.

76 John Wesley (1703–91) and his brother Charles (1707–88) started the 'Holy Club' at the University of Oxford. The way in which they conducted their lives was mocked as 'methodist' by students. John took this title, 'methodist', he 'owned' it and thus turned it into a title of honour. Initially, the Methodists wished for reform within the Church of England but the gap widened. Women were allowed authority as leaders, but that fell away after 1790.

77 WT Stead, William Thomas Stead (1849–1912) was passionate about political and social change. He was Editor of the *Pall Mall Gazette* from 1883 until 1889.

78 Charles Cruft (1852–1938). Among his dogs was a St Bernard and he promoted the breed. He ran dog shows in France from 1878 and his first in London took place in March 1886. Believe it or not, Lord Alfred Paget (see Preface) was one of the patrons. Cruft ran his first Cruft's dog show in 1891 and organised forty-five more national shows until his death.

79 Mesmerism, a word used from the nineteenth century to refer to the theories of Franz

Mesmer (1734-1815) who posited that natural energy transference took place between animate and inanimate objects. He had termed it 'animal magnetism'.

80 By Jove (or 'by Jupiter') originally referred to the Roman deity and has been used in English language since the sixteenth century. It became a way of using a euphemism instead of blaspheming against a god.

81 Condy's Fluid was a disinfectant first developed by Henry Bollmann Condy, chemist and industrialist, in 1857. Made in Battersea, London between 1867 and 1897, it was a popular product for external and internal use.

82 Julius Caesar (100 BC–44 BCE) wrote about the Gaul's practice of holding inquests in his account of their culture *Commentarii de bello Gallico VI.19.3.*

83 Dr Thomas Stevenson (1838–1908) was an English toxicologist and forensic chemist, an analyst for the Home Office and an expert witness in many well-known poisoning cases, including Maybrick.

84 *Encyclopaedia Britannica.*

85 Sir James Young Simpson (1811–70) was a Scottish obstetrician with wide-ranging interests and expertise, including his role in the study of the history of medicine. He emphasised the importance of midwives in hospitals. His use of chloroform had a huge influence on its use as an anaesthetic in surgery. It is still used in medical practice, and in the preparation of samples for DNA testing; also as an industrial chemical.

86 Linda Stratmann (born 1948) is a British writer specialising in historical true crime, biography and crime fiction. She left school after O levels and trained as a chemist's dispenser before taking various paths and obtaining a first-class honours degree in psychology. She was commissioned to write *Chloroform: The Quest for Oblivion,* her first book, in 2002. Kate Clarke's *In the Interests of Science: Adelaide Bartlett and the Pimlico Poisoning* has an excellent foreword by Stratmann.

87 *Cornish Telegraph,* 11 February 1886.

88 *ibid.*

89 *Beverley Recorder And General Advertiser,* 20 February 1886.

90 *ibid.*

91 *Alcester Chronicle,* 20 February 1886.

92 The Reverend Marmaduke Riggall went on to become General Secretary of the Wesley Historical Society from 1902–04.

93 *Standard,* 19 February 1886.

94 Alice Fulcher also gave evidence in April: see Day Two of the Trial.

95 The newspapers included the *Devon and Exeter Daily Gazette,* 20 February 1886.

96 *Bradford Daily Telegraph,* 20 February 1886.

97 *Liverpool Mercury*, 22 February 1886.

98 *Wigan Observer and District Advertiser*, 22 February 1886, one of those newspapers in which the details about Edwin were printed.

99 *Devon and Exeter Daily Gazette*, 5 March 1886.

100 *Philadelphia Times*, 28 February 1886.

101 *Newcastle Daily Chronicle*, 6 March 1886.

102 *ibid*

103 *Aberdeen Evening News*, 6 March 1886.

104 *Newcastle Daily Chronicle*, 6 March 1886.

105 *Salisbury Times and South Wilts Gazette*, 13 March 1886

106 Newgate Prison was built in the twelfth century into a gate on the old Roman wall. Renowned for its terrible conditions for over 600 years it was rebuilt many times, finally in 1782, and closed down in 1902.

107 Article by Dr John A Vickers, *George Dyson Alias John Bernard Walker* (Methodist History, 41:1. October 2002)

108 *Manchester Courier and Lancashire General Advertiser*, 8 March 1886.]

109 To read the Trial in full online see: archive.org. Full text of *The Trial of Adelaide Bartlett for Murder, held at the Central Criminal Court from Monday April 12 to Saturday April 17, 1886* by Edward Beal. All quotes are (unless otherwise stated in Endnotes) from Beal. See Bibliography: Edward Beal.

110 The road was by the ancient fortified wall, or bailey, of the City of London. The Old Bailey has various names: Justice Hall, Sessions House, Criminal Central Court. For some reason it took almost thirty years to complete the new Old Bailey building and its formal opening was not until 1907.

111 *Cornishman*, 22 April 1886.

112 *Daily News*, 13 April 1886.

113 Charles Arthur Russell (1832–1900) was an Irish statesman, knighted and appointed Attorney General early in 1886. He was raised to the peerage as Baron Russell of Kilowen in 1894. That same year he became Lord Chief Justice of England, the first Roman Catholic to serve as such since the Reformation in sixteenth-century England.

114 Edward George Clarke (1841–1931) was an English barrister and politician, one of the leading advocates of the Victorian era. In *R v Staunton; Staunton, Staunton and Rhodes*, in an 1877 case known as The Penge Murder, Clarke defended Patrick Staunton, a brother of Harriet Staunton, who had died in Penge, apparently of starvation. Harriet's baby son also died and

may have been a victim. The Defendants were convicted and sentenced to death, but that was commuted to penal servitude.

Clarke was appointed Solicitor-General in the Conservative government, just months after the Trial of Adelaide Bartlett.

In *Wilde v Queensbury*, 1895, and *R v Wilde*, 1895, Clarke represented Oscar Wilde – and blamed himself for tactics used in the first Trial. Hence he undertook Wilde's defence in the second Trial without charging a fee.

115 The Judge, Mr Justice Wills. Sir Alfred Wills (1828–1912) was a judge of the High Court of England and Wales from 1884 to 1905. He and his father William Wills co-authored *An essay on the principles of circumstantial evidence: illustrated by numerous cases* (1905) a valued text, still cited. Certainly he heard much evidence of a circumstantial nature during the Trial of Adelaide.

116 Kate Summerscale, *The Suspicions of Mr Whicher or The Murder at Road Hill House: A Shocking Murder and the Undoing of a Great Victorian Detective* (Walker & Company, 2008). That sub-title was used for the hardcover edition; the paperback version's title was *The Suspicions of Mr Whicher, or, The Murder at Road Hill House* (Bloomsbury, 2009). The author won the Samuel Johnson Prize for Non-fiction in 2008.

117 *Buckinghamshire Advertiser, Uxbridge and Watford Journal*, 17 April 1886.

118 *Cornishman*, 22 April 1886.

119 *Buckinghamshire Advertiser, Uxbridge and Watford Journal*, 17 April 1886.

120 *People's Weekly Journal*, 17 April 1886.

121 *Cornishman*, 22 April 1886.

122 *Cornishman*, 22 April 1886.

123 *Cornishman*, 22 April 1886.

124 *Buckinghamshire Advertiser, Uxbridge and Watford Journal*, 17 April 1886.

125 *ibid.*

126 *Guardian*, 17 April 1886.

127 The *Graphic* newspaper, stated on 17 April that the Wimbledon photography studio may have been 'Russell & Sons' on the corner of Worple Road.

128 Dr Hubert Montague Murray performed a post-mortem in 1900 at Charing Cross Hospital, on a young man who died of pulmonary fibrosis having worked for fourteen years in an asbestos textile factory. In 1906, Dr Murray reported on that death for a government inquiry, observing that care should be taken to prevent inhalation of the dust – but no full study of the terrible dangers of asbestos was undertaken until 1928.

129 Millbank Street Mortuary, near the Thames in Westminster, was used during investigations of the murders of women in the 'Jack the Ripper' cases around Whitechapel in London, 1888.

130 Charles Meymott Tidy (1843–92) began in his father's medical practice in Hackney and went on to become a professor of chemistry and forensic medicine. An official analyst to the Home Office, he also had an interest in sanitary reform and public health.

131 *Daily News*, 17 April 1886.

132 Steven Arthur Pinker (born 1954), Canadian-American cognitive psychologist and linguist.

133 *Daily Telegraph*, 19 April 1886.

134 *Cambridge Independent Press*, 24 April 1886.

135 'Fools rush in where angels fear to tread' is a famous line from the poem *An Essay on Criticism* published in 1711 by the English writer, Alexander Pope (1688–1744). 'Fools Rush in (Where Angels Fear to Tread)' is a song which uses that line. Lyrics by Johnny Mercy and music by Rube Bloom (1940).

136 *Cambridge Independent Press*, 24 April 1886.

137 *Warwick & Warwickshire Advertiser & Leamington Gazette*, 24 April 1886.

138 Letter from 'A Barrister', *St James's Gazette*, 19 April 1886.

139 *The Historical Review*, Vol 82, Issue 5, December 1977, page 1237. Kathleen E McCrone (University of Windsor, Ontario, Canada).

140 *Lowestoft Journal*, 24 April 1886.

141 *Eddowes's Shrewsbury Journal*, 21 April 1886.

142 *Daily Telegraph*, 19 April 1886.

143 Edward Clarke in *The Story of my Life* also stated that at some key point in her Trial, his client Adelaide passed to him a note. 'Monsieur, I am very grateful to you although I do not look at you.' Whether she did use the French word, or just wrote Sir, is not known.

144 *Lloyd's Weekly London Newspaper*, 25 April 1886.

145 *Eastern Daily Press*, Norwich, 21 April 1886.

146 In England and Wales, unanimous verdicts were required until the Criminal Justice Act 1967.

147 Emile Edouard Charles Antoine Zola (1840–1902). French novelist, political activist and critic. The cycle of twenty novels (published from 1871 to 1893 and highly influential within the French naturalism literary movement): *Les Rougon-Macquart*, subtitled *Histoire naturelle et sociale d'une familie sous le Second Empire (Natural and social history of a family under the Second Empire)*.

148 Mary S Hartman (born 1941) instituted many nationally acclaimed programmes for women's education and women's studies. In 1995, she became Director of the Institute for Women's Leadership at Rutgers, The University of New Jersey, USA.

149 Edgar Lustgarten, *The Murder and the Trial* (New York: Scribner, 1958). Edgar Lustgarten

(1907–1978) esteemed British broadcaster and crime writer, died while reading the *Spectator*, a weekly magazine, in the Marylebone Library, London.

150 Derek Walker-Smith and Edward Clarke, *The Life and Famous Cases of Sir Edward Clarke* (London: Eyre & Spottiswoode, 1939).

151 *Hampshire Telegraph and Sussex Chronicle*, 24 April 1886.

152 *Folkestone Express*, 24 April 1886, one of many newspapers which featured this 'London Letter'.

153 The abridged version of the letter from Adelaide to Clarke was published in Sir John Hall (ed.), *Notable British Trials Series, Trial of Adelaide Bartlett* (London: William Hodge & Company Ltd, 1927) and in Kate Clarke, *The Pimlico Murder: The Strange Case of Adelaide Bartlett* (London: Souvenir Press, 1990)

154 *The Life and Famous Cases of Sir Edward Clarke*. Derek Walker-Smith and Edward Clarke (Eyre and Spottiswoode, 1939).

155 *The Lights o' London* was a melodrama by George R Sims and was first performed in 1881. The music was composed by Michael Connelly, published by Hopwood & Crew of 42 New Bond Street and the song sung by Miss Mary Eastlake. The melodrama had a long, successful run at the Princess's Theatre in London; it was also performed in Australia, for example.

156 'Tietjens': Therese Tietjens (b 1831, Hamburg – d 1877, London) was an opera and oratario soprano, considered one of the finest sopranos of the second half of the nineteenth century. Her career in London from the 1860s was a fine one, but she died relatively young from cancer.

'Grisi': Carlotta Grisi was born in Visinada, Istria (now Visinada, Croatia) in 1819. A ballet dancer, she was well-known in London, particularly for her performances in *Giselle*. Also a singer, she died in 1899.

'Malibran': Maria Malibran (b 1808, Spain – d 1836) was one the most famous opera singers of the first half of the nineteenth century, sang contralto and soprano parts with huge power and range and had a dramatic life to match. Sadly she died at only twenty-eight.

'Albani': Dame Emma Albani, DBE (born some time between 1847 and 1852; died in 1930) was a leading soprano from the late nineteenth century into the twentieth century, the first Canadian opera singer to become internationally famous.

157 *The Times*, 19 April 1886.

158 *Eastern Daily Press*, 11 April 1886.

159 Reynold's 'Waxworks and Exhibition' opened in 1858 at 12 Lime Street in the city of Liverpool, north-west England. It became one of the most prominent venues in the north, with attractions based on Madame Tussauds in London.

160 *Western Gazette*, 30 September 1892.

161 Alfred Leach (1856–92) LRCS, LSA, LM. *The British Medical Journal*, 24 September, 1892; Obituary. *The Letter H: Past, Present, and Future (London: Griffith & Farran, 1880)*.

162 Jeannette Hensby, *Edwin, Adelaide & George: The Bizarre Bartlett Poisoning* (Jeannette Hensby, 2016)

163 *Northampton Mercury*, 1 May 1886.

164 Created in 1867 for the British magazine *Judy*, Alexander 'Ally' Sloper was the eponymous fictional character in the comic strip *Ally Sloper*. He was one of the first, recurring comic-strip characters in Britain, initially written and drawn by Charles H Ross, then illustrated by Emilie de Tessier, Ross's French wife. She used the pseudonym 'Marie Duval' or Marie du Val. It was very rare for a woman to be a comic-strip artist at that time. From 1884, the character had his own weekly comic, *Ally Sloper's Half Holiday* and was drawn by William Baxter, until the latter died in 1888. 'Half holiday' referred to the practice of workers in Victorian times generally being off work from lunchtime on Saturday until Monday morning.

165 *St Stephen's Review of Facts and Fancies, Thoughts, Realities and Shams* was published in London from 1883 until 1892 and included the work of political cartoonists and satirists.

166 Complete and revised Report, edited by Edward Beal, BA, Cantab. With a preface by Edward Clarke, QC, MP, *The trial of Adelaide Bartlett for murder, held at the Central Criminal Court from Monday, April 12, to Saturday, April 17, 1886*, (London: Stevens and Haynes, 1886).

167 *The Pimlico Murder*, Kate Clarke, 1990.

168 Edward Jolley Crooke went on to become a member of the Legislative Council and a minister without portfolio in the Australian government in 1901–02.

169 *Launceston Examiner* [Tasmania], 23 January and 16 February 1880.

170 *Gippsland Times*, 22 January 1880.

171 *Gippsland Times*, 20 February 1880.

172 John King (1820–1895) was a grandson of Governor Philip Gidley King, who had arrived from England with the First Fleet in 1788. John was born in Parramatta, near Sydney, went to England to finish his education and returned to Sydney at the age of seventeen. After the death of his first wife, he married again in England. The 1871 England Census, Penge, Surrey shows John, second wife Antoinette and family. They left for Australia in 1872 and lived at Nambrok, Rosedale, in Gippsland.

173 *Gippsland Times*, 21 January 1887.

174 Henry Hunt, *A peep into a prison, or, The inside of Ilchester Bastille: dedicated, without permission, to William Hanning, esq., high sheriff, and the magistrates of the County of*

Somerset (London: Thomas Dolby, 1821).

175 Henry 'Orator' Hunt (1773–1835) campaigned vigorously around England for parliamentary reform in the early nineteenth century. He believed that reform and political change would only be brought about through massive public support and participation.

176 *Peterloo* (2018) a film directed by Mike Leigh. The Bicentenary of the Massacre was on 16 August 2019.

177 Alexandre Dumas (1802–70) born Dumas Davy de la Pailleterie, also known as Alexandre Dumas père. His father was an army general, born in the French colony of Saint-Domingue (now Haiti). Alexandre's grandmother was a black slave, Marie-Cessette Dumas. Dumas' collaborator, Auguste Maquet, worked with him from 1838 and received payments for his work – but the publishers would not include Maquet's name on the title pages. Dumas' novels and chronicles included *Georges* (1843); *The Three Musketeers* (1844); *The Count of Monte Cristo* (1844–46).

178 John A Vickers, in his May 2006 article from Proceedings of the Wesley Historical Society.

179 Verdict on Dyson, George, WM probationer, 42:122; 47:140. Wesley Historical Society; General Index to the Proceedings Vols 31–50, compiled by John A Vickers. See *Conference Journal* (Methodist Archives, John Rylands University Library of Manchester).

180 The term 'by golly' appears to date back to the eighteenth century in England, as a euphemism for 'by God'.

181 *Scientific American*, the oldest monthly magazine continuously published in the USA, was first published in 1845.

182 The National Security League (NSL) was founded by SS Menken, an attorney, and General L Wood, encouraged by AP Gardner, a US Representative. In addition to its promulgation of national preparedness for the ensuing war in Europe, the NSL supported various key initiatives including the Americanisation of immigrants, a comprehensive interstate highway system and the universal conscription of men. The NSL attracted support from people with a range of political views but in 1918 its influence declined.

183 In this context, a niche is a shallow recess in a wall, with an urn on display. A columbarium is a place for the (usually) public storage of an urn which contains the remains of a deceased person. The word derives from the Latin word '*columba*' (dove) and originally referred to the nesting boxes for doves (and pigeons) in a dovecote.

184 Helen McKenny, *A City Road Diary 1885–1888*, ed. Alfred Binney and John A Vickers, 1978, 15, 105.

185 *Daily Free Press*, Carbondale, 21 August 1916.

186 *Des Moines News*, 20 August 1916; the news item was from United Press.

187 *Lincoln Sunday Star*, 20 August 1916.

188 New York, Wills and Probate Records 1659–1999, concerning Ernestine V Walker.

189 J Bernard Walker, quoted by the Washington correspondent to the *Sheffield Daily Telegraph*, 4 May 1917.

190 William Roughead, *Murder: Murder And More Murder* (Sheridan House, 1939).

191 'Mrs Belloc Lowndes' was Marie Adelaide Elizabeth Rayner nèe Belloc (1868–1947). She married Frederick Lowndes in 1896 and, writing as Marie Belloc Lowndes, was well-respected for her skills in combining exciting occurrences with psychological insights. She was born in Marylebone, London and brought up in La Celle-Saint-Cloud, near Versailles, France, the daughter of the English feminist Bessie Parkes and Louis Belloc, a French barrister. Her younger brother was Hilaire Belloc, a prolific writer who covered a wide range of subjects from religion to comedy.

192 Article by Dr John A Vickers, *George Dyson Alias John Bernard Walker* (Methodist History, 41:1. October 2002) and also an article by Dr John A Vickers, *A 'Distressing Poisoning Case' and its aftermath* (Wesley Historical Society Proceedings, Part 5, May 2006). Described as 'new material which recently surfaced on the involvement of the Rev George Dyson in the case of Adelaide Bartlett and his subsequent career in America'.

193 Articles by J Bernard Walker in the *Scientific American* cover a huge range of subjects including submarines, the Panama Canal, transatlantic steamships and the following selected titles: *The Racing Aeroplane of the Future – A Study,* 22 October 1910; *The Government and the Railroads,* 6 April 1918; *Saving St Paul's Cathedral,* 1 May 1925; *Giant Floating Aircraft Bases,* 1 August 1926; *The Post-War Navies,* 1 December 1927; *A Two Hundred Mile-Per-Hour Car,* 1 June 1927.

194 Books by 'J Bernard Walker' include:

J Bernard Walker, Editor of the *Scientific American*: *An Unsinkable Titanic: Every Ship Its Own Lifeboat* (New York, Dodd, Mead and Company, 1912). Published just three months after the Titanic sank.

J Bernard Walker, Editor of the *Scientific American*: *America Fallen! The Sequel to the European War* (New York: Dodd, Mead and Company, 1915).

195 *Victorian Murderesses: A True History of Thirteen Respectable French and English Women Accused of Unspeakable Crimes.*

196 *New York Times,* 19 April 1886.

197 Christianna Brand (1907–88) was born Mary Christianna Milne and, among her varied occupations, was a crime writer and children's author (she wrote *Nurse Matilda,* which Emma Thompson adapted for the film *Nanny McPhee* (2005). The quote about chloroform is from: https://www.historyextra.com/period/the-truth-behind-10-historical-mysteries/ the official website for BBC History Magazine and BBC World Histories Magazine.

198 Rachel Yehuda (born 1959) has qualifications which include biological psychology,

biological psychiatry and neurochemistry. She is a leader in the field of traumatic stress studies and her research has included the study of children of Holocaust survivors.

199 Angela Bourke, *The Burning of Bridget Cleary* (Pimlico, 1999)

ACKNOWLEDGEMENTS

Thank you to everyone who helped me during the process of writing this book, by way of friendship and family kindnesses, writing spaces and encouragement, including: Gemma, Larissa, Tom, Alina, Faye, Heather, Linda Bentley, Norah, Alison C, Rosie W and the late Roger Veale. To Jennifer Mahlberg for diligence and skill, typing and shaping it into a manuscript, and Luke Storkey for the cover design and drawings. To all of you (and anyone I have omitted to mention) I send much love and gratitude.

Thank you also to Damien for a chance encounter; Gillian D; Richard N Ether of 131st New York Volunteer Infantry Web Page, Facebook, for invaluable knowledge of the Civil War in the States and Gregory Tavormina for information concerning Rodolphe; Linda Barraclough, one of the administrators of Gippsland History Facebook page, for her crucial publication 'Gippsland Legends: George de Thouars and the Holey Plain holdup of 1880' (published 11 January 2018) and her advice; Lucy Roeber for an editing consultation.

My sincere apologies in advance for any errors I have made.

On a Greek island in 2019, at a Murder/Mystery Writing Workshop I was paired for a short exercise with a Frenchman; we had never met before.

I asked if he was 'writing anything': yes, researching the history of the Genovese, Venetians and French who had been in that region of Greece. Pricking up my ears at the word 'French' I asked if there was a particular French family name that featured. He wrote on the exercise sheet 'de la Tremouaille'. A shiver went up and down my spine; of course, I then told him that 'de la Tremouille' was one of the key surnames of the family (was that Adolphus' true name?) about which I was writing! I don't know the odds of two people meeting in that chance way and having such an unusual subject surname in common, but the odds must be sky high.

And on 26 January 2022 I opened an email from Linda Barraclough in Australia and shouted with excitement when I saw that George de Thouars' marriage certificate included his mother's maiden name: Chamberlain. Thus I knew he was *the* Freddy, who became George and had a traumatic life in Australia.

Those are just two examples of the delight I felt when researching, writing and editing this book.

1 February 2022

BIBLIOGRAPHY

Edward Beal, *The Trial of Adelaide Bartlett for Murder, held at the Central Criminal Court from Monday, April 12, to Saturday, April 17, 1886. Complete and Revised Report* (London, Stevens and Haynes, 1886).

Yseult Bridges, *Poison and Adelaide Bartlett* (Hutchinson, 1962).

Edward Clarke, *The Story of my Life* (London, John Murray, 1918).

Kate Clarke, *The Pimlico Murder: The Strange Case of Adelaide Bartlett* (Classic Crime Series, Souvenir Press Ltd, 1990).

Kate Clarke; foreword by Linda Stratmann, *In the Interests of Science: Adelaide Bartlett and the Pimlico Poisoning* (Mango Books, 2015).

Anne de Courcy, *The Fishing Fleet: Husband-Hunting in the Raj* (Great Britain: Weidenfeld & Nicolson, 2012).

William Dalrymple, *The Anarchy: The Relentless Rise of the East India Company* (Bloomsbury, 2019).

Mary S Hartman, *Victorian Murderesses: A True History of Thirteen Respectable French and English Women Accused of Unspeakable Crimes* (USA, Schocken Books, 1976).

Jeannette Hensby, *Edwin, Adelaide & George: The Bizarre Bartlett Poisoning* (Jeannette Hensby, 2016).

Michelle Lovric, *The Book of Human Skin* (Bloomsbury Publishing, 2010).

Steven Pinker, *The Sense of Style: The Thinking Person's Guide to Writing in the 21st Century* (United States: Viking Penguin, 2014 and Great Britain: Allen Lane, 2014).

James Ruddick, *Death at the Priory: Sex and Murder in Victorian England* (London: Atlantic Books, 2001).

George Saunders, *Lincoln in the Bardo* (United States, Random House, 2017).

Jean L Silver-Isenstadt, *Shameless: the Visionary Life of Mary Gove Nichols* (United States: Johns Hopkins University Press, 2002).

Julian Symons, *Sweet Adelaide: A Victorian Puzzle Solved* (Great Britain, Collins Crime Club, 1980).

Linda Stratmann, *Chloroform: The Quest for Oblivion* (UK, Sutton Publishing Ltd, 2003).

Kate Summerscale, *The Suspicions of Mr Whicher: A Shocking Murder and the Undoing of a Great Victorian Detective* (Walker & Company, 2008). Hardcover.

Kate Summerscale, *The Suspicions of Mr Whicher, or, The Murder at Road Hill House* (Bloomsbury Publishing, 2009). Paperback.

Richard Whittington-Egan, *William Roughead's Chronicles of Murder* (Moffat, Scotland, Lochar Publishing, 1991).

OTHER SOURCES   Ancestry; Findmypast; FamilySearch; National Archives: UK and Australia. Local records office: Orleans, France.

FINIS